Searching for the Future in the Past

T&T Clark Renewing Feminist Theology as Inclusive Radical Praxis

Series editors
Keun-joo Christine Pae
Kathleen T. Talvacchia

Searching for the Future in the Past

Reclaiming Feminist Theological Visions

Edited by
Keun-joo Christine Pae and
Kathleen T. Talvacchia

t&tclark
LONDON • NEW YORK • OXFORD • NEW DELHI • SYDNEY

T&T CLARK
Bloomsbury Publishing Plc
50 Bedford Square, London, WC1B 3DP, UK
1385 Broadway, New York, NY 10018, USA
29 Earlsfort Terrace, Dublin 2, Ireland

BLOOMSBURY, T&T CLARK and the T&T Clark logo are trademarks of Bloomsbury Publishing Plc

First published in Great Britain 2024

Copyright © Keun-joo Christine Pae and Kathleen T. Talvacchia, 2024

Keun-joo Christine Pae and Kathleen T. Talvacchia have asserted their right under the Copyright, Designs and Patents Act, 1988, to be identified as Editors of this work.

Cover design: Ben Anslow

All rights reserved. No part of this publication may be reproduced or transmitted in any form or by any means, electronic or mechanical, including photocopying, recording, or any information storage or retrieval system, without prior permission in writing from the publishers.

Bloomsbury Publishing Plc does not have any control over, or responsibility for, any third-party websites referred to or in this book. All internet addresses given in this book were correct at the time of going to press. The author and publisher regret any inconvenience caused if addresses have changed or sites have ceased to exist, but can accept no responsibility for any such changes.

A catalogue record for this book is available from the British Library.

Library of Congress Cataloging-in-Publication Data
Names: Pae, Keun-Joo Christine, editor. | Talvacchia, Kathleen T., editor.
Title: Searching for the future in the past : reclaiming feminist theological visions / Keun-joo Christine Pae, Kathleen T. Talvacchia.
Description: London ; New York : T&T Clark, 2024. | Series: T&T Clark renewing feminist theology as inclusive radical praxis |
Includes bibliographical references and index.
Identifiers: LCCN 2024011011 (print) | LCCN 2024011012 (ebook) |
ISBN 9780567712196 (pb) | ISBN 9780567712202 (hb) |
ISBN 9780567712219 (epdf) | ISBN 9780567712226 (epub)
Subjects: LCSH: Feminist theology.
Classification: LCC BT83.55 .S4466 2024 (print) | LCC BT83.55 (ebook) |
DDC 230.082–dc23/eng/20240605
LC record available at https://lccn.loc.gov/2024011011
LC ebook record available at https://lccn.loc.gov/2024011012

ISBN: HB: 978-0-5677-1220-2
PB: 978-0-5677-1219-6
ePDF: 978-0-5677-1221-9
ePUB: 978-0-5677-1222-6

Series: T&T Clark Renewing Feminist Theology as Inclusive Radical Praxis

Typeset by Newgen KnowledgeWorks Pvt. Ltd., Chennai, India
Printed and bound in Great Britain

To find out more about our authors and books visit www.bloomsbury.com and sign up for our newsletters.

CONTENTS

Acknowledgement vii

Introduction: Why Renew Feminist Theologies? 1
Kathleen T. Talvacchia and Keun-joo Christine Pae

Part One: The Praxis of Embodied Living

1 Can Feminist Theology Be Queer? 13
   Kathleen T. Talvacchia

2 Embodiment, Identity, and Sexuality: Reproductive and Sexual Justice and Theological Anthropology 29
   Toni M. Bond

3 Challenging the Notion of Presumptive Motherhood 47
   Margaret D. Kamitsuka

4 Policing Black Womanhood: Sin, Respectability, and Abolitionist Sanctuaries 67
   Nikia Smith Robert

5 A Tale of "Two" Marys 85
   Charlene Sinclair

6 Reclaiming Disabilities Theologically, Envisioning Just Flourishing 95
Heike Peckruhn

Part Two: The Praxis of Living Relationally

7 Traveling between Mountains and White Doves: Spiritual Rhythms of *Runa* Feminisms 121
Mónica A. Maher with Samay Cañamar M.

8 An Embodied Feminist Theology of Peace as Radical Praxis 143
Keun-joo Christine Pae

9 Decolonizing Dialogues: Bridging Ecofeminism, Religion, and the Decological Path Forward 163
Elaine Nogueira-Godsey

10 Re-membering Interdependency 189
Esther Parajuli

11 Queer Intimacies and Art as the Necessary Work of the Soul 205
Su Yon Pak and Alicia R. Forde

List of Contributors 229
Index 233

ACKNOWLEDGEMENT

A village of feminist theologians and allies helped us conceive and produce this book. As the title suggests, *Searching for the Future in the Past*, is the collection of intergenerational, interreligious, and cross-national dialogue and feminist theological reflections. We are deeply grateful all the contributors who passionately and graciously participated in this dialogue and produced critical feminist theological discourses and praxis. Our deep gratitude goes to Dr. Mary Hunt who read our book proposal and offered valuable comments. Mary has shown what sisterhood looks like in a theological world.

This book project was possible thanks to the initiation of Anna Turton from T&T Clark. Anna's affirmation of feminist theology in today's academia and society gave us renewed energy to embark on editing this anthology. We also owe big thanks to Anna's team at T&T Clark.

K. Christine Pae wants to express thanks to her students and colleagues at Denison University. David Woodyard generously supported this project in many ways. John Jackson has been Christine's conversation partner, who stimulates her intellectual curiosity. Christine's colleagues in the Women's and Gender Studies Program have been her source of academic friendship and solidarity. Of course, her students inspire her to continue to produce feminist theological ethics. She particularly thanks Ali and Greta whose activism for peace and justice in the time of war on Gaza. Their nonviolent activism helped her imagine a feminist theology of peace in a new generation.

Her thanks also go to Kwok Pui-lan for generously sharing transnational feminist theological perspectives. She deeply thanks Jin Young Choi, Atalia Omer, Laura Bothwell, MT Davilla, Kelsi Morrison-Atkins, Isis Nusair, Hoda Yusuf, and Hosna Sheikholeslami for their friendship and intellectual challenge; and

Marc H. Ellis for his Prophetic Jewish theological inspiration and Mitri Raheb for embodying the persistence of Palestinian Christian liberation theology. She thanks all the anti-war feminist theologians, especially those in conflict zones—Palestine, Palestinian diasporas, Ukraine, Iraq, Afghanistan, Sudan, the Republic of Congo, African diasporas and Korea.

Christine's family in South Korea and in the United States has a special place in her heart. She sends deep gratitude to her parents and two sisters in Korea and her partner, Jinwoo, and precious children, Juahn Julian and Jubin Lucas, for sustaining her through the tumultuous journey of this anthology.

Kathleen T. Talvacchia expresses her thanks to both the foremothers of feminist and womanist theologies and the ongoing generations of women and women identified persons who continue to create new theologies for inspiring her journey. Their courage and clarity have strengthened her own vision of an authentic, diverse, and effective theological praxis that empowers and includes the experience of all.

She also sends deep appreciation and love to the Talvacchia Family and the Pak Family for their ongoing love and support through the many stages of this project; to her children Jocelyn and Chloe and their families for their encouragement and affirmation; and to her grandchildren, Isobel and Isla, who keep her grounded in what is truly real. As always, she sends deep gratitude to her partner Su whose love, support, and commitment to her journey is a blessing and a gift.

Introduction: Why Renew Feminist Theologies?

Kathleen T. Talvacchia and Keun-joo Christine Pae

In times of various crises, ranging from climate change to gender-based violence and war, where can we begin to renew and reimagine life-affirming feminist theologies—the theologies that still make the hearts of people of faith beat in excitement and yearning for wholeness? As feminist theology has done since its inception, we begin with women's experiences. More so, feminist theology has argued that women's experiences are not only to be included, but they are also *authoritative* and, therefore, a necessary aspect of genuine "theologizing."

However, in its history, feminist theology has not always lived out the inclusive understandings of women's experiences that it intended. For example, in the late 1980s, womanist ethicist Katie Cannon claimed the legitimacy of the lived experience of Black women as a source of theological ethics that challenged white and patriarchal norms. In *Black Womanist Ethics*, she wrote: "Black women live out a moral wisdom in their real-lived context that does not appeal to the fixed rules or absolute principles of the white-oriented, male structured society."[1] Thus, feminist theology should

---

[1] Katie Cannon, *Black Womanist Ethics* (Atlanta, GA: Scholar's Press, 1988), 4.

be interrogated, challenged, and critiqued for the ways it served (consciously or unconsciously) to universalize the experiences of white, heterosexual, cisgender, and able-bodied women as representing the "hegemonic" norm of women's experience. As Namsoon Kang argues, "The invisible structure of [the] 'absence' of the 'who-am-I' question, the absence of an adjective describing one's identity becomes the ground of its power. By absenting its overt specificity (i.e. gender, race, ethnicity, sexual orientation, etc.) it is simply assumed to be universal and normative."[2] As it developed, feminist theology understood more deeply the ways that an authentically inclusive feminist theology begins from an understanding of the diversity and particularity of women's experiences and that the authority of those particular experiences impacts and influences the ways in which we "do" theology.

Importantly, speaking from lived experience and claiming the authority of that voice is not simply an act of self-reflection or an effort to raise the consciousness of racial, gender, and sexual oppression, but rather, it is a political act that challenges the power structures that have constantly excluded those who are on the margins. The sociologist Tressie McMillan Cottom argues for the legitimacy and necessity of the personal essay as a political act of embodied resistance to an unjust system's attempt to silence and make disregarded groups invisible and their experiences of injustice trivialized or ignored. She states that, "In a modern society, who is allowed to speak with authority is a political act."[3] Thus, feminist theology at its core is a deeply political act that makes space for voices that have not been heard and claims them as essential to the work of theology.

As editors, we locate the necessity of a renewed feminist theology in our present social context—a feminist theology that is rooted in inclusivity and grounded in an intersectional understanding of women's diverse experiences due to their varied social locations created by the political economic system. Specifically, we *ex*claim

---

[2]Namsoon Kang, "Transethnic Feminist Theology of Asia: Globalization, Identities, and Solidarities," in *The Oxford Handbook of Feminist Theology*, ed. Mary McClintock Fulkerson and Sheila Briggs (New York: Oxford University Press, 2012), 110.
[3]Tressie McMillan Cottom, *Thick: And Other Essays* (New York: New Press, 2019), 19.

a desire to *re*claim feminist theological vision as a project that can embrace the authority of diverse women's experiences as resources for the creation of theology from and of religious and spiritual communities.

We approach this project with a bold assumption: in our current social, political, and environmental context, we need an inclusive, creative, audacious, and radical feminist theology for life, peace, and justice even more now than when it was first developed in the 1960s. The persistence of gender-based and racialized violence, heteronormativity and white supremacy, the feminization of global poverty, the gendered impact of climate change, public disputes over women's reproductive justice, women's bodies, and the resurgence of religious fundamentalism across the globe are just a few of the issues that express the urgency of this moment in the lives of all women-identified persons. Women experience the impacts of these realities differently from male-identified persons and from one another as their experiences are rooted in specific contexts and social locations. Understanding the variety of experiences among women can help us see more clearly how normative heteropatriarchal culture has shaped the relations of ruling through various legal apparatuses (i.e., treaties, immigration laws, and citizenship), domestically and globally, and how these relations of ruling bind together global populations. Feminist theology begins when women's survival wisdom and courageous activism arise to confront injustice in the relations of ruling through different historical contexts.

This anthology was developed from the conviction that the voices and experiences of all women and women-identified persons— understood in all of our intersectional and inclusive diversity— must be a fundamental and integral aspect of the authoritative theological expressions of religious communities and that these voices are imperative to understanding the larger community outside of themselves. It seeks to embody the political action of speaking with authority about diverse religious and ethical experiences in Christian traditions from a stance that is inclusive of the experiences of all women-identified persons and actively seeks to promote the work of justice in an unjust society through radical praxis.

The project begins with a crucial belief: inclusive and progressive theological and religious perspectives, nurtured from the heritage and voices of feminist theological traditions, have a critical and distinctive contribution to make to an analysis of the challenging issues facing communities in the twenty-first century. While religion and spirituality are critical resources for many women's communities to resist unjust social structures, envision an alternative future, and experience healing from the violence, women's and gender studies and sexuality studies often overlook them. Women's faith-based activism is also an important source of feminist theologies. Hence, as this anthology aims to recover women's theological voices, we intentionally sought out and included new methodological approaches from activist, community-based, and academic writers in our desire to reimagine how feminist theologies grounded in religious traditions and communities might be constructed.

From their beginnings, feminist theologies have aspired to be the communal production of women's communities that critically reflect on their experiences in the contexts of culture, social standpoint, religious practices and beliefs, and the imagination of the Feminine Divine. As stated previously, despite its aspirational aims, feminist theologies could be myopic universalizing women's experiences if they do not critically analyze social injustice that diversifies those experiences. With this text, we endeavor to create theologies that reflect the material realities of women-identified persons as they exist within intersectional structures of dominance and marginalization. In creating their distinctive voices, the writers each find a connection to the heritage conversations of feminist theology that have proven useful for the development of their voice to engage the critical issues of today to forge new perspectives. The book seeks to create an intellectual and discursive space where feminist theologians in all of their diversity renew and reclaim the rich legacies of the feminist theological tradition through intergenerational, racially diverse, and transnational conversation.

The womanist, feminist, and queer theologians in this anthology articulate with critical rigor their responses to contemporary political, cultural, economic, and racial issues. As they make a concerted effort to create cross-racial, transnational, transdisciplinary, inter-religious, and intergenerational dialogue, the contributors reclaim the rich legacies of feminist theology by rereading, retelling, and reinterpreting womanist and feminist foremothers' scholarships and activism.

With a focus on the variety among women's experiences, the writers engage with the question: *How can feminist theology be renewed in a way that creates a more inclusive discursive analysis and, therefore, greater relevance to the twenty-first century?* More specifically, in reclaiming feminist theology as inclusive radical praxis, this anthology offers critical views on *how to think about women's experiences, how to produce diverse theological knowledge from these experiences, and how to let women express their methodological diversity.*

Reclaiming a feminist theological method of critically engaging women's experiences is a fundamental component of these processes. Specifically, we seek to enact a necessary subversion of traditional academic models that too often value the methods, voice, and concerns of cis-heteronormative white male perspectives. How to think about women's experiences, how to produce diverse theological knowledge from these experiences, and how to let women express their methodological diversity can help reclaim feminist theology as inclusive radical praxis. Inclusive radical praxis underscores the inseparability between spiritual/religious renewal and social/political changes with concrete experiences of bodies (i.e., raced, gendered, sexed, classed, differently abled bodies, etc.). Our aim is to renew and reclaim the rich legacies and wisdom of feminist theology through inclusive discourses, across various social and cultural differences, that speak to the critical issues and multiplicities facing women-identified persons.

Among the various and often contesting definitions of feminism, this anthology underscores feminism as a political movement—"political" meaning every human relationship is a power relation. The power relations that have often created what are considered acceptable forms of expression and methods of investigation—often rooted in white supremacist, patriarchal, heteronormative, and disembodied belief systems—must be challenged for a renewed and reclaimed feminist theology to have authenticity. These challenges disrupt the traditional boundaries of the academy and create new ways to analyze, understand, and articulate the experiences of all women-identified persons. From this perspective, the contributors endeavor to renew theories and methods in producing feminist theology generally in three areas: (1) expressing methodological diversity, (2) renewing feminist differences, and (3) resurging radical praxis.

Expressing methodological diversity: Women's experiences remain as critical for feminist theology. In all of their nuance and particularity, creative and transdisciplinary methods of analysis need to be used. The methodological diversity expressed in the chapters highlights the variety of ways in which womanist and feminist theologians engage and understand women's experiences with the Sacred, social activism, oppression, historical memories, and power relations. With this methodological diversity, we seek to challenge and reimagine the ways that theology can be constructed and expressed.

Renewing feminist differences: Also, the contributors seek out innovative methods of reimagining cross-racial and cross-border feminist theologies and diverse approaches to solidarity for peace with justice across sexual and religious differences. The convergence of intersectionality feminism and transnational feminism in many of the chapters expands the discursive space for intergenerational, transnational, interracial, and interreligious feminist theology.

Resurging radical praxis: Finally, understanding that feminist theology has been historically responding to critical issues in its time, this anthology reclaims and elaborates on feminist theology as radical praxis. The contributors retell, reinterpret, and renew twentieth-century feminist theologies, offering new theological perspectives on the radical social movements and renewing theological discourses informed by these movements.

Each writer approaches their chapter considering the following questions: (1) What intersectional feminist perspectives, grounded in diverse lived experiences, should be incorporated to create genuinely inclusive renewed feminist theologies? (2) What, if any, aspects of the history and traditions of feminist theologies are useful base points for creating a renewed vision? (3) What might radical praxis mean and look like within the concerns discussed in the chapter? (4) What is the new vision and direction for creating a renewed feminist theology in the twenty-first century?

From these questions for reflection, the contributors articulate their experiences in ways that felt compelling and real to them. To be sure, these experiences are not simply personal but also communal and political. Some find an artistic method to be the way to capture and make sense of their experiences. For others, autoethnography or sermonic methods seem most appropriate. Yet others use a more traditional academic style to disrupt and subvert its methodological and subject exclusions of women's experience. Using innovative approaches, the contributors forge new ways to pose issues of difference across the intersections of differences. All of the writers understand the implications of their ideas and analysis for changes in all women-identified persons' lives on a material as well as on a spiritual level.

Searching for the Future in the Past consists of two interrelated parts. Part One considers the praxis of embodied living, seeking to theologize from the lives of women. Speaking from her context as a queer, feminist, practical theologian, Kathleen T. Talvacchia asks the question of whether feminist theology can be queer, arguing that it can be, provided that it is able to successfully devise better strategies of (a) representation of diverse experiences and (b) inclusive theological construction. Toni M. Bond, using the principles of reproductive and sexual justice (of which she is a co-originator), examines embodiment, identity, and sexuality as avenues in the development of a theological anthropology that is responsive to the demands of reproductive and sexual justice. Margaret D. Kamitsuka interrogates conservative Christian theologies that promote what she refers to as "presumptive motherhood" for cisgender women. She seeks to raise the suppressed voices within the tradition who have challenged this notion, with the aim of creating greater freedom for women's choices to embrace other forms of generativity and mothering beyond the cisgender experience. Nikia Smith Robert examines the ways in which the church doctrines of sin and deviance, along with "respectability politics," serve to police the lives of Black women. She argues for a womanist theological ethic of abolition as a justice response. In dialogue with biblical accounts of Mary, the mother of Jesus, and Mary Magdalene, Charlene Sinclair offers a reflection of the truth of her experience of being a teenage parent as a way to challenge and disrupt the expected notions of what it means to be a womanist theo-ethicist. Heike Peckruhn challenges feminist theologies to engage intentionally with the work of secular disabilities justice movements, which are providing important interventions that promote embodied flourishing.

The chapters in Part Two examine the praxis of living relationally in community, transnationally, interpersonally, with interreligious engagement, and in connection to the environment. Mónica A. Maher, with her colleague Samay Cañamar M., using the intersectional, intergenerational, intercultural, and transnational lens, invites readers to engage with the Andean ancestral spirituality of its women practitioners and its implications for Christian theology. Keun-joo Christine Pae argues for a feminist theology of embodied peace as radical praxis that takes seriously transnational women's wisdom related to peace-building while critically analyzing the sexual and gender-based labor imposed on women that military engagement and war demand. For Elaine Nogueira-Godsey, the threats of ecological destruction facing both the Global North and the Global South require creating new ways for feminist theologians to engage each other. She argues for a "decological dialogue" that consists of decolonial analysis, ecological commitments, and pedagogical intentions. Esther Parajuli examines the global rise of exclusionary politics that are expressed with patriarchal and racist rhetoric and articulates the challenges it creates for postcolonial feminist commitments for liberation. She advocates a postcolonial feminist theology of relationship that remembers our common interdependence. Su Yon Pak and Alicia R. Forde explore their reimagining of feminist theological praxis in the context of an artistic process. Using a method of creative nonfiction, they ask the questions: How do we practice new feminist praxis in our ordinary and everyday lives? What are the roles of art and intimacy in feminist praxis?

In her articulation of a postcolonial view of Christianity, feminist theologian Kwok Pui-lan has stated, "The future of feminist Christianity is not located at the center of the bureaucratic church, but at the margins and in other subversive spaces."[4] It is in that spirit that the writers of this anthology search for the future in the past—reclaiming the emancipatory aspects of heritage feminist and womanist theologies and disrupting and disturbing its limitations to speak to the concerns of this time. Employing new methods of inquiry, envisioning diverse and inclusive theological and ethical constructions, and engaging embodied radical praxis, we work to create a new feminist theological vision for a new generation and a new time that so urgently needs its wisdom.

---

[4]Kwok Pui-lan, "A Postcolonial Feminist Vision for Christianity" in *New Feminist Christianity: Many Voices, Many Views*, ed. Mary E. Hunt and Diann L. Neu (Woodstock, VT: Skylight Paths, 2010), 5.

Bibliography

Cannon, Katie G. *Black Womanist Ethics*. Atlanta, GA: Scholar's Press, 1988.

Cottom, Tressie McMillan. *Thick: And Other Essays*. New York: New Press, 2019.

Kang, Namsoon. "Transethnic Feminist Theology of Asia: Globalization, Identities, and Solidarities." In *The Oxford Handbook of Feminist Theology*, edited by Mary McClintock Fulkerson and Sheila Briggs, 109–30. New York: Oxford University Press, 2012.

Kwok, Pui-lan. "A Postcolonial Feminist Vision for Christianity." In *New Feminist Christianity: Many Voices, Many Views*, edited by Mary E. Hunt and Diann L. Neu, 3–10. Woodstock, VT: Skylight Paths, 2010.

PART ONE

The Praxis of Embodied Living

1

Can Feminist Theology Be Queer?

Kathleen T. Talvacchia

When I was in high school (in the 1970s!), one of the teachers, who was a religious sister, came up to me one day after school while I was in the midst of some student activity. She said to me, "Stand up straight and take smaller steps when you walk! You walk like you're on the basketball court!" I remember being both irritated at her (who asked her to comment on my posture and gait?) and embarrassed because she said it in front of a couple of other students. On a deeper level, though, I felt a slight panic and fear because, in fact, that was exactly how I carried myself both on and off the court. She was correctly observing something about me but gave it an interpretation that indicated that it was a problem. And, more to the point, that it was a problem in the way I presented myself as a woman. It was one thing to be athletic, but at least by puberty, girls are expected to feminize into more traditional gender roles. It was confusing because I actually had a good relationship with this teacher, who was in many ways a progressive, nontraditional, Catholic nun, a kind of early feminist in a religious community, you might say. If she noticed it, what did others see? What she noticed was something that I had been observing in myself and struggling with: how exactly is a woman supposed to look, act, feel, and, yes, walk?

As a child, I was what was described then as a "tomboy"—very rough-and-tumble, the type of little girl who preferred sports to dolls, and (to my mother's dismay) liked to run around testing my jumping capacities.[1] Adults would say to me as I stopped for a breath, "What are you? A boy?" to which I instinctively pushed back and said, "No! I'm a girl!" I was insistent that being a girl meant that I could do those things. At the same time, I know I absorbed the message that there was something not quite right about the kind of girl I was and was becoming. My bearing and behaviors were too boyish for the expectations that society had for me about growing into womanhood. I remember the many times I would stand in front of the mirror as a preteen and teen, trying to figure out how a girl was expected to stand and move and whether I could teach myself to imitate the conforming behaviors of that heteronormative standard. When I came out as a lesbian[2] in my mid-twenties, I came to understand more deeply some of the reasons why I felt so different from the descriptions of normative womanhood that had been a part of my maturing experiences—and why I needed to stand in front of the mirror to try to figure them out.

In what ways did feminist theology help me to navigate the complexities of my nonnormative sexual life? Feminist theology helped me to critique the white patriarchal constructs of the Christian theology of my heritage, it helped me to understand the ways in which the constructions of gender were embedded in my theological analyses, and it helped me to begin to think about the role of eros in developing constructive theological thinking that can embrace passion and desire. However, I was also engaging in

---

[1] For an interesting analysis of the concept of the tomboy, see Lisa Selin Davis, *Tomboy: The Surprising History and Future of Girls Who Dare to Be Different* (New York: Hachette, 2020).

[2] Naming the identifications that we embrace in ourselves is a dynamic and evolving process, and this is especially true in LGBTIQ+ communities. When I first came out, I named myself as lesbian, and then over time, while not disengaging from that naming, I found that naming myself as queer expressed many more of the nonnormativities that I lived. In this chapter, you will see me use both identifications to describe my own experience, as well as a variety of naming conventions that are in use in LGBTIQ+ communities.

what it meant to be a white cisgender woman, nonconforming to expected gender presentation, and negotiating the targeting and discrimination that was a result of choosing to stay in the world of theology both personally and professionally. In those ways, I found feminist theology not particularly helpful and turned to secular gender and sexuality studies as well as theological and ethical thinking from LGBTIQ+ perspectives. Perhaps it was just me, limitations in my own vision, but I have a sense that others might be able to relate to my experience. For me, as a cisgender queer woman, the disconnect was obvious and unsettling; for trans* and nonbinary persons, the disconnect was, likely, even more jarring.

As I reflect upon what a feminist theology that is more open to and engaged with the embodied expression of queer life—in all of its intersectionality and diversity—might look like, I realize that it is a journey that I myself have been engaging in for the over thirty years that I have both lived a queer life and been a theologian who is deeply influenced by feminist principles. A feminist theology that embraces the lived experiences of embodied queer life has been missing for me. I am looking for a renewed feminist theology as inclusive radical praxis that speaks to LGBTIQ+ experiences in a way that does not ignore the realities of queer bodies, queer desires, and the practices of queer life.

I believe that feminist theology from a queer perspective is both necessary and possible: that is, it can both better attend to the lived experiences of queer lives and disrupt social structures that support and enforce cisgender heteronormativity. As a way to move forward toward this goal, I would like to suggest two strategies for a renewed feminist theology as inclusive radical praxis that can create a theology that is more responsive to queer bodies, sexualities, and lived experiences. First, feminist theology can devise better *strategies for the representation of diverse experiences*, creating opportunities for queer persons to articulate their embodied living and their images of God from the location of their lived religious experience of gender and sexual nonnormativity in all of their intersectionality and diversity. Second, feminist theology can devise better *strategies for inclusive theological construction*, developing more intersectionally diverse queer images of God that unmask the cis-heteronormative structures and beliefs that undergird feminist theological constructions. Such unmasking can open feminist theology to encounter a greater plurality of constructions and experiences, responsive to the diverse realities of queer lives existing outside of heterosexual normativities. If this sounds like where feminist theology began its work decades ago, then I suppose you could say that I am seeking a return to the radical roots of feminist theology's disruptive instincts. I am seeking a feminist theology that commits itself to creating new theological thinking from queer lives, queer bodies, and queer desires.

We need to be clear about the challenges inherent to this effort. There are significant tensions with which to contend. Who defines what it means to be a woman? How far can theological thinking go in engaging gender and sexuality issues before it bumps up against the doctrines and traditions of religious communities that are in opposition and increasingly hostile to even discussing the questions? There are real reasons why many LGBTIQ+ persons reject religion and find religious communities unwelcoming. And yet, in specific traditions and in cultures and communities for whom religion is the center of their formative experiences, LGBTIQ+ persons exist in those spaces that are their spiritual heritages or spiritual homes. The choice should not be between feminist theology and queer theology—or no theology—as a way of reconciling these realities. In this important way, faith and theology are engaging each other in necessary and holistic ways to support and sustain queer lives. Working at the intersections of feminist and queer theology as a way to support queer faith experiences is the work of intersectional inclusion that the praxis of justice must embrace. Feminist theology, as a theology rooted in the lived reality of all women-identified persons, embraces LGBTIQ+ experiences of gender and sexuality and makes it an intersectional and integrated aspect of feminist theologizing. In this inclusive form, feminist theologizing can be a concrete praxis of justice that both challenges a tradition and supports a community's faith.

Methodological Base Points

The work of Marcella Althaus-Reid, which lives in the intersection of feminist and queer theologizing, provides an important methodological grounding for this exercise in practical theological thinking.³ Her work is useful to this project in large part because of her fundamental assumption that all of theology is constructed from heteronormative sexual assumptions. She states, "Based on sexual categories and heterosexual binary systems, obsessed with sexual behavior and orders, every theological discourse is implicitly a sexual discourse, a decent one, an accepted one."⁴ For Althaus-Reid, liberatory feminist analysis sets itself in opposition to the sexual discourses that have been fundamental to creating heteronormative structures that prevent the full inclusion of women, particularly poor women, in images of God and moral norms. I will use her methods of "indecenting" (deconstructing heterosexually normative understandings of women) and queering (unmasking sexual ideologies that are at the heart of theology) to partner with these practical strategies of inclusion. First, Althaus-Reid's method of "indecenting" can be a helpful component of strategies to increase the representation of women's experiences to include the experiences of all women-identified persons that includes their experiences of sex and gender. Second, Althaus-Reid's method of queering theology seeks to disrupt the ideological sexual binaries that prevent theologies from engaging more diverse experiences of loving. This involves celebrating the diverse ways of knowing God and, through indecency as a constructive method, making space for various theologies and sexualities to emerge, thus contributing to a strategy of inclusive theological construction.

Additionally, I will engage pieces of my autobiographical experience as another methodological base point. In using my own journey, I am seeking to contextualize my thinking in lived experience without seeking to universalize it to make claims about all women's experiences. As I ask readers to engage my experiences in their positionality, I also invite readers to consider their own experiences and positionality in relation to feminist theology.

---

³For another theological analysis that engages the work of Marcella Althaus-Reid as an example of the intersection of feminist theology and queer theology, see Linn Marie Tonstad, *Queer Theology: Beyond Apologetics* (Eugene, OR: Cascade Books, 2018).
⁴Althus-Reid, *Indecent Theology*, 22.

Creating Space for Queer Experiences of Gender and Sexuality in Feminist Theology

One strategy for creating a feminist theology that is more responsive to queer lives—strategies for the representation of diverse experiences—actively seeks to include the bodies, desires, and lives of all women-identified persons. This involves bringing to the work not only the analyses of gender and sexuality but also an openness to engaging the ways in which the tradition is deeply queer in its transformative instincts.

I came to a fuller understanding of myself as a lesbian, queer woman—I came out—through the Spiritual Exercises of Saint Ignatius of Loyola, a spiritual practice of my Roman Catholic heritage. In a previous writing, I wrote about this experience, concluding with a very queer claim: "The tradition itself holds the power of transgression and transformation within its own practices."[5] It is a radical claim to make today, but it was an even more radical claim to make and live in 1984 when I embraced my difference. At that time, I was in my mid-twenties and deeply engaged with the heritage feminist theology of that period. However, as I stated earlier, feminist theology was helpful to my formation in many ways but left out significant pieces of my experience of being a sexual body that was fundamental to my journey. It would have made a difference for me if feminist theology had been better able to engage my experience of queerness—to have better strategies for the representation of diverse experiences—so that I could understand more fully what it meant to theologize from the experience of women, in this instance, as a white queer cisgender woman.

One entry point for me in this process was Carter Heyward's erotic theology, which was an essential first step for me in finding feminist theology that I could relate to my experiences.[6] I read

---

[5]Kathleen T. Talvacchia, "Disrupting the Theory-Practice Binary," in *Queer Christianities: Lived Religion in Transgressive Forms*, ed. Kathleen T. Talvacchia, Michael F. Pettinger, and Mark Larrimore (New York: New York University Press, 2015), 194.
[6]See Carter Heyward, *Touching Our Strength: The Erotic as Power and the Love of God* (San Francisco, CA: Harper & Row, 1989). For further information on the larger

Touching Our Strength: The Erotic as Power and the Love of God with an eye toward finding something of my experience as a lesbian with which to identify. Heyward's understanding of the erotic as "power in right relation"[7] and her connection of this relationality to her understanding of the Sacred ("God is our relational power"[8]) showed me that I could use the categories of my experience to understand something about God and our lives in the community. Also, Heyward's discussion about sexual theology inspired me to think about what it meant to theologize from my experience of sexuality. She writes, "Our shared experience of relational power, our sacred experience of sensual power, our erotic experience of the power of God, is the root of our theological epistemology. It is the basis of our knowledge and love of God."[9] Her thinking opened up the possibilities for me of engaging sensuality as an important aspect of my theologizing.

How can feminist theology today, though, create opportunities for queer women to articulate their embodied experiences and images of God? Althaus-Reid's method of indecency is particularly useful as a strategy of inclusion. Based on the belief that all theology is sexual theology steeped in heterosexual ideology, Althaus-Reid's method of *indecenting* interrogates and unmasks the heteronormative ideologies at the center of Christian theological paradigms. She proposes an Indecent Theology, "which problematizes and undresses the mythical layers of multiple oppression in Latin America," by questioning the traditional notions of sexual decency and indecency.[10] She examines these layers of sexual ideology as they are embodied in the structures of the church, theologies, politics, and sexual norms, critiquing the ways that they exclude the most marginalized.

Althaus-Reid challenged feminist theology, and liberation theology in general, to interrogate and reveal the oppressive heterosexual ideologies (we would now say heteronormative ideologies) and discourses of power that regulate women's lives.

---

genre of erotic theology, see Elizabeth Stuart, *Gay and Lesbian Theologies: Repetitions with Critical Difference* (Burlington, VT: Ashgate, 2003), 51–63.
[7] Heyward, *Touching Our Strength*, 3.
[8] Heyward, *Touching Our Strength*, 24.
[9] Heyward, *Touching Our Strength*, 99.
[10] Althaus-Reid, *Indecent Theology*, 2.

It requires sexual honesty to engage the concrete embodied lives of women (especially poor women) when doing theology. For Althaus-Reid, engaging the embodied lives of women—attending to real bodies, especially excluded bodies—means to engage their sexual experience and for these experiences to become part of the contextual thinking that we bring to constructing theology. "Indecenting," then, seeks to find God outside of heterosexual theological constructs of the Christian tradition; it is a praxis the main function of which is to "destabilize the decent order, that is a constructed political, social and sexual order which has been ideologically sacralized, and whose moralizing objective is based on the dyadic reflection on a dyadic God."[11]

How might "indecenting" make queer experiences more visible in the practices of religious communities? A simple practice from the heritage of feminist traditions is telling the stories of women. In the context of religious communities, where heteronormative ideology suffuses the traditions, the simple act of speaking the truth of all women-identified persons in all of our queer experiences—of telling our stories—is a radical act of transgression. It is the radical activism of saying, "We exist," "We are here," and "We will not be pushed away from the faith that sustains us."

In the face of interpretations and doctrines that claim queer is an abomination and sinful, to claim that identification as one rooted in an experience of the Holy *formed in that tradition* is deeply disruptive and radically unsettling of people's experience of heteronormative ideologies that infuse theologies. It forces the experience of contradiction that is essential to the opening of the Spirit of God. That contradiction can make space for compassion and openness to difference. It forces the upheaval: if I see this person as a spiritual person, a child of the faith tradition formed in its ways, and I see that this person is sincere in their conviction, then I must try to make sense in some way of what I have been taught to understand is "indecent."

A powerful example of an inclusive representation of women-identified persons comes from trans scholar Joy Ladin. In *The Soul of the Stranger: Reading God and Torah from a Transgender Perspective*, she engages in reading the Jewish scriptures from

---

[11] Althaus-Reid, "Queer I Stand," 101.

the perspective of her experience as a transgender woman. For her, there was no inherent contradiction between the female she knew herself to be and the God with whom she had a personal relationship: "I'm often asked how I reconcile being religious with being transgender. For me, there has never been a conflict between them. For as long as I can remember, I felt that I was female, and for as long as I can remember, I have sensed God's presence."[12] As she reads through the Torah, she discovers not only the ways in which the Torah can illuminate trans lives but also the ways in which trans lives bring new insights to the Torah. As she engages scripture from her experiences of being female, she enlarges our understanding of what it means to be a woman and our understanding of our relationship with God:

> Male-centered and feminist theologies draw our attention to ways in which God can be understood by analogy to human maleness and femaleness. By extension, expanding our definition of humanity to include transgender people draws our attention to ways in which God can be understood by analogy to transgender lives—the lives of those who, like God, do not fit traditional roles and categories.[13]

For Ladin, the reading of the Torah through the lens of her experience provides the opportunity to expand representation so that a broader and more inclusive understanding of women can be brought to the work of inclusive theologizing.

Unmasking Cis-Heteronormative Theology and Developing New Images

The second strategy for creating a feminist theology that is more inclusive and responsive to queer experiences—strategies for inclusive theological construction—actively generates queer images of God that can be embraced in the practices of religious

---

[12] Joy Ladin, *The Soul of the Stranger: Reading God and Torah from a Transgender Perspective* (Waltham, MA: Brandeis University Press, 2019), 1.
[13] Ladin, *The Soul of the Stranger*, 8.

communities. This task is a major work of deconstruction that requires feminist theology to be in connection with LGBTIQ+ experiences on economic, theological, cultural, and sexual levels. It is the fruit of the type of inclusion for which I am advocating.

For Althaus-Reid, this type of disruption involves queering theology, challenging its heterosexual ideological stance, and creating the opportunity for new theological descriptions to emerge. Queering, as a method of unsettling heteronormative theology, becomes a tool of inclusion that creates the possibility that theology can be in better conversation with the plurality of lived experiences that people have as sexual and social beings. Queering theology builds upon the work of indecency critiques and deconstruction. It requires not just an unmasking of theology but also the honesty and courage of the theologian to unmask those same dynamics of heteronormativity in themselves: "By theological queering, we mean the deliberate questioning of heterosexual experience which has shaped our understanding of theology, the role of the theologian and hermeneutics."[14] To queer theology, according to Althaus-Reid, is to reflect upon the realities of queer love, bodies, and desires. It forces theology to "un-shape Totalitarian Theology (T-Theology) [theology as ideology] while re-shaping the theologian."[15]

As I reflect upon my journey as a feminist queer practical theologian, there is one consistent thread that has helped me to indecent and queer Christian theology and thereby create new images of God. It is a thread that is both traditional and radical at the same time: the wisdom of the spiritual traditions and discernment methods. A consistent and lively engagement with the inner life of the spirit has fueled my capacity to indecent and queer the oppressive elements of heteronormative Christian theology. That statement is in itself deeply disruptive and destabilizing! Spiritual traditions have often been used as a tool to perpetuate and reinforce the heteronormative ideological frameworks of theology. But, in the same way that Christian theology can be domesticated from its radical intent when paired with an oppressive theological construct, embracing its radical message of inclusion, freedom, and love can empower critique and resistance to exclusive heteronormative theologies.

---

[14] Marcella Althaus-Reid, *The Queer God* (New York: Routledge, 2003), 2.
[15] Althaus-Reid, *The Queer God*, 8.

Through an engaged and vibrant awareness of the life of the Spirit, nurtured and lived out in the community, I found an understanding of God's acceptance of me and, just as importantly, my acceptance of myself through the integration of spirituality, sexuality, and gender. This has been foundational. In essence, through the practices of spiritual discernment, I found my acceptance and a place with God—if not with the church—that supported my efforts to indecent and queer the tradition. I experienced the freedom to take a critical stance that challenged the exclusivity of the oppressive theological constructs of T-Theology and created a new image of God that fuels my theological perspectives and actions. This is the constructive aspect of indecenting. It is the ability to expand theology and to facilitate the emergence of varying theologies and sexualities based in lived experiences. As Thia Cooper interprets Althaus-Reid, "Indecency shows us that our realities and our frameworks do not match; hence, we need to prioritize reality ... Rather than craft theology and then repeatedly fail to enact it, since it does not relate to reality, we should begin with our realities, analyzing how we relate to God."[16]

The Queer Icons of artist Gabriel Garcia Roman are powerful images of theological construction that is inclusive of queer bodies, experiences, and lives.[17] Drawing on diverse queer and trans persons and their experiences, the artist transforms these figures by imaging them in the style of religious icons. This representation of queer and trans lives upends our traditional notion of saints that includes queerness in sacred imagery. This work makes space in the tradition to reimagine the lives of LGBTIQ+ persons in religious traditions in our imagery of the sacred.

Embracing Queer Desire as a Praxis of Justice

In her discussion of Althaus-Reid as a feminist, queer theologian, Linn Marie Tonstad comments, "If theology told the truth, it would

---

[16] Thia Cooper, *Queer and Indecent: An Introduction to the Theology of Marcella Althaus-Reid* (London: SCM Press, 2021), 105.
[17] Gabriel Garcia Roman, *Queer Icons*, http://www.gabrielgarciaroman.com/about (accessed April 7, 2024).

speak of bodies, of flesh."[18] Althaus-Reid's work pushes theology to tell the truth about bodies, sexuality, and desire, using this as a way to understand the God who is revealed to us in and through those embodied experiences. She views this as a "coming out" experience: "an Indecent Theology should also come from sexual transgression, or 'Coming Out' stories; the experience of finding one's own sexual identity in community."[19] A renewed feminist theology as inclusive radical praxis seeks to create representation and develop inclusive theological constructions that can "come out" to include the stories of all women-identified persons in all of their diverse intersectionality and lived experiences.

Queer persons navigate and negotiate the complexities of disclosure of their identities within contexts where the assumptions are heteronormative. This dynamic reality is foundational in the lived experience of many LGBTIQ+ persons. I have described this dynamic as "embracing a fluid understanding of the constant movement between being out and being in the closet, disclosure and hiddenness, revelation and covering."[20] Our capacity to speak and act with truthfulness and authenticity anchors our fluid movements between disclosure and hiddenness in our lived experience. Coming out, then, is not a declaration of a category of identity but rather "an erotic ethical practice of truth-telling" and, therefore, articulates an ethical action that is based in our body, passion, and sexuality.[21] I have named this understanding of coming out as "disruptive coherence," an action of embodied truth-telling that disrupts heteronormative structures, while also creating a greater sense of wholeness and coherence in a person's life.[22]

What did I come to know about the God who was revealed to me through my embodied queer experience? In order to reflect on this question, I will return to my coming out experience that

---

[18] Tonstad, *Queer Theology*, 78.
[19] Althaus-Reid, *Indecent Theology*, 21.
[20] Kathleen T. Talvacchia, *Embracing Disruptive Coherence: Coming Out as Erotic Ethical Practice* (Eugene, OR: Cascade Books, 2019), 3.
[21] Talvacchia, *Embracing Disruptive Coherence*, 5–6.
[22] "[A] transgressive action of embodied truth-telling that is formed from moral convictions for the purpose of resisting normative discourses that perpetuate injustice." See Talvacchia, *Embracing Disruptive Coherence*, 85.

I spoke about earlier in this chapter. In that experience, I discovered a God that could speak to my queer experience, one who embraces transgressive truth-telling, affirms our queerness, and provides the grace to live lives of "disruptive coherence" for the work of justice.

In many ways, it was a fairly unusual experience to come out through the Spiritual Exercises of Saint Ignatius, a normative spiritual tradition of my Roman Catholic heritage. I am typically greeted with shocked disbelief when I tell people of my experience; this makes complete sense to me. As Althaus-Reid articulates, theology is thoroughly infused with heterosexual assumptions, normativities, and expectations. Queer persons have been hurt, damaged, and at times brutalized by homophobic and transphobic religious interpretations and actions. Yet, the core intention of the Spiritual Exercises is to comprehend your sense of who you are in relation to God and in relation to freedom. From that perspective, it seems quite possible and not especially unusual for me to have had this experience. This fact gave me an important awareness that God is not bound to ideologies of gender and sexuality that suppress queer experiences; rather, God embraces transgressive truth-telling and authenticity that challenges heteronormative pressures. In the process of wrestling with my identity, it became very clear to me that God affirmed me as I was created, and not only did God not condemn me, but embraced me even more deeply as I came to understand myself and accept its transgressive implications and ramifications more fully. In this way, telling the truth about my body, desires, and passions for love revealed to me a God who was not afraid to disrupt and transgress norms and, thus, would partner with me in living that truth.

The God who embraces us in our transgressive truth-telling also affirms us in our queerness. This is another disruptive and unusual aspect of my coming out experience. I did not go through a process of wrestling with guilt and shame about my identity that often comes with the homophobic and transphobic interpretations of the tradition. At the time that I came out, I had completed several years of theological study in which I learned the tradition and also learned to reflect critically on it. In this sense, feminist theology gave me a perspective that deconstructed patriarchy, and from that base, I could begin to think critically about the structures of cisgender heterosexuality that were so deeply embedded in tradition. Additionally, because I came out from a positive and affirming spiritual experience within Catholicism, I felt empowered through religion, rather than disempowered.

To make such a statement is completely indecent in the way that Althaus-Reid suggests. To believe in a God who affirms our queerness is to unmask the sexual ideologies of gender and sexual heteronormativity that theology has perpetuated. Rather than experiencing a God who would condemn me for my nonconforming gender presentation and my nonnormative sexuality, I came to understand a God who affirms that difference and views it as a sacred aspect of my personhood. And in that awareness, I understood that my queer life helped me to affirm something new about how we come to know God in the human community. There is an irony here: to be seen as queer in heteronormative structures is to be seen *as* indecent (an ethical characteristic); to thrive in that transgression as an affirmation of God and as a new image of God is *to* indecent (the method of deconstruction). God works with what the world views as normal and upends it in order for justice to flourish.

Finally, choosing to live openly as a queer person helped me to know a God who provides grace to live lives of "disruptive coherence" for the work of justice. Coming out helped me to experience a God who wants me to thrive in my queerness, to be empowered to use my difference to participate in the work of justice. Living authentic lives and telling the truth about our bodies, desires, and experiences is an action of resistance against heteronormative structures that oppress. Ladin states it beautifully:

> God knew who and what I was. God had created me, fitting my mismatched body and soul together ... We were an odd couple, me struggling with a body that didn't feel like mine, God existing beyond all that is, was, and will be. But when it came to relating to human beings, God and I had something in common: neither of us could be seen or understood by those we dwelt among and loved.[23]

This is the power of a God who provides the grace to live "disruptive coherence" for the work of justice—to work for the ability to be

---

[23]Ladin, *The Soul of the Stranger*, 3.

seen, understood, and treated with respect by those with whom we live.

I want to close with a return to the question in the title of this chapter: Can feminist theology be queer? The answer for me is *yes*, provided it is willing to radically expand its understanding of whose experiences and which bodies are represented and its images of God. A feminist theology that can embrace the gender and sexual diversity of queerness—and that can embrace all excluded bodies—as integral to its theologizing is a theology of radical inclusive praxis.

Bibliography

Althaus-Reid, Marcella. *Indecent Theology: Theological Perversions in Sex, Gender and Politics*. New York: Routledge, 2000.
Althaus-Reid, Marcella. *The Queer God*. New York: Routledge, 2003.
Althaus-Reid, Marcella. "Queer I Stand: Lifting the Skirts of God." In *The Sexual Theologian: Essays on Sex, God and Politics*, edited by Marcella Althaus-Reid and Lisa Isherwood, 99–109. New York: T&T Clark, 2004.
Cooper, Thia. *Queer and Indecent: An Introduction to the Theology of Marcella Althaus-Reid*. London: SCM Press, 2021.
Davis, Lisa Selin. *Tomboy: The Surprising History and Future of Girls Who Dare to Be Different*. New York: Hachette, 2020.
Heyward, Carter. *Touching Our Strength: The Erotic as Power and the Love of God*. San Francisco, CA: Harper & Row, 1989.
Ladin, Joy. *The Soul of the Stranger: Reading God and Torah from a Transgender Perspective*. Waltham, MA: Brandeis University Press, 2019.
Stuart, Elizabeth. *Gay and Lesbian Theologies: Repetitions with Critical Difference*. Burlington, VT: Ashgate, 2003.
Talvacchia, Kathleen T. "Disrupting the Theory Practice Binary." In *Queer Christianities: Lived Religion in Transgressive Forms*, edited by Kathleen T. Talvacchia, Michael F. Pettinger, and Mark Larrimore, 184–94. New York: New York University Press, 2015.
Talvacchia, Kathleen T. *Embracing Disruptive Coherence: Coming Out as Erotic Ethical Practice*. Eugene, OR: Cascade Books, 2019.
Talvacchia, Kathleen T. *Queer Christianities: Lived Religion in Transgressive Forms*. Co-edited with Michael F. Pettinger, and Mark Larrimore. New York: New York University Press, 2015.
Tonstad, Linn Marie. *Queer Theology: Beyond Apologetics*. Eugene, OR: Cascade Books, 2016.

2

Embodiment, Identity, and Sexuality: Reproductive and Sexual Justice and Theological Anthropology

Toni M. Bond

The relationship between human embodiment, human identity, and reproduction and sexuality are interconnected within the context of human's relationship with God. The theoretical framework of reproductive and sexual justice (RSJ) provides us with a roadmap to reclaiming individual embodiment rather than being subjects owned by parents, spouses, governments, or other private actors. I elaborate upon the RSJ framework below and connect it to a theological, anthropological doctrine of RSJ.

An Overview of Reproductive and Sexual Justice

In July 1994, I, along with eleven other Black women, coined the term "Reproductive Justice" in Chicago while attending a gathering sponsored by the Ms. Foundation for Women and the Illinois Pro-Choice Alliance.[1] The focus of the conference was the Clinton administration's proposed Health Security Act of 1993 to reform the US health care system. Health care reform was one of three midterm election issues put forth by the Clinton administration, all with far-reaching racial and economic implications for people of color and young people. The other two were a complete overhaul of the welfare system and a crime bill that allocated massive amounts of federal dollars to mass incarceration efforts.

We knew the impact of the two-tiered health care system that existed in the United States through the stories of Black women we advocated on behalf of the communities around the country and from our individual personal struggles to access adequate health care. Unfortunately, the Clinton administration's proposed plan maintained that two-tiered health care system. Although health care reform was the focus of the conference, abortion access took center stage. We were frustrated with mainstream white feminists who continued to prioritize abortion as the primary reproductive health issue that all women faced. We strategized around a course of action that would put federal legislators on notice about the unique reproductive and sexual health concerns of Black women. The result of that meeting was a full-paged signature ad in the *Washington Post* and *Roll Call*.[2] Over a two-month period, we collected the signatures of 836 Black women, including prominent women like Alice Walker, Angela Davis, Supermodel Veronica Webb, and all the current Black female federal legislators.

Calling ourselves the Women of African Descent for Reproductive Justice (WADRJ), we found ourselves on the brink

---

[1]The founding mothers of the reproductive justice movement and their affiliations at the time are Loretta Ross (Center for Democratic Renewal), Toni Bond (Chicago Abortion Fund), Winnette Willis (Chicago Abortion Fund), Terri James (Illinois American Civil Liberties Union), Cynthia Newbille (Black Women's Health Imperative), Reverend Alma Crawford (Religious Coalition for Reproductive Choice), Bisola Marignay (Black Women's Health Imperative), Kim Youngblood (Black Women's Health Imperative), Evelyn Field (National Council of Negro Women), Cassandra McConnell (Planned Parenthood of Greater Cleveland), "Able" Mable Thomas (Pro-Choice Resource Center), and Elizabeth Terry (National Abortion Rights Action League of Pennsylvania).
[2]*Roll Call* is a Washington, DC, newspaper reporting on legislative news on Capitol Hill.

of a pivotal moment for organizing and mobilizing Black women. Reproductive justice caused a paradigm shift in how women of color would add their collective voices to the fight for reproductive autonomy and freedom.[3] After years of trying to collaborate with reproductive health and rights movements, we decided to center ourselves. Centering ourselves set the groundwork for Black women to no longer remain on the margins of the reproductive health and rights movements. Instead, we centered our lived experiences and positioned ourselves as leaders in a new movement that places the spotlight on the lives of women of color. The name WADRJ "spoke to the injustices of the current health system that denied women of color full services due to compounded issues of race, class, and gender."[4] WADRJ also reflected our awareness that Black women needed access to comprehensive reproductive health care, including safe, affordable abortion services, but that abortion access was one of a host of reproductive and sexual health issues confronting Black women.[5] We coined the phrase "reproductive justice" from the concepts of reproductive rights, social justice, and human rights as a way of centering the specific lived experiences of Black women when neither the mainstream women's rights movement or the civil rights movement was able to adequately address the reproductive health experiences that Black women face. As the theory was further developed, an intersectional and Black feminist lens was applied to the analysis to better illustrate how race, class, and gender functioned simultaneously to produce an integrative form of reproductive and sexual oppression.

In addition to the call for comprehensive reproductive health care, our statement also demanded that any health care plan must (1) include universal coverage and access to health services, (2) be comprehensive, and (3) provide protection from discriminatory practices that deny health care on the basis of race, class, gender, or sexual

---

[3]Toni Bond Leonard, "Laying the Foundation for a Reproductive Justice Movement," in *Radical Reproductive Justice: Foundation, Theory, Practice, Critique*, ed. Loretta Ross, Lynn Roberts, Erika Derkas, Whitney Peoples, and Pamela Bridgewater (New York: Feminist Press, 2017), 40.
[4]Bond Leonard, "Laying the Foundation," 40.
[5]Bond Leonard, "Laying the Foundation," 40.

orientation.⁶ Finally, we demanded that Black women be represented on local, state, and national bodies involved in the planning, review, and decision-making processes about health care reform.⁷

RSJ centers the lived experiences and human rights of all individuals on reproductive and sexual autonomy and liberation as its goal. Grounded in Black feminist thought and the human rights framework, RSJ recognizes the particularities of the individual and, at the same time, is applicable to everyone. Black women developed the concept of RSJ as a strategy to challenge and dismantle white supremacy and population control. Reproductive and sexual autonomy includes the agency to be self-governing over one's body, which is inclusive of the moral agency to decide to have a child, to not have a child, and to experience sexual pleasure. RSJ theory in practice prioritizes the bodily and sexual autonomy of the individual and acknowledges them as a moral agent with reasoning capabilities and the free will to be self-determining about their reproductive and sexual lives.⁸

RSJ is abolitionist work. The work not only encompasses ending reproductive and sexual oppression but also advocates for the dismantling of systemic racism, white supremacy, Christian nationalism and exceptionalism, and other forms of systemic oppression that impede access to the socioeconomic supports that many communities lack, especially Black, Indigenous, and people of color. The theory rests upon four key pillars.

Four Core Principles of Reproductive Justice

- The Right to Have a Child

    The right to have a child is equally as important as the right to decide not to have a child. RSJ addresses the impact of structural racism and white supremacy that preclude women

---

⁶Bond Leonard, "Laying the Foundation," 42.
⁷Bond Leonard, "Laying the Foundation," 42.
⁸Loretta J. Ross, "Conceptualizing Reproductive Justice: A Manifesto for Action," in *Radical Reproductive Justice: Foundation, Theory, Practice, Critique*, ed. Loretta J. Ross, Lynn Roberts, Erika Derkas, Whitney Peoples, and Pamela D. Bridgewater (New York: The Feminist Press at the City University of New York, 2017), 171.

from having healthy pregnancies, delivery outcomes free of complications, and even infertility issues. It challenges the dominant cultural and social expectations about motherhood and parenthood that rely on middle-class ideals of who should reproduce. The right to have a child includes women and pregnant-capable people being able to make key decisions about their birthing experiences, the right to receive support from a doula or midwife, access to pre- and post-natal care, postpartum care, and access to various forms of assisted reproductive technologies to support them to have a child.

- The Right Not to Have a Child

    Like the right to have a child, the second principle of RSJ is also much more comprehensive than just the right to have an abortion. It includes access to person-controlled, barrier methods of contraception and the ability to access those methods free of force or coercion. The US history of sterilization abuse of women of color has taken on myriad forms and has been especially egregious. From the targeting of women deemed mentally incompetent and Latina immigrants to using sterilization and long-acting reversible contraception (LARC) methods as financial incentives to welfare recipients to control their childbearing, governmental and private actors have sought to rob poor women and women of color of their procreative ability. At the same time, the Supreme Court's June 24, 2022, decision in the *Dobbs v. Jackson Women's Health Organization* further robbed women and pregnant-capable persons of their reproductive and sexual autonomy by overturning *Roe v. Wade*, a 50-year precedent that protected the federal right to obtain an abortion. The overturning of *Roe* set the stage for trigger bans on abortion in some states and for anti-choice legislators to pass abortion restrictions in other states as early as six weeks.[9]

---

[9] As of August 23, 2023, Alabama, Arizona, Arkansas, Florida, Georgia, Idaho, Indiana, Kentucky, Louisiana, Mississippi, Missouri, Nebraska, North Carolina, North Dakota, Oklahoma, South Carolina, South Dakota, Tennessee, Texas, Utah, West Virginia, and Wisconsin have either restricted or banned abortion. See Oriana González, "Where Abortion Has Been Banned Now That *Roe v. Wade* Is Overturned," *Axios*, August 23, 2023, https://www.axios.com/2022/06/25/abortion-illegal-7-states-more-bans-coming (accessed April 7, 2024).

The RSJ framework also connects pregnancy prevention to the prevention of HIV/AIDS and other sexually transmitted infections. Reproductive justice advocates have argued that an unintended pregnancy is one risk factor in the reproductive lives of women. They stress the importance of dual contraception, especially given the high rates of HIV/AIDS among certain populations. However, until recently, reproductive health and rights activists have focused their attention on reducing unintended pregnancies with little regard for the fact that most women, especially adolescents and younger women, do not dual-contracept. When they do use a dual method of contraception, such as internal and external condoms, it is still used to provide additional protection to prevent an unintended pregnancy and not to reduce the risk of contracting a sexually transmitted infection.[10]

Finally, the second RSJ principle advocates for access to both surgical and medical abortion. RSJ recognizes that access to safe abortion is not merely about the "right" or "choice" to have an abortion. *Roe v. Wade* may have affirmed the constitutional right to have an abortion, but rights without access placed abortion out of reach for poor women, women of color, many undocumented immigrants, and young women.

- The Right to Parent the Child(ren) One Already Has

The right to parent the child(ren) one already has encompasses providing families with the social and economic support they need so that families can do more than just survive but also thrive. This includes receiving living wages, access to clean water, healthy food, and affordable housing. It also includes living in areas that are free from environmental toxins.

From 2019 to 2021, 15 percent of children in the United States lived in food insecure homes—meaning their families

---

[10] Julie Lemoine, Stephanie B. Teal, Marissa Peters, and Maryam Guiahi, "Motivating Factors for Dual-Method Contraceptive Use among Adolescents and Young Women: A Qualitative Investigation," *Contraception* 96, no. 5 (2017), https://doi.org/10.1016/j.contraception.2017.06.011.

lacked the financial resources to purchase enough food to meet the family's nutritional needs.[11] Working families that do not qualify for governmental food assistance programs experience some of the greatest challenges to accessing food. Several factors can plunge a family into a food insecurity situation. A layoff or being fired, a major illness befalling a working family member, or an unexpected expense like a car repair or major medical bills can plunge a family into economic insecurity.

- The Right to Sexual Pleasure
RSJ activists began to expand the theory to include the right to sexual pleasure with SisterSong Women of Color Reproductive Justice Collective's second national conference in Chicago called "Let's Talk About Sex."[12] One of the central themes of the conference was the right to have sexual pleasure without procreation. Because abortion and family planning had been the primary foci of the reproductive health and rights movements, activists wanted to expand RSJ theory to include the human right to sexual pleasure and create a pro-sex space within the reproductive health, rights, and justice movements.[13] Younger RSJ activists have broadened the right to sexual pleasure analysis to include fluidity of sexuality and gender nonconformity. Groups like SisterLove and Black Women for Reproductive Justice (BWRJ),[14] an organization that was based in Chicago, prioritized sex education and sexual pleasure as core strategies of their missions.

---

[11] The Annie E. Casey Foundation, "Nearly 11 Million Kids Face Food Insecurity as Statistic Dips to 20-Year Low," *KIDS COUNT® Data Book*, Baltimore, MD (2022).
[12] Headquartered in Atlanta, GA, the SisterSong Women of Color Reproductive Justice Collective is a national organization dedicated to reproductive justice for women of color.
[13] Loretta Ross, "Understanding Reproductive Justice: Transforming the Pro-Choice Movement," *Off Our Backs* 36, no. 4 (2006): 14–19, http://www.jstor.org/stable/20838711.
[14] Founded in 1996 by Toni Bond and Winnette Willis, the Black Women for Reproductive Justice was the first Black women's reproductive justice organization in the country. The organization closed its doors in September 2011 due to lack of funding. Black Women for Reproductive Justice, "BWRJ Health Education," https://bwrj.wordpress.com/category/ssex/.

Individual Human Rights and Governmental Obligations

Reproductive justice theory offers RSJ activists a framework for expanding the discourse beyond what they are against and, instead, discusses what conditions are needed to ensure that people are able to be reproductively and sexually healthy, have healthy families, and live in healthy communities. The four human rights values of RSJ—the right not to have a child, the right to have a child, the right to parent the child(ren) one already has, and the right to sexual pleasure and bodily autonomy—are based on the human right to make personal decisions about one's life and the obligation of governments and societies to ensure that the conditions exist for individuals to realize the human rights values of RSJ.[15] For example, reproductive justice theory sees the right to have a child through access to safe abortion as both a negative and a positive human right. The state has a negative duty not to interfere with an individual's right to decide not to have a child. But merely the right to use contraceptives to control one's fertility and the right to decide to have an abortion are not enough. A key aspect of the human right to control one's fertility places a negative duty on the government that goes beyond not interfering with an individual exercising their right not to have a child. For sure, the overturning of *Roe* violates this right because the right to choose to have an abortion is no longer protected under the US Constitution. Through the lens of RSJ, the government has a positive duty to create the enabling conditions that support individuals' reproductive autonomy and, thus, an obligation through regulations to make abortion services safe, affordable, and accessible. It also has a negative duty not to interfere with that right through undue and burdensome government restrictions that make it impossible for women and pregnant-capable persons to realize that right. The decision of the Supreme Court of the United States to overturn

---

[15] Loretta J. Ross, Lynn Roberts, Erika Derkas, Whitney Peoples, and Pamela D. Bridgewater, eds., *Radical Reproductive Justice: Foundation, Theory, Practice, Critique* (New York: The Feminist Press at the City University of New York, 2017), 14.

Roe places an undue burden upon women and pregnant-capable persons and impedes their ability to be reproductively autonomous. The RSJ analysis argues that there are both positive and negative duties and rights that must be applied around the human right to have a child. Black women die of pregnancy-related causes at a rate that is three times higher than for white women.[16] While the government cannot tell a woman to become pregnant, it does have a responsibility to make sure maternal health care is safe, affordable, and accessible. Through an RSJ analysis, the government has not only failed in fulfilling its positive duty to investigate why conditions that contribute to Black maternal health disparities exist but also failed to correct them.

The third pillar of reproductive justice addresses the right to raise children with the social and economic support they need to not just survive but also to thrive and live free from fear of violence by governmental and private actors. Again, this third pillar is viewed by RSJ advocates as both a positive and a negative right. The excessive monitoring and surveillance of Black and brown people, the stop-and-frisk laws that target young Black and brown men, and the targeted incarceration of people of color all violate the negative rights of individuals to live their lives without interference from the government in ways that violate their personal liberties.

In the fourth and last pillar of RSJ, advocates argue that every human being has the right to sexual pleasure and bodily autonomy. The right to sexual pleasure can likewise be seen as both a positive and a negative right. In fulfilling its duty to ensure a minimal standard of health care, the state, thus, has a positive obligation to provide comprehensive, evidence-based sexuality education that includes information and education about sexual pleasure as a part of human sexuality. According to the Guttmacher Institute, only thirty-nine states and the District of Columbia mandate some form of sex education and/or HIV education.[17]

---

[16] Centers for Disease Control and Prevention, "Working Together to Reduce Black Maternal Mortality," April 3, 2023, https://www.cdc.gov/healthequity/features/maternal-mortality/index.html.

[17] Guttmacher Institute, "Sex and HIV Education," February 18, 2020, https://www.guttmacher.org/state-policy/explore/sex-and-hiv-education.

Race Used to Deny Black Women's Embodied Existence

Somebody owned our flesh, and decided if and when and with whom and how our bodies were to be used. Somebody said that Black women could be raped, held in concubinage, forced to bear children year in and year out, but often not raise them. Oh yes, we have known how painful it is to be without choice in this land … . Now once again somebody is trying to say that we can't handle the freedom of choice … . Somebody's saying that we should not have the freedom to take charge of our personal lives and protect our health, that we have limited rights over our bodies.[18]

The human right to be self-governing over one's body has been elusive to women of color, especially Black women in the United States. While Black women are not a homogenous group, the relationship of the United States to Black women has historically been one of control and ownership of Black women's sexuality and reproduction through enslavement, punitive welfare measures, the erosion of governmental safety net support, and violence by governmental and other private actors. Black women have been challenged to fully experience what it means to be an embodied

---

[18] "We Remember: African American Women Are for Reproductive Freedom," Planned Parenthood, https://100years.plannedparenthood.org/content/images/era-4/WeRememberBrocure.pdf. In 1989, incensed by the court's sanctioning of governmental interference in women's reproductive decision-making, sixteen Black women issued a public statement in response to the *Webster* decision with a pamphlet entitled, "We Remember: African American Women Are for Reproductive Freedom." Coordinated by political strategist, Donna Brazile (the then executive director of the National Political Congress of Black Women (NPCBW) and written by Marcia Ann Gillespie (the then editor-in-chief of *Ms. Magazine*), the pamphlet gave Black women permission to talk about their abortions without shame or judgment. Powerful Black women like Rev. Willie Barrow (Operation Push), Shirley Chisholm (NPCBW), Faye Wattleton (Planned Parenthood Federation of America), and Illinois US Congresswoman Cardiss Collins signed on to the statement. "We Remember" outlined Black women's historical struggle for reproductive freedom and discussed the racial and economic impact of the government's efforts to regulate their wombs.

being, fully embracing our conscious selves because our humanity has been denied. Catholic theologian M. Shawn Copeland relates the body and its inscription within a theological, anthropological context that examines the relationships between the social and physical body. Copeland offers that the body "is an essential quality of the soul."[19] Copeland situates the body as the site of divine revelation.[20] There is an ontological correlation between the social and physical body that calls for freedom and human sacrament.

Yet, the Black body, especially the bodies of Black women, has never been recognized as autonomous, free, or sacred. To experience embodiment, one must be able to feel ownership over the embodied self. The European Enlightenment period bestowed the white male with the attributes of rational thinking and reasoning capabilities. Enlightenment thinkers prioritized individual freedoms and rights, and at the same time, sanctioned (or at best were neutral or ambiguous about) colonial domination and propagated notions of race and racism. Philosopher Charles Mills argues that Enlightenment thinkers like Immanuel Kant, for example, played a pivotal role in substantiating whiteness as a "prerequisite for full personhood" and assigning subhuman status to nonwhites.[21] In *Physische Geographie*, Kant notes that

> The race of the Negroes, one could say, is completely the opposite of the Americans; they are full of affect and passion, very lively, talkative and vain. They can be educated but only as servants (slaves), that they allow themselves to be trained. They have many motivating forces, are also sensitive, are afraid of blows and do much out of a sense of honor.[22]

The Christian church codified this conceptualization of humans and whiteness in the likeness of the *imago Dei*. Thus, there is no

---

[19] M. Shawn Copeland, *Enfleshing Freedom: Body, Race, and Human Being* (Minneapolis, MN: Fortress Press, 2010), 7.
[20] Copeland, *Enfleshing Freedom*, 8.
[21] Charles W. Mills, *Black Rights/White Wrongs the Critique of Racial Liberalism* (New York: Oxford University Press, 2017), 92–3.
[22] Mills, *Black Rights/White Wrongs*, 92–3.

escaping the fact that the Enlightenment or Age of Reason laid the groundwork for the conceptualization of scientific racism.

Indeed, humans are imbued by God with free will, and because of that free will, we can make moral decisions. We are moral agents favored with the free will to make decisions about our lives and our bodies. Where the biblical text says that God created humankind in God's own image, male and female, there is no wording that says God created men to have dominion over women.[23] As it is written, the implication is that God created male and female, man and woman, equally. Meaning, that man and woman each have free will and agency, both are in the likeness of the *imago Dei*, have the ability to make moral decisions, and both are moral agents. Correspondingly, in the likeness of the *imago Dei* is without the social construct of race.

What does becoming human mean in a world where racial, socioeconomic, gender, and morality constructs dictate the lived realities of humanity, especially that of Black women and pregnant-capable persons and other people of color? What does it mean to be free to enjoy one's embodiment? In the Christian tradition, perspectives about sexual pleasure and passion tend to be more conservative, feeding into a soul versus body duality, which is counterintuitive to the nature of the relationship between the *imago Dei* and humanity. Religious and theological anthropology scholar Marc Cortez points out that sexuality is a core aspect of human existence and "a natural and essential aspect of humanity."[24] Humans, as subjects of our own sexuality, have reproductive and sexual autonomy, the right to give consent and the obligation to seek it, the right to utilize our individual conscience and reasoning to engage in processes of discernment about our reproductive and sexual activity, and the right to assess individual risks and to exercise fairness in sexual encounters.

God imbues us with free will at birth, which, once we are born, connects with our ability to be self-determining and to exercise free will. Irenaeus of Lyons argued that God imbues humans with all that they are and all that they will become. He writes,

---

[23]Gen. 1:27, New Revised Standard Version.
[24]Marc Cortez, *Theological Anthropology: A Guide for the Perplexed* (New York: T&T Clark International, 2010), Kindle.

How, then, shall he be a God, who has not as yet been made a man? Or how can he be perfect who was but lately created? How, again, can he be immortal, who in his mortal nature did not obey his Maker? For it must be that you, at the outset, should hold the rank of a man, and then afterwards partake of the glory of God. For you did not make God, but God you.[25]

Therefore, a theological, anthropological doctrine of RSJ connects God's creation of humans to the free will imbued within them to their ability to consent. It recognizes the humanity of every individual and that every individual has been created by and fashioned in the image of God.

Our personhood and fashioning in the *imago Dei* is inclusive of autonomy, self-determination, and the ability to consent. These three aspects are at the very core of who we are as humans, in God's image, and in relationship with God and the free will with which we are imbued. In the case of reproductive and sexual autonomy, humans were created with sexual organs to experience and enjoy sexual pleasure. As we mature, we gain knowledge about God, ourselves, and our relationship to the divine. It is our God-given free will that enables us to make decisions about and consent to not only our sexual encounters but also to be self-determining about whether to birth a child or to terminate a pregnancy. To that end, RSJ, with its grounding in human rights, recognizes the whole individual as an embodied being with moral agency and authority. In the section that follows, I outline the aspects of a theological, anthropological doctrine of RSJ that further codifies humans as embodied sexual beings created in the image of God with moral agency and the free will to be self-determining about their reproductive and sexual lives.

A Theological, Anthropological Doctrine of Reproductive and Sexual Justice

A theological, anthropological doctrine of RSJ must consider what it means to violate our status as humans made in the image of God. At the same time, it must also consider those individuals who lack

---

[25]Irenaeus, *Against Heresies*, XXXIX.2 (*ANF* 1:522).

the mental capacity to make decisions about whether and how they give consent to a sexual encounter or decide whether to have a child.

A theological, anthropological doctrine of RSJ requires the following:

1. An acknowledgment and valuing of individual human identity, human existence, and personhood.
2. An affirmation of sexuality as fundamental to human existence.
3. An affirmation that human sexuality and reproduction must not be forced or coerced. It recognizes the potential for abuses of power and exploitation and identifies the sinfulness of those acts.
4. An understanding that sexuality and relationality are connected. Consent must be sought in order to authentically fulfill the fundamental need to be in a relationship with another, with the understanding that a sexual encounter is just one of many ways to be in the relationship.
5. Nonconsensual sexual activity defiles an individual's humanity. When there is consent, there is no intent to harm in the sexual encounter and no desire to exercise power over or subjugate another individual. Lack of consent and the desire to subjugate another individual is sinful because it alienates humans from each other and the community.
6. Impeding individual self-determination and autonomy also defiles individual humanity and is counterintuitive to the free will humans are imbued with when they are created by God.
7. Each individual has been created in the divine image of God, to be in a relationship with God and the community. It is sinful to force, coerce, or mislead humans about their reproduction and sexuality because it devalues them and God and disrupts the sacred relationship between the individual and God. Force, coercion, and deception also alienate humans from each other and the community.
8. It acknowledges that with respect to teenage sexuality, the levels of maturity may vary. Not everyone matures at the same level. Teenagers, like adults, are fully human and sexual beings who also have a fundamental need to be in a relationship

with another. Sometimes, that fundamental need is to connect through a sexual relationship or encounter.
9. There is no one way to express human sexuality. Human sexuality fulfills humans' need to be in a relationship with another. Fulfillment of the human need for relationality may be through encounters that are heterosexual or LBGTQIA+. Denigration of sexual acts that do not fit within the confines of heteronormativity is sinful because it devalues the individual human identity that each human is created by God.
10. The fundamental need of humans to be sexual and to be in a relationship with another does not rest upon the requirement that sex is only in a marital relationship between a man and a woman, nor only for the purposes of procreation. To require the above is sinful because it affirms a gender essentialism that denies that God created humans as sexual beings and the fundamental need of humans to be sexual and experience their full embodiment.

Notwithstanding the above, there remains the issue of when there is no consent and sexual autonomy has been violated, which we have identified as a sinful act. Thus, a theosis or transformative process is required to restore individuals to the image of God (*imago Dei*) and wholeness. Again, guidance can be found in Irenaeus and his recapitulation theory of atonement. Irenaeus writes,

> For I have shown that the Son of God did not then begin to exist, being with the Father from the beginning; but when He became incarnate, and was made man, He commenced afresh the long line of human beings, and furnished us, in a brief, comprehensive manner, with salvation; so that what we had lost in Adam—namely, to be according to the image and likeness of God—that we might recover in Christ Jesus.[26]

For the purposes of constructing a theological, anthropological doctrine of RSJ, Irenaeus' recapitulation theory of atonement, which focuses on Christ's atonement as a way to reverse the wrongs of humanity to rightness and reconnect humans with the *imago Dei*,

---

[26] Irenaeus, *Against Heresies*, XVIII.2 (*ANF* 1:446).

does not go far enough because it does not explicitly address the harm realized by others as a result of humanity's sins. A theological, anthropological doctrine of RSJ affirms reproductive and sexual autonomy and also acknowledges the suffering experienced through forms of reproductive and sexual oppression in order to fully realize restoration to wholeness for the individual and the broader community.

Sexual activity is not just relegated to the physical act between individuals. It also includes experiencing the sensation of pleasure and circles back to the body as a sight and source of pleasure of the individual through self-pleasuring acts like masturbation, as well as through engaging in sexual activity with another to fulfill the human desire to be in a relationship with another. Cortez posits that relationality is connected to sexuality.[27] Humans have a fundamental need to connect with each other. Our sexuality is one way of expressing and fulfilling that need for relationality. It is important to note, however, that the relationality that humans seek is not just satisfied through sexual encounters, but it can also be satiated through nonsexual relationships as well.

Conclusion

A theological, anthropological doctrine of RSJ moves humanity toward reproductive and sexual liberation, autonomy, and self-determination. It recognizes that just as young people have the moral capacity to exercise agency around their sexuality, teenage girls also have the capacity to parent a child if provided the support outlined in the RSJ theoretical framework. It counters the guilt that has been associated with premarital sex, teenage pregnancy and teenage sexuality, abortion, and/or the use of contraception and assisted reproductive technologies with sinlessness. It situates shame where it belongs, with oppressive theology. Guilt and shame are, thus, clarified as tools of oppression to keep sexual beings from being reproductively and sexually liberated. Realizing the full humanity that God created humans with recognizes that women and pregnant-capable people have the moral agency to make decisions about their

---

[27]Cortez, *Theological Anthropology*, Kindle.

procreative liberty, free from human interferences that attempt to stand in the way of their reproductive and sexual autonomy. This holds especial significance for Black women whose humanity has historically been denied and, as a result, have had their ability to exercise procreative liberty to be in creative partnership with God around their pregnancies disrupted. Any corruption of human reproductive and sexual self-determination and autonomy disrupts the relationship between humans and God and is, thus, sinful.

Bibliography

The Annie E. Casey Foundation. "Nearly 11 Million Kids Face Food Insecurity as Statistic Dips to 20-Year Low." *KIDS COUNT® Data Book*, Baltimore, MD, 2022.

The Ante-Nicene Fathers: Translations of the Writings of the Fathers Down to A.D. 325. Edited by Alexander Roberts and James Donaldson. 10 vols. 1885–7. Reprint. Grand Rapids, MI: Eerdmans, 1989.

Black Women for Reproductive Justice. "BWRJ Health Education." https://bwrj.wordpress.com/category/ssex/.

Centers for Disease Control and Prevention. "Working Together to Reduce Black Maternal Mortality," April 3, 2023. https://www.cdc.gov/healthequity/features/maternal-mortality/index.html.

Copeland, M. Shawn. *Enfleshing Freedom: Body, Race, and Human Being*. Minneapolis, MN: Fortress Press, 2010.

Cortez, Marc. *Theological Anthropology: A Guide for the Perplexed*. New York: T&T Clark International, 2010. Kindle.

González, Oriana. "Where Abortion Has Been Banned Now That *Roe v. Wade* Is Overturned," *Axios*, August 23, 2023, https://www.axios.com/2022/06/25/abortion-illegal-7-states-more-bans-coming, accessed April 7, 2024.

Guttmacher Institute. "Sex and HIV Education," February 18, 2020. https://www.guttmacher.org/state-policy/explore/sex-and-hiv-education.

Lemoine, Julie et al. "Motivating Factors for Dual-Method Contraceptive Use among Adolescents and Young Women: A Qualitative Investigation." *Contraception* 96, no. 5 (2017), https://doi.org/10.1016/j.contraception.2017.06.011.

Leonard, Toni Bond. "Laying the Foundation for a Reproductive Justice Movement." In *Radical Reproductive Justice: Foundation, Theory, Practice, Critique*, edited by Loretta Ross, Lynn Roberts, Erika Derkas,

Whitney Peoples, and Pamela Bridgewater, 39–49. New York: Feminist Press, 2017.

Mills, Charles W. *Black Rights/White Wrongs the Critique of Racial Liberalism.* New York: Oxford University Press, 2017.

Planned Parenthood. "We Remember: African American Women Are for Reproductive Freedom." https://100years.plannedparenthood.org/content/images/era-4/WeRememberBrocure.pdf.

Ross, Loretta. "Conceptualizing Reproductive Justice: A Manifesto for Action." In *Radical Reproductive Justice: Foundation, Theory, Practice, Critique*, edited by Loretta J. Ross, Lynn Roberts, Erika Derkas, Whitney Peoples, and Pamela D. Bridgewater, 170–232. New York: The Feminist Press at the City University of New York, 2017.

Ross, Loretta. "Introduction." In *Radical Reproductive Justice: Foundation, Theory, Practice, Critique*, edited by Loretta J. Ross, Lynn Roberts, Erika Derkas, Whitney Peoples, and Pamela D. Bridgewater. New York: The Feminist Press at the City University of New York, 2017.

Ross, Loretta. "Understanding Reproductive Justice: Transforming the Pro-Choice Movement." *Off Our Backs* 36, no. 4 (2006): 14–19. http://www.jstor.org/stable/20838711.

3

Challenging the Notion of Presumptive Motherhood

Margaret D. Kamitsuka

Motherhood is the hardest of all jobs.[1] Mothers appreciate it when people acknowledge their challenging, lifelong, and unpaid labor of gestating, giving birth, and raising children. So profound is the work of mothering that it functions as an evocative metaphor for theological reflection.[2] Feminist theology finds resources deep in the Christian tradition that analogize the generative and life-shaping nature of motherhood to divine creativity. Medieval mystic Julian of Norwich asserted: "To the quality of motherhood belongs natural love, wisdom and knowledge—and this is God."[3] To speak of motherhood is to gesture toward the divine.

---

[1] An early version of this chapter was presented as a keynote lecture at the American Academy of Religion 2020 workshop on "Motherhood and Religion." My thanks to the conference organizers, Florence Pasche Guignard and Pascale Engelmajer. Eleanor Barkhorn, "There's No Tougher Job Than Being a Mom: The Long History of a Ubiquitous Statement," *Atlantic*, July 11, 2013.
[2] Activities associated with mothering are also done by childfree "other mothers." Stephanie R. Buckhanon Crowder, *When Momma Speaks: The Bible and Motherhood from a Womanist Perspective* (Louisville, KY: Westminster John Knox, 2016), 11–13.
[3] Julian of Norwich, quoted in Lyn Holness, "Motherhood and Spirituality: Faith Reflections from the Inside," *Agenda* 18, no. 61 (2004): 66.

In conservative Christian circles, however, motherhood is seen differently: less as a window on God's nature, more as a window on the womb. Motherhood is hailed as a woman's divinely intended nature because "a woman's physical capacity to give birth points to [her] spiritual purpose and calling ... . what God has 'hardwired' women to do."[4] A pious, fertile wife should prioritize using her body for procreative purposes. The phrase "motherhood is the hardest of all jobs" may entail an unspoken pronatalist sentiment among conservative family-values Christians. Procreation, in these Christian communities, is something few married women are praised for avoiding. Once a mother, she rarely finds support for wanting to be relieved of those duties. The pregnant believer is shamed for ending her mothering responsibilities before she gives birth.

Conservative Christianity's views on motherhood are linked to their views on fetal personhood. Prolife theologians interpret God as "creatively involved from the very beginning" of human conception—meaning, "every human being thus receives a divine call from the first moment he or she begins ... as a newly conceived embryo."[5] That supposedly divinely ordained, personhood-constituting event determines the woman's moral obligation to bring the so-called preborn child to birth, at the very least, and, optimally, to devote her life to its care.

While theologians and ethicists debate the metaphysics of personhood, real women face material realities. Motherhood is not just a demanding job; it entails risks. Pregnancy on the road to motherhood means precarity. Maternal mortality has not disappeared, even in countries with advanced medical care. The rate of maternal mortality in the United States is alarmingly high, especially in states that have implemented restrictive abortion laws after the *Dobbs* Supreme Court decision overturning *Roe v. Wade*.[6] Forced motherhood due to a denied abortion is linked

---

[4]Mary A. Kassian and Nancy Leigh DeMoss, *True Woman 101: Divine Design* (Chicago, IL: Moody, 2012), 188.
[5]David Albert Jones, *The Soul of the Embryo: An Inquiry into the Status of the Human Embryo in the Christian Tradition* (London: Continuum, 2004), 17. See my critique of this position in Margaret D. Kamitsuka, *Abortion and the Christian Tradition: A Pro-Choice Theological Ethic* (Louisville, KY: Westminster John Knox, 2019), 63–8.
[6]"The U.S. Maternal Health Divide: The Limited Maternal Health Services and Worse Outcomes of States Proposing New Abortion Restrictions," Commonwealth

to wealth inequities, meaning mothers in poverty will struggle to meet their family's most basic needs.[7] An intersectional analysis reveals how African American mothers carry the additional burden of the cultural stereotype of being a strong Black maternal figure, who self-sacrifices without complaint and to the detriment of her own well-being.[8] Black mothers also shoulder the painful ancestral knowledge that their enslaved foremothers bore children through violence and under conditions of exploitation and abuse by white masters and mistresses.[9]

Contrary to the conservative Christian assumption that maternity is a believing wife's highest spiritual calling, there are good reasons for women wanting or needing to delay, avoid, or leave mothering duties altogether. Motherhood can be one of the most treasured, meaningful, and spiritual experiences for many believers, but women's stories across the centuries reveal how complicated and even treacherous the idea of presumptive motherhood is.

Part One of the chapter adopts a genealogical method of tracing how suppressed historical women's voices challenge presumptive motherhood in Christianity. That women rejected or abandoned mothering to pursue other spiritual callings provides evidence that when the subaltern does speak (even if sporadically in history),[10] their words coalesce into an "insurrection of subjugated knowledges."[11] This eruption of counter-stories still reverberates

---

Fund (December 14, 2022), https://www.commonwealthfund.org/publications/issue-briefs/2022/dec/us-maternal-health-divide-limited-services-worse-outcomes (accessed March 30, 2023).

[7] "The Harms of Denying a Woman a Wanted Abortion: Findings from the Turnaway Study," ANSIRH, https://www.ansirh.org/sites/default/files/publications/files/the_harms_of_denying_a_woman_a_wanted_abortion_4-16-2020.pdf.

[8] Chanequa Walker-Barnes, *Too Heavy a Yoke: Black Women and the Burden of Strength* (Eugene, OR: Cascade, 2014).

[9] Dorothy E. Roberts, *Killing the Black Body: Race, Reproduction, and the Meaning of Liberty* (New York: Vintage, 1999).

[10] The allusion is to Gayatri Chakravorty Spivak, "Can the Subaltern Speak?" in *Marxism and the Interpretation of Culture*, ed. Cary Nelson and Lawrence Grossberg (London: Macmillan, 1988). Spivak addresses subalternity in the postcolonial setting, but the subaltern can be a metaphor for other identities silenced by hegemonic discourses and excluded from political or economic self-determination.

[11] Michel Foucault, "Two Lectures," *Michel Foucault Power/Knowledge: Selected Interviews and Other Writings 1972–1977*, trans. and ed. Colin Gordon et al. (New York: Pantheon, 1980), 81–2. Genealogy is "the attempt to emancipate historical

in Christian circles today. Part Two discusses two contemporary examples of Christian mothers who transgressed or failed the norms of Christian mothering. The attempt to label these mothers as *bad* and as exceptions to the virtuous maternal rule is another instance of how the myth of presumptive motherhood polices pregnancy-capable people today.

Christian discourses of motherhood weigh heavily on pregnant people—especially those who are labeled as, or themselves wish to comply with, the identity of *woman*. From Simone de Beauvoir to Judith Butler, the term "woman" has been exposed as a construct, but a powerfully constraining one with deep cultural roots.[12] The same is true of the concept of *mother*. Other histories, geographies, subaltern identities, and gender performativities exist, some of which contest the very category of mother. While the body of this chapter analyzes the impact of presumptive motherhood for cisgender women, the conclusion discusses emergent discourses pointing to new avenues for feminist scholarship on diversity in mothering and parenting in the years to come.

Presumptive Motherhood and Women's Historical Counter-Stories

The church has papered over the labor, sacrifice, and historical traumas of mothering and has promoted childbearing as a married woman's essential calling, no matter what her circumstances. Things were not always thus in Christian communities historically. In fact, presumptive motherhood is more a construct than a practice with strong roots in Christianity's origins. The genealogical work of reading between the lines, from ancient hagiography and Apocrypha to early modern women's spiritual autobiography, reveals two competing types of counter-stories: women skirting or leaving maternal roles in favor of a life consecrated to God and

---

knowledges ... to render them ... capable of opposition and of struggle against the coercion of a theoretical, unitary, formal and scientific discourse" (85).
[12]See Simone de Beauvoir, quoted in Judith Butler, *Gender Trouble: Feminism and the Subversion of Identity*, 10th anniv. ed. (New York: Routledge, 2002), 3.

women's resistance to the repeated resurgence of presumptive motherhood.

Leaving Maternal Duties Behind

One set of discourses contesting motherhood intersects with tales of martyrdom in the early church. Persecution of Christians in the Roman Empire was sporadic, but these stories had a great impact.[13] One of the most famous martyr texts recounts the death of two early-third-century young Christian mothers, Perpetua and Felicitas. Sitting in her jail cell, intent on dying for her faith, Perpetua rejected pleas to recant and return home to care for her child.[14] Felicitas gave birth to her infant in prison, proceeding "from the blood and from the midwife to the gladiator."[15] The church praised their faithful sacrifice. Apparently, martyrdom took precedence over presumptive motherhood.

Thecla, the (real or invented) protagonist of the second-century "Acts of Paul and Thecla," rejected overtures to marriage. She set her cap, instead, on taking up a ministry like that of the apostle Paul.[16] She even dressed in men's clothing to facilitate her vocation as an itinerant preacher—a life that also ended in a martyr-like death.[17] While this apocryphal text may have been too radical for inclusion in the New Testament canon, the veneration of Thecla was widespread into the fifth century, not despite her rejection of marriage and motherhood but because of it.[18] Again, presumptive motherhood was not always the norm for female believers.

---

[13] Candida R. Moss, *Ancient Christian Martyrdom: Diverse Practices, Theologies, and Traditions* (New Haven, CT: Yale University Press, 2012).
[14] "Then her father laid [Perpetua's] son upon her shoulder ... . But she threw the infant from her and repulsed her parents, saying: 'Get away from me, you enemies of God, because I do not know you!'" Julia Weitbrecht, "Maternity and Sainthood in the Medieval Perpetua Legend," in *Perpetua's Passions: Multidisciplinary Approaches to the* Passio Perpetuae et Felicitatis, ed. Jan N. Bremmer and Marco Formisano (New York: Oxford University Press, 2012), 162.
[15] "The Acts of Perpetua and Felicitas," VI.1, trans. Roberts-Donaldson, https://www.earlychristianwritings.com/text/tertullian24.html (accessed January 7, 2023).
[16] "Acts of Paul and Thecla," 6:13, trans. Jeremiah Jones, available at: https://sourcebooks.fordham.edu/basis/thecla.asp (accessed January 7, 2023).
[17] "The Acts of Perpetua and Felicitas," 9:25.
[18] Stephen T. Davis, *The Cult of Saint Thecla: A Tradition of Women's Piety in Late Antiquity* (Oxford: Oxford University Press, 2001).

Motherhood means sex. Women's sexuality, in particular, vexed the sex-phobic early church. Eminent church theologians praised the piety of their Christian mothers, separate from and almost in spite of their status as women-who-had-sex-and-became-mothers. Gregory of Nyssa, whose theological discussions with his ascetic, unmarried sister are recounted in his *Life of Macrina*, spoke glowingly of their mother's faith. Her virtue resided in the fact that "she herself 'did not voluntarily choose marriage'" (though once married, she did obediently submit to her husband and to procreative obligations).[19] Gregory's text implies not a presumption of but a concession to sex in marriage. Motherhood was deemed a vocation of lesser spiritual status than the celibate asceticism at which his sister Macrina so excelled.

The church's acceptance and institutionalizing of celibate women living in enclosed religious communities beginning in the fifth and sixth centuries marked the ascendance of the religious life over that of marriage and family. Celibacy as a woman's religious calling was not only extolled by the church hierarchy but also embraced from the grassroots. Women refused marriage (or remarriage after widowhood) and lived celibate lives of enclosure in their family homes or in cloisters.[20] The biblical notion that women would be "saved by childbearing" (1 Tim. 2:15) and the instruction for young widows to marry and have children (1 Tim. 5:4), apparently fell by the wayside in favor of the ideal of a consecrated religious life.

It is safe to assume that ordinary believers having children throughout church history outnumbered those who took the path of celibacy, not to mention martyrdom. Their stories are mostly lost to history since, for the most part, "mothers did not write about motherhood."[21] Mothering for the vast majority of non-elite, premodern women was grindingly hard and endlessly worrisome. Many women died in childbirth or, if they survived, suffered health complications. They watched most of their children perish

---

[19] Davis, *The Cult of Saint Thecla*, 64.
[20] Eliana Magnani and Lochin Brouillard, "Female House Ascetics from the Fourth to the Twelfth Century," in *The Cambridge History of Medieval Monasticism in the Latin West*, ed. Alison I. Beach and Isabelle Cochelin (Cambridge: Cambridge University Press, 2020), 213–31.
[21] Clarissa W. Atkinson, *The Oldest Vocation: Christian Motherhood in the Medieval West* (Ithaca, NY: Cornell University Press, 1991), 26.

in infancy.²² Dutiful mothering came with few church accolades, which were reserved for those consecrated virgins who, through asceticism, attempted to transcend sexuality and the signs of their female fleshiness—and thereby avoided motherhood.²³

Resistance to the Resurgence of Presumptive Motherhood

The Reformation instituted a shift from women's celibacy to marriage and motherhood. Monasteries and convents were disbanded in many Protestant-controlled areas in Europe, leaving former nuns free (and burdened with the obligation) to forge a new life path out in the world on their own. The path of marriage, motherhood, and mistress of one's household may have been welcome for some, such as Katharina von Bora, the indomitable former nun and wife of reformer Martin Luther. However, foreclosing the option of convent life also "stripped women of the opportunities their all-female environment allowed them of higher education and self-expression."²⁴ The window for women pursuing education, writing, teaching, the arts, and liturgical expression was shuttered. The reformers agreed that it was better for women to marry and remain in the domestic sphere where they could fulfill their natural and God-given maternal duties.

The higher the estimation of motherhood as godly, the more demanding and constricting it became. Virtue accrued from the degree of motherly self-sacrifice. Luther, knowing intimately the risks and difficulties of pregnancy,²⁵ nevertheless, did not hesitate to promote motherhood's ultimate sacrifice: "Remember that you are a woman, and that this work of God in you is pleasing to him ... . Work with all your might to bring forth the child. Should it mean

---

[22] Jennifer Lawler, *Encyclopedia of Women in the Middle Ages* (Jefferson, NC: McFarland, 2001), see "Medicine and Health," 121–4.

[23] Teresa M. Shaw, *The Burden of the Flesh: Fasting and Sexuality in Early Christianity* (Minneapolis, MN: Fortress, 1998), chapter 6.

[24] Kirsi Stjerna, *Women and the Reformation* (Malden, MA: Blackwell, 2011), 23–4.

[25] Luther's wife Katharina gave birth to six children between 1526 and 1534 and nearly died from a miscarriage in her forties; see Stjerna, *Women and the Reformation*, 58.

your death, then depart happily, for you will die in a noble deed and in subservience to God."²⁶

Even if one reads this statement charitably (not as a prescription but as Luther's reluctant description of pregnancy risks), the elevation of maternal sacrifice in this way constituted a toxic imposition of presumptive motherhood upon pious Protestant women. This viewpoint continued to resurge and arguably has filtered down to the present day.²⁷

The expectation for procreation in marriage remained strong in Roman Catholic communities, alongside well-established institutionalized celibacy. However, wives did kick against the goad of presumptive and repeated childbearing. Margery Kemp, an early-fifteenth-century English mystic, wife, and reluctant mother of fourteen living children, found herself in deep despair over becoming pregnant—again. She prayed to Christ, bemoaning her condition, saying, "Lord! It is to me a great pain and great distress."²⁸ After her first traumatic experience with childbirth, Margery felt called to lead a celibate lay religious life as a spiritual mother of fellow pilgrims. Margery submitted reluctantly for many years to conjugal obligations, all the while begging her husband to allow her to live chastely devoted to God.

Margery and her husband eventually agreed upon a celibate marriage, which was a premodern wife's principal form of birth control. Abstinence, however, has a poor success rate even for the pious, and a late pregnancy did occur. Margery recounts that Christ appeared to her in a vision and promised that he himself would arrange for someone to care for the infant and her other children so that Margery would be free to leave home and embark on her spiritual pilgrimages.²⁹ In other words, Christ encouraged her to prioritize her spiritual calling over her mothering duties. It took a mystical revelation for Margery to break free from the expectation

---

[26] Amy Marga, "Martin Luther and the Early Modern Beginnings of a Feminist Maternal Theology," *Religions* 11, no. 3 (2020): 115.

[27] Catholicism has its version of self-sacrificial motherhood, as exemplified by the death of the now-canonized Gianna Beretta Molla. See her biography at https://www.vatican.va/news_services/liturgy/saints/ns_lit_doc_20040516_beretta-molla_en.html (accessed January 7, 2023).

[28] *The Book of Margery Kempe*, trans. and ed. Lynn Staley (New York: Norton, 2001), 36.

[29] *The Book of Margery Kempe*, 36.

that the biblical command to be fruitful and multiply was her wifely lot in life.[30]

In seventeenth-century France, the recently widowed Marie Martin relinquished her weeping eleven-year-old son to the care of his uncle so that she could enter an Ursuline convent. Even the lofty calling of the religious life did not shield her from her family's condemnation and societal disapproval. In her memoirs, she reflected on the difficulty of that day—especially the cries of her inconsolable son. However, she remained resolute, saying that "God was dearer to me than all that ... I bid adieu to him joyfully."[31] After taking the veil, Marie de l'Incarnation—literate and driven by talent, piety, and ambition—embarked on a missionary career. She founded an Ursuline community in Canada, opened a girls' school, and translated the catechism into several First Nations languages. She eventually began to correspond with her adult son back in France and begged his forgiveness for the abandonment. She explained that she had to "yield to the force of divine love" that made her into the "cruelest of all mothers" for the sake of Christ.[32]

Margery's and Marie's startling stories of maternal abandonment were admitted into the Roman Catholic Church's hagiographical canon for the purpose of inspiring women's piety.[33] The tradition makes these two women's tales all about leaving sex behind (their deserted children are an unfortunate footnote). A feminist reading, however, discerns the subversive subtext in their stories. Religious callings—any callings—trump the claim of biology-as-destiny.

These two women did not have the resources and the options for easy travel and long-distance communication that women use today when their jobs take them away from their families for long periods. Nevertheless, Margery and Marie, if allowed to speak through their texts, can be recognized as self-aware, thoughtful, and spiritually guided decision-makers regarding their sexual,

---

[30] Margery pushed back on the meaning of the biblical call to procreate (Gen. 1:22), arguing that it could mean producing not biological children but virtues. *The Book of Margery Kempe*, 89.

[31] Mary Dunn, *The Cruelest of All Mothers: Marie de l'Incarnation, Motherhood, and Christian Tradition* (New York: Fordham University Press, 2015), 5.

[32] Dunn, *The Cruelest of All Mothers*, 2.

[33] Marie was canonized in 2014. Cindy Wooden, "Laval, Marie de l'Incarnation Decreed Saints," *Catholic Register*, April 3, 2014.

reproductive, and religious lives. The spirit of their counter-stories resonates with contemporary women managing life's demands and opportunities in relation to mothering.

Presumptive Motherhood Today

Life is precarious—especially during and after pregnancy. This precarity can sometimes intersect with mothering in tragic ways. Some mothers are unexpectedly caught up in mental health crises or unanticipated life-changing tragic events. These cases may be less common for mothering generally, but they function as canary-in-the-coalmine reminders of what can happen if mothering pressures build up too much. Feminist scholarship on mothering cannot afford to pass over without comment Christianity's bias (witting or not) toward compliant, sacrificial, indefatigable mothers.

Mental Health and Mothering Tragedies

The death of a child is shattering. Child murder appalls. Mothers who kill their own children are considered evil and beyond the pale. These stories are shocking, but they happen—even to Christians.

In 2001, a stay-at-home, churchgoing, white mom, Andrea Yates, took her five children, one by one, ages seven years to six months old, and drowned them in the bathtub of their Houston home.[34] The news story stunned the country. One recoils at the horror of what this monstrous mother did. One feels relief that she was committed to a mental institution, away from society.[35]

Societies have mechanisms that delineate boundaries regarding people and actions deemed profane, taboo, and evil. Society abjects that which it fears and does not understand.[36] However, abjecting

---

[34] Faith McLellan, "Mental Health and Justice: The Case of Andrea Yates," *Lancet* 368, no. 9551 (2006): 1951–4.
[35] Kait Hansen, "Andrea Yates, Who Drowned Her 5 Kids, Declines Release Hearing from Mental Hospital, Again," *Today*, April 6, 2022.
[36] Julia Kristeva, *Powers of Horror: An Essay on Abjection*, trans. Leon S. Roudiez (New York: Columbia University Press, 1982).

Andrea Yates means a missed opportunity to probe further into how frighteningly thin the wall is between this horrific event and so-called normal motherhood. Try as one might to deny it, the monstrous hovers perilously close to the normal for beleaguered mothers. Few speak of it, but many parents know well the unbidden thoughts that intrude in those zero-dark-thirty moments after walking the floor for hours with a colicky baby. Yates's actions were beyond the pale, but to marginalize her as a mad and evil mother[37] is to ignore a maternal reality that is not uncommon and should not remain unspoken.[38]

Yates's story begins with the familiar. High school class valedictorian and registered nurse, she married in her mid-twenties, eager to have children. With each pregnancy, she began suffering from postpartum depression. She soldiered on, homeschooling the children. Her depression worsened with bouts of self-harming, hallucinations, and suicide attempts. Even so, her husband and extended family thought she could pull it together and continue to care for her children, which she did, alone, in the trailer home where they lived.

Then the unimaginable happened. Something triggered a psychotic break, which led to the fateful day when she murdered her children. After all the children lay dead, she called her husband: "'It's the kids,' Andrea said. He inquired which one. She said, 'All of them.'"[39]

While psychosis is not common after parturition, postpartum depression is. As many as one in eight women experience postpartum depression symptoms in the year after giving birth.[40] Had Yates's family and her doctors taken her postpartum depression more seriously, had she been treated for it more aggressively, this tragedy

---

[37] See Sarah LaChance Adams, *Mad Mothers, Bad Mothers, and What a "Good" Mother Would Do: The Ethics of Ambivalence* (New York: Columbia University Press, 2014), 1–4.
[38] Cheryl L. Meyer, Tara C. Proano, Michelle Oberman, Kelly White, and Priyahelle Batra, *Mothers Who Kill Their Children: Understanding the Acts of Moms from Susan Smith to the "Prom Mom"* (New York: New York University Press, 2001).
[39] Deborah W. Denno, "Who Is Andrea Yates? A Short Story about Insanity," *Duke Journal of Gender Law and Policy* 10, no. 1 (2003): 35.
[40] "Depression among Women," Centers for Disease Control and Prevention, https://www.cdc.gov/reproductivehealth/depression/index.htm (accessed March 30, 2023).

may have been averted. Yates's depression was not extraordinary but, in fact, ordinary, common, and treatable. The monstrosity is not only Yates's actions but also society's refusal to recognize and respond to the burdens of motherhood.

Andrea Yates was deeply religious. She and her husband were associated with an almost cultish, fundamentalist Christian preacher who spouted a fire-and-brimstone view of salvation and damnation. This preacher claimed that working women are evil daughters of Eve, children should be homeschooled to protect them from evil influences, and wives should submit to their husbands.[41] Yates repeated this extreme religious rhetoric in her interviews with the prison psychiatrists, saying that she killed her children to save their souls from Satan.[42] One can easily retreat into the reductive explanation that Yates came under the influence of a crackpot type of fundamentalist Christianity, which aggravated her fragile mental state—as if such a scenario would not happen to anyone without mental health issues and situated in a more established Christian denomination. However, the premise that otherwise healthy believers in mainline churches do not suffer from postpartum depression is flawed and dangerous.[43] Religion played a problematic role in Yates's suicidal and murderous ideations. However, despite her religiously linked psychosis, Yates retained a clear self-awareness that she was maxed out in terms of caring alone for her five children. She actually was still competent in assessing that she had come to the end of her mothering rope and was no longer a safe mother. She knew she needed to be at a safe distance from her children. She needed someone to listen to her. Traditional Christian communities, not just extreme fundamentalist ones, are guilty of making it difficult for mothers to voice when they need to walk away from mothering duties—for their own and their children's well-being.

---

[41]Denno, "Who Is Andrea Yates," 31–2.
[42]Denno, "Who Is Andrea Yates," 37, 43.
[43]For a compelling theological account of postpartum mental illness, see Elizabeth Allison-Glenny, "The Disembodiment of Birthing and the Incapacity to Theologically Reflect: A Perspective from Perinatal Mental Illness in Ministry," unpublished paper delivered at the British and Irish Association for Practical Theology Annual Conference (July 13, 2022).

Motherhood on the Margins of the Prolife-Prochoice Binary

Shannon Dingle, a mother of six, including several special needs children, discovered she was pregnant a mere one week after a freak accident took the life of her husband in 2019. Up to that point, she was active in Christian prolife circles, writing and speaking on disability and the sanctity of life. Grieving and battling her own medical complications, she began making plans to have an abortion.

Then she miscarried. The miscarriage made abortion unnecessary but did not change the fact that Dingle had come to a new appreciation for pregnant women's moral agency. She says she is "not pro-life anymore, not in the political sense." Dingle went public with the details of this painful period of her life in order to counter distorting prolife caricatures about reproductive decision-making. Such caricatures "make for good propaganda but terrible policy. People, real people, become pregnant" and may need not to be pregnant. As Dingle writes, "I knew I couldn't have this baby."[44] She was a mom, making a mothering decision—seriously and prayerfully—about a living being, that could be born as her seventh child.[45]

Miscarriage and abortion intersect in Dingle's story, which is neither a prolife nor a prochoice one. It would be a mistake to read her miscarriage as a divinely authorized pregnancy ending in binary opposition to the morally dubious abortion she was planning to have. It would also be a mistake to think that the moral of Dingle's story is that some pregnancies happen in such tragic contexts and to such otherwise exemplary mothers that they meet some narrow casuistic criteria for a morally permissible abortion—even for a prolife person. Looking at miscarriage and abortion together underlines the importance of moral agency in light of the complexities of pregnancy and motherhood.[46] Binaries (miscarriage

---

[44] Shannon Dingle, "I Was in the Pro-Life Movement. But Then, Widowed with 6 Kids, I Prepared for an Abortion," *USA Today*, Opinion (October 11, 2020).

[45] For more on abortion as a mothering decision, see Kamitsuka, *Abortion and the Christian Tradition*, chapter 5.

[46] Statistics show that the majority of women who have abortions in the United States self-identify as Christian, and 13 percent are evangelical Christians. "Induced Abortion in the United States," Guttmacher Institute (2019), https://www.guttmacher.org/fact-sheet/induced-abortion-united-states# (accessed March 30, 2023).

versus abortion, or good mother versus bad mother) do not support pregnant people as they navigate difficult decision-making that occurs in real reproductive and mothering lives. Binaries marginalize and silence the so-called bad mothers—that is, those who succumb to mental health crises or who actively choose their well-being in opposition to the presumption that every conception should be allowed to come to birth.

Future Paths for Feminist Theologies of Motherhood

These stories of motherhood share the theme of pregnancy-capable believers wanting or needing the option of resisting the myths and pressures of presumptive motherhood. Spiritual callings interrupted mothering duties for early church martyrs, medieval lay spiritual teachers, and women with aspirations for consecrated religious life and missionary work. The church extols their chaste piety; feminist theology recognizes the submerged insurrectional message of women's agency. With the Reformation's emphasis on marriage over celibacy, women were pressured to marry and become mothers. In many Christian circles today, Protestant and Catholic women still feel the pressure to try to have children, to bring every pregnancy to birth, and to continue mothering no matter what difficulties they face. The above counter-stories only scratch the surface of how the presumptive motherhood myth adversely affects women.

Feminist theology's renewal depends on letting even more and varied marginalized mothering voices be heard.[47] Intersectional methods facilitate a deeper understanding of the imbricating elements that impact mothering, including race, class, nationality, degree of able-bodiliness, and so on.[48] Scholars are also contesting

---

[47]Literature can provide a compelling window into mothering. Four now-classic contemporary novels are Buchi Emecheta, *The Joys of Motherhood* (Oxford: Heinemann, 1994); Cherríe Moraga, *Waiting in the Wings: Portrait of a Queer Motherhood* (Ithaca, NY: Firebrand Books, 1997); Toni Morrison, *Beloved* (New York: Penguin, 1997); Amy Tan, *The Joy Luck Club* (New York: Putnam, 1989); Alice Walker, *The Color Purple* (New York: Harcourt Brace Jovanovich, 1982).

[48]For an intersectional approach to motherhood, see Lynn O'Brien Hallstein, Andrea O'Reilly, and Melinda Vandenbeld Giles, eds., *The Routledge Companion to Motherhood* (New York: Routledge, 2019); Claire Bischoff, Elizabeth O'Donnell

how the very term *mother* is linked to heteronormative cisgender female bodies.

Queer studies have opened the door to new theories of gender and sexuality that make possible the recognition of bodies and desires outside of compulsory reproductive heterosexuality.[49] Queering the concept of motherhood is in full swing in secular feminist and queer scholarship.[50] In religious studies circles, the scholarly literature is growing regarding how church practices and traditional Christian theologies marginalize and harm LGBTQ persons.[51] LGBTQ individuals get pregnant, have miscarriages, need abortion healthcare, have babies, raise children, and face parenting challenges.[52] Some of these people are church-goers. Future research into their experiences will reveal how normative Christian views of motherhood bear dangerously upon their lives.

Motherhood, it turns out, is less a secure harbor of spiritual or biological identity and more a ship battling stormy seas. By asserting their own agency regarding their sexual, reproductive, and family lives, people with uteruses can weather the storm. Christian mothers throughout church history and to the present have turned away from mothering duties (or contemplated doing so). Some navigated their way to other callings and identities. Their compelling, tragic, heroic, subversive, and agonizing stories of wanting and needing to postpone or extricate themselves from motherhood serve as

---

Gandolfo, and Annie Hardison-Moody, eds., *Parenting as Spiritual Practice and Source for Theology* (New York: Palgrave Macmillan, 2017).

[49] Adrienne Rich, "Compulsory Heterosexuality and Lesbian Existence," *Signs: Journal of Women in Culture and Society* 5, no. 4 (1980): 631–60.

[50] Margaret F. Gibson, *Queering Motherhood: Narrative and Theoretical Perspectives* (Bradford, ON: Demeter, 2014); Shelley M. Park, "Queering and Querying Motherhood," and Alisa Grigorovich, "Pregnant with Meaning," in *The Routledge Companion to Motherhood*, ed. Lynn O'Brien Hallstein, Andrea O'Reilly, and Melinda Vandenbeld Giles (New York: Routledge, 2019); Christa Craven, *Reproductive Losses: Challenges to LGBTQ Family-Making* (New York: Routledge, 2019).

[51] Austen Hartke, *Transforming: The Bible and the Lives of Transgender Christians* (Louisville, KY: Westminster John Knox, 2018); Bridget Eileen Rivera, *Heavy Burdens: Seven Ways LGBTQ Christians Experience Harm in the Church* (Grand Rapids, MI: Brazos, 2021).

[52] The reproductive justice movement is attuned to an intersectional approach to abortion healthcare, including in LGBTQ communities. See "Reproductive Justice," SisterSong, https://www.sistersong.net/reproductive-justice (accessed April 5, 2023).

cautionary tales. The ongoing renewal of feminist theology depends on letting these voices—past and present—be heard.

There are many reasons, conscious and unconscious, why people feel the call to motherhood or parenting identities. Those who eagerly and wholeheartedly respond to the call to nurture new life deserve thanks and recognition. Those who diligently fulfill their maternal duties amid great adversity deserve support and understanding. But thanks, recognition, support, and understanding for mothering should also be extended to those people who challenge the pressures of presumptive motherhood.

Bibliography

"Acts of Paul and Thecla." Translated by Jeremiah Jones. https://sourcebooks.fordham.edu/basis/thecla.asp, accessed January 7, 2023.

"Acts of Perpetua and Felicitas." Translated by Roberts-Donaldson. https://www.earlychristianwritings.com/text/tertullian24.html, accessed January 7, 2023.

Adams, Sarah LaChance. *Mad Mothers, Bad Mothers, and What a "Good" Mother Would Do: The Ethics of Ambivalence.* New York: Columbia University Press, 2014.

"After Abortion Fell: Abortion Laws by State." Center for Reproductive Rights. https://reproductiverights.org/maps/abortion-laws-by-state/.

Allison-Glenny, Elizabeth. "The Disembodiment of Birthing and the Incapacity to Theologically Reflect: A Perspective from Perinatal Mental Illness in Ministry." Unpublished paper presented at the British and Irish Association for Practical Theology Annual Conference, July 13, 2022.

Atkinson, Clarissa W. *The Oldest Vocation: Christian Motherhood in the Medieval West.* Ithaca, NY: Cornell University Press, 1991.

Barkhorn, Eleanor. "There's No Tougher Job Than Being a Mom: The Long History of a Ubiquitous Statement." *Atlantic.* July 11, 2013.

Bianchi, Tracey. *Mom Connection: Creating Vibrant Relationships in the Midst of Motherhood.* Grand Rapids, MI: Revell, 2012.

Bischoff, Claire, Elizabeth O'Donnell Gandolfo, and Annie Hardison-Moody, eds. *Parenting as Spiritual Practice and Source for Theology.* New York: Palgrave Macmillan, 2017.

The Book of Margery Kempe. Translated and edited by Lynn Staley. New York: Norton, 2001.

Butler, Judith. *Gender Trouble: Feminism and the Subversion of Identity*, 10th anniversary ed. New York: Routledge, 2002.

Craven, Christa. *Reproductive Losses: Challenges to LGBTQ Family-Making.* New York: Routledge, 2019.
Crowder, Stephanie R. Buckhanon. *When Momma Speaks: The Bible and Motherhood from a Womanist Perspective.* Louisville, KY: Westminster John Knox, 2016.
Davis, Stephen T. *The Cult of Saint Thecla: A Tradition of Women's Piety in Late Antiquity.* Oxford: Oxford University Press, 2001.
Denno, Deborah W. "Who Is Andrea Yates? A Short Story about Insanity." *Duke Journal of Gender Law and Policy* 10, no. 1 (2003): 1–60.
"Depression among Women." Centers for Disease Control and Prevention. https://www.cdc.gov/reproductivehealth/depression/index.htm, accessed March 30, 2023.
Dingle, Shannon. "I Was in the Pro-Life Movement. But Then, Widowed with 6 Kids, I Prepared for an Abortion." *USA Today*, Opinion, October 11, 2020.
Dunn, Mary. *The Cruelest of All Mothers: Marie de l'Incarnation, Motherhood, and Christian Tradition.* New York: Fordham University Press, 2015.
Emecheta, Buchi. *The Joys of Motherhood.* Oxford: Heinemann, 1994.
Foucault, Michel. *Power/Knowledge: Selected Interviews and Other Writings, 1972–1977.* Translated and edited by Colin Gordon et al. New York: Pantheon, 1972.
"Gianna Beretta Molla (1922–1962)." The Vatican. https://www.vatican.va/news_services/liturgy/saints/ns_lit_doc_20040516_beretta-molla_en.html, accessed January 7, 2023.
Gibson, Margaret F. *Queering Motherhood: Narrative and Theoretical Perspectives.* Bradford, ON: Demeter, 2014.
Grigorovich, Alisa. "Pregnant with Meaning." In *The Routledge Companion to Motherhood*, edited by Lynn O'Brien Hallstein, Andrea O'Reilly, and Melinda Vandenbeld Giles, 63–76. New York: Routledge, 2019.
Hansen, Kait. "Andrea Yates, Who Drowned Her 5 Kids, Declines Release Hearing from Mental Hospital, Again." *Today*. April 6, 2022.
"The Harms of Denying a Woman a Wanted Abortion: Findings from the Turnaway Study." ANSIRH. https://www.ansirh.org/sites/default/files/publications/files/the_harms_of_denying_a_woman_a_wanted_abortion_4-16-2020.pdf.
Hartke, Austen *Transforming: The Bible and the Lives of Transgender Christians.* Louisville, KY: Westminster John Knox, 2018.
Holness, Lyn. "Motherhood and Spirituality: Faith Reflections from the Inside." *Agenda* 18, no. 61 (2004): 66–71.
"Induced Abortion in the United States." Guttmacher Institute, 2019. https://www.guttmacher.org/fact-sheet/induced-abortion-united-states#.

Jones, David Albert. *The Soul of the Embryo: An Inquiry into the Status of the Human Embryo in the Christian Tradition.* London: Continuum, 2004.

Kamitsuka, Margaret D. *Abortion and the Christian Tradition: A Pro-Choice Theological Ethic.* Louisville, KY: Westminster John Knox, 2019.

Kassian Mary A., and Nancy Leigh DeMoss. *True Woman 101: Divine Design.* Chicago, IL: Moody, 2012.

Kristeva, Julia. *Powers of Horror: An Essay on Abjection.* Translated by Leon S. Roudiez. New York: Columbia University Press, 1982.

Lawler, Jennifer. *Encyclopedia of Women in the Middle Ages.* Jefferson, NC: McFarland, 2001.

Ludy, Leslie. *Set-Apart Motherhood: Reflecting Joy and Beauty in Family Life.* Np: Nav, 2014.

Mackey-Kallis, Susan, and Dan F. Hahn. "Questions of Public Will and Private Action: The Power of the Negative in the Reagans' 'Just Say No' Morality Campaign." *Communication Quarterly* 39, no. 1 (1991): 1–17.

Magnani, Eliana, and Lochin Brouillard. "Female House Ascetics from the Fourth to the Twelfth Century." In *The Cambridge History of Medieval Monasticism in the Latin West*, edited by Alison I. Beach and Isabelle Cochelin, 213–31. Cambridge: Cambridge University Press, 2020.

Marga, Amy. "Martin Luther and the Early Modern Beginnings of a Feminist Maternal Theology." *Religions* 11, no. 3 (2020): 115.

McLellan, Faith. "Mental Health and Justice: The Case of Andrea Yates." *Lancet* 368, no. 9551 (2006): 1951–4.

Meyer, Cheryl L., Tara C. Proano, Michelle Oberman, Kelly White, and Priyahelle Batra. *Mothers Who Kill Their Children: Understanding the Acts of Moms from Susan Smith to the "Prom Mom."* New York: New York University Press, 2001.

Moraga, Cherríe. *Waiting in the Wings: Portrait of a Queer Motherhood.* Ithaca, NY: Firebrand, 1997.

Morrison, Toni. *Beloved.* New York: Penguin, 1997.

Moss, Candida R. *Ancient Christian Martyrdom: Diverse Practices, Theologies, and Traditions.* New Haven, CT: Yale University Press, 2012.

Park, Shelley M. "Queering and Querying Motherhood." In *The Routledge Companion to Motherhood*, edited by Lynn O'Brien Hallstein, Andrea O'Reilly, and Melinda Vandenbeld Giles, 63–76. New York: Routledge, 2019.

"Reproductive Justice." SisterSong. https://www.sistersong.net/reproductive-justice, accessed April 5, 2023.

Rich, Adrienne. "Compulsory Heterosexuality and Lesbian Existence." *Signs: Journal of Women in Culture and Society* 5, no. 4 (1980): 631–60.

Rivera, Bridget Eileen. *Heavy Burdens: Seven Ways LGBTQ Christians Experience Harm in the Church*. Grand Rapids, MI: Brazos, 2021.

Roberts, Dorothy E. *Killing the Black Body: Race, Reproduction, and the Meaning of Liberty*. New York: Vintage, 1999.

Shaw, Teresa M. *The Burden of the Flesh: Fasting and Sexuality in Early Christianity*. Minneapolis, MN: Fortress, 1998.

Spivak, Gayatri Chakravorty. "Can the Subaltern Speak?" In *Marxism and the Interpretation of Culture*, edited by Cary Nelson and Lawrence Grossberg, 24–8. London: Macmillan, 1988.

Stjerna, Kirsi. *Women and the Reformation*. Malden, MA: Blackwell, 2011.

Tan, Amy. *The Joy Luck Club*. New York: Putnam, 1989.

"The U.S. Maternal Health Divide: The Limited Maternal Health Services and Worse Outcomes of States Proposing New Abortion Restrictions." Commonwealth Fund. December 14, 2022. https://www.commonwealthfund.org/publications/issue-briefs/2022/dec/us-maternal-health-divide-limited-services-worse-outcomes, accessed March 30, 2023.

Walker, Alice. *The Color Purple*. New York: Harcourt Brace Jovanovich, 1982.

Walker-Barnes, Chanequa. *Too Heavy a Yoke: Black Women and the Burden of Strength*. Eugene, OR: Cascade, 2014.

Weitbrecht, Julia. "Maternity and Sainthood in the Medieval Perpetua Legend." In *Perpetua's Passions: Multidisciplinary Approaches to the Passio Perpetuae et Felicitatis*, edited by Jan N. Bremmer and Marco Formisano, 150–66. New York: Oxford University Press, 2012.

Wooden, Cindy. "Laval, Marie de l'Incarnation Decreed Saints." *Catholic Register*, April 3, 2014.

4

Policing Black Womanhood: Sin, Respectability, and Abolitionist Sanctuaries

Nikia Smith Robert

Introduction

This chapter explores the interplay of punitive theologies and the policing of Black womanhood. I argue that interpretations of sin and social constructions of deviance coalesce to preserve the innocence and immunity of deplorable white men but punish Black women who transgress respectable norms for merely trying to survive. I support this thesis by highlighting three Black women—Rosie McIntyre, Niko Quinn, and Ophelia Williams—and their fraught experiences with State and sexual violence by Detective Roger Golubski and the Kansas City Police Department. The connection of Black women's lived realities with carceral punishment compounded by condemnatory church teachings in western Christianity of sin and sacrifice signify an exigent moral crisis that needs an urgent intervention. Ergo, I construct an abolitionist theological and ethical framework that turns to nonwestern religious traditions in eastern orthodoxy and African diasporic interpretations of divination to construct Black women's agentic survival practices, not as deviant, but as an embodiment of the divine.

Policing Black Womanhood

On September 16, 2022, a grand jury federally indicted sixty-nine-year-old retired police captain and detective Roger Golubski on six counts that could carry a life sentence.[1] On November 14, 2022, the Department of Justice announced three additional indictments for conspiracy to kidnap and sexually assault teenagers.[2] Golubski served as a Kansas City, Kansas, police officer for three and a half decades. Michael Harriot, a journalist for the *Root*, who broke this story, declared this case as "one of the widest-ranging examples of state-sponsored terror against Black women this country has ever seen."[3] As a decorated officer and civil employee paid by local tax dollars, Golubski raped, kidnapped, terrorized, and extorted the Black communities he vowed to protect, notwithstanding Black women.

A 2018 lawsuit alleged that Golubski sexually abused Rosie McIntyre. When McIntyre refused further sexual advances, Golubski extorted another Black woman, Niko Quinn, to give false witness framing McIntyre's son for double murder. At the time, Lamont McIntyre was only seventeen years old. He spent twenty-three years in prison for a crime he did not commit.[4] Quinn was coerced into her false testimony by the state prosecutor, Terra Moorehead, who was allegedly having an affair with the

---

[1] Juan Cisneros, Tia Johnson, Makenzie Koch, and Regan Porter, "FBI Arrests Former KCKPD Detective Roger Golubski," *Fox News Kansas City*, September 15, 2022, https://fox4kc.com/news/fbi-arrest-former-kckpd-detective-roger-golubski/ (accessed April 9, 2024).
[2] "KCKPD Corruption," KCKPD Corruption, https://kckcorruption.info (accessed March 22, 2023).
[3] Michael Harriot, "A Criminal Injustice: How a City Ignored the Rape, Murder and Terrorism of Black Women for Four Decades," *The Root*, May 27, 2021, https://www.theroot.com/a-criminal-injustice-how-a-city-ignored-the-rape-murd-1846883970 (accessed March 22, 2023).
[4] Cisneros et al., "FBI Arrests Former KCKPD Detective Roger Golubski."

District Judge J. Dexter Burdette and presider over the hearing. In 2024, the Kansas Disciplinary Board disbarred Moorhead for framing McIntyre.[5] Actors in both the criminal and legal systems conspired against these two Black women and their families, forcing them to participate in state terror against one another or risk being targeted themselves by its violence. The immunity and putative innocence of a corrupt white police officer hanged in the balance.

Further investigation into this story revealed other reports of Black women who were mysteriously murdered and dubbed as "Golubski girls." Ophelia Williams gave an interview with CBS affiliate and local network, KCTV, recounting her story from twenty years ago when Golubski stopped by her house unannounced.[6] In a slow labored cadence, Williams shared that she invited Golubski inside her home under false pretenses. She thought Golubski was there on official police business related to her imprisoned sons. However, after sitting on the couch and feeling Golubski's hands creep up her skirt, Williams quickly learned that he was there to do harm. Fighting off his advances, Golubski pinned down Williams on the couch by her hands and proceeded to rape her. He continued to sexually assault Williams several more times after that.

The stories of these three Black women—Rosie McIntyre, Niko Quinn, and Ophelia Williams—reveal a startling tale of America's investment in the innocence of whiteness. The legal and criminal system conspired to cover up corruption by protecting Roger Golubski and instead demoralized, demonized, and discredited the Black women whom he harmed. Rather than interrogate the missteps of the Kansas City Kansas Police Department and the complicity of the courts, the system blamed Black women for their

---

[5]Peggy Lowe, "Kansas Prosecutor who Framed Innocent Man Surrenders Law License, Will Soon Be Disbarred," *KCUR - Kansas City News and NPR*, April 16, 2004, https://www.kcur.org/news/2024-04-16/notorious-kansas-prosecutor-surrenders-law-license-will-soon-be-disbarred (Accessed May 15, 2024).
[6]Angie Ricono and Cyndi Fahrlander, "KCK Woman Outraged That Disgraced Cop Golubski Allowed to Go Home," KCTV5, September 29, 2022, https://www.kctv5.com/2022/09/29/kck-woman-outraged-that-disgraced-cop-golubski-allowed-go-home/ (accessed March 22, 2023).

own victimization and, even worse, the system, at times, ignored their cries for help altogether. This imbalance of power unearths a moral crisis of policing that is rooted in racism, misogynoir, and economic inequities. False constructions of Black women as deviant and undeserving increase vulnerability to state violence and bolster a carceral system of domination that assigns immunities and protections to white men.

There is an uncanny relationship between policing Black womanhood and theological interpretations of sin. At the heart of both secular and sacred surveilling of Black womanhood is the policing of their bodies by jurisprudence and religious doctrine to judge, punish, and disqualify individuals who deviate from dominant norms. Hence, in the next section, I explore the policing of Black womanhood as not only a social prescription but also as a theological problem.

Sin and Stereotypes of Deviance

The religious overture to punishment is undeniable and rooted in the conceptions of sin that parallel racialized and gendered constructions of deviance. Dominant definitions of sin have historically and contemporarily justified the oppression of marginalized groups—including the gas chambers at Auschwitz, the lynching tree in the Antebellum South, the colonization and stolen land of Indigenous people, and the 2 million Americans in prisons with a disproportionate population of Black and brown people. Today, a dangerous cocktail of Christian nationalism, American exceptionalism, racial capitalism, and white supremacy continues to perpetuate America's evils against marginalized groups. This nefarious foundation creates systems that punish marginalized individuals like McIntyre, Quinn, and Williams for transgressing normative boundaries. Importantly, society uses hegemonic appraisals of human worth to protect whiteness, demonize Blackness, and evade the root causes of social problems in the process.

During the rise of the Roman Empire in the fourth century, Saint Augustine (Aurelius Augustinus), an African bishop of the early church, first conceptualized the theological category of original sin.[7] In 412, Augustine responded to the Pelagian controversy that debated whether humanity is born perfect or as inherit sinners. Augustine compelled the church to condemn Pelagius and his followers with heresy for upholding the possibility of human perfection. In contradistinction to his adversaries, Augustine believed that sin is inescapable and inherited. Augustine, therefore, emphasized the importance of God's grace. The fall of humanity that followed Adam and Eve's disobedience required divine grace to free humanity from sin. Shifting from a cosmic struggle with the devil to an individual warring with morality, Augustine held that personal or lived experiences, as early as birth or involuntarily, produced sin. Augustine turned to grace to repair and restore humanity from the fallen state of sinfulness, which is made possible by God's incarnation and Christ's sacrificial atonement.

The doctrine of sin and its connectedness to punishment by atonement is apparent during the scholastic period in the works of Saint Anselm of Canterbury. Anselm interpreted original and personal sin to defend the purity of Christ. For Anselm, there is an important distinction between humanity's corruption and Jesus, who was borne by a human but not stained by sin. For Anselm, like Augustine, sin is corruption and separates fallen humanity from divine purity, which only divine grace can repair and restore. Anselm's notion of sin is inextricably linked to his conception of sacrifice. Anselm believed in Christ's death as an atoning for sinful humanity by paying a debt to God.[8] Sin, then, is the cause of debt and an affront to God that only Jesus, who is fully human and fully divine, can give recompense. This substitutionary sacrificial atonement theory maintains that Christ's death is the sacrifice for human sin. Importantly, the response to humanity's fall and sin is punishment, thereby producing a precarious relationship to preserve purity or the ideals of innocence.

During the reform period, John Calvin, a trained lawyer, applied a juridical lens to interpretations of sin. For Calvin, sin is the distance

---

[7]Matthew Fox, *Original Blessing: A Primer in Creation Spirituality: Presented in Four Paths, Twenty-Six Themes, and Two Questions* (New York: Jeremy P. Tarcher/Putnam, 2000).
[8]Lisa Sowle Cahill, "Quaestio Disputata the Atonement Paradigm: Does It Still Have Explanatory Value?" *Theological Studies* 67 (2007): 418.

between humanity and God. In *Institutes of the Christian Religion*, Calvin defines original sin "as the hereditary corruption and depravity of our nature that extends to every part of our soul."[9] Sin is rebellion and the source of shame and justifies divine punishment. Calvin states, "Through Adam we have not only derived punishment, but have a pollution instilled in us for which punishment is justly due."[10] According to Calvin, God justly punishes human actions in the manner of judging a heinous crime to dispense divine wrath and condemnation. Calvin uses concupiscence to describe the ways in which humanity is wholly inclined to sin.

Reinhold Niebuhr examined the morality of humanity against the immorality of society. Niebuhr states, "Sin is, in short, the consequence of man's inclination to usurp the prerogatives of God, to think more highly of himself than he ought to think, thus making destructive use of his freedom by not observing the limits to which a creaturely freedom is bound."[11] Niebuhr is a strong proponent of original sin, which he defines as an inherited corruption. Additionally, Niebuhr states, "the Christian doctrine of original sin with its seemingly contradictory assertions about the inevitability of sin and man's responsibility for sin is a dialectical truth which does justice to the fact that man's self-love and self-centeredness is inevitable, but not in such a way as to fit into the category of natural necessity."[12] Niebuhr contrasted the involuntary nature of original sin at birth from the nature of humanity and individual sin. According to Niebuhr, individual sin is grounded in humanity's pride, which is the source of injustices that reinforce oppressive powers antithetical to God's love and require self-responsibility and moral accountability. Here, Niebuhr turns away from Augustinian conceptions of original sin and an emphasis on individual responsibility to collective accountability that is aligned with constitutions of social sin traced to the social gospel.

---

[9]John Calvin, *Institutes of the Christian Religion* (Peabody, MA: Hendrickson, 2008), 2.1.8.
[10]Calvin, *Institutes of the Christian Religion*, 2.1.8.
[11]Reinhold Niebuhr, *Faith and History: A Comparison of Christian and Modern Views of History* (New York: Scribner, 1949), 21, https://kinginstitute.stanford.edu/king-papers/documents/theology-reinhold-niebuhr#fn8 (accessed April 9, 2024).
[12]Reinhold Niebuhr, *The Nature and Destiny of Man: A Christian Interpretation* (Louisville, KY: Westminster John Knox Press, 1996), 263.

The social gospel grounds religious responses to social inequities and serves as the catalyst for social transformation as a theological and moral imperative. In *The New Abolition: W. E. B. Du Bois and the Black Social Gospel*, social ethicist Gary Dorrien argues for the church's historic radicality to respond to racial discrimination and support social justice. Dorrien asserts, "the Black social gospel affirmed the dignity, sacred personhood, creativity, and moral agency of African Americans and responded to racial oppression. It asked what a new abolitionism should be and what role the churches should play within it."[13] In sharp contrast to the religious doctrine of sin used to promote individual responsibility and punish people for their misfortune, social sin holds accountable the structural injustices that create oppressive conditions that make it hard for marginalized people to secure freedom and flourishing.

Interpretation of social sin highlights oppressive systems that undermine the civil and human rights of marginalized groups, particularly Black women. A shift from original sin to social sin moves away from the constructions of Black people as inherently bad and guilty *a priori* a claim made by Kelly Brown Douglas to understanding society's malignant and reproachable wrongdoings that perpetuate harm.[14] Rather than the function of sin to cast individual blame, social sin provides a rationale for the ways in which society is complicit in the evil reproductions that create a social hierarchy between the good who are deserving and the bad who are undeserving of human dignity.

In *Womanist Ethics and the Cultural Production of Evil*, Emilie Townes describes the Welfare Queen as a trope used to label and punish Black mothers with burdensome policies. Townes points out that studies such as the Moynihan report labeled Black women as doubly deviant, raising criminal sons, emasculating fathers, and destroying the Black family.[15] At the center of punitive welfare policies is the pathology of Black women as bad mothers who dominant society views as blameworthy. Townes concludes that a fantastic

---

[13]Gary J. Dorrien, *The New Abolition: W. E. B. Du Bois and the Black Social Gospel* (New Haven, CT: Yale University Press, 2015), 2.
[14]See Kelly Brown Douglas, *Stand Your Ground: Black Bodies and the Justice of God* (Maryknoll, NY: Orbis Books, 2015).
[15]Emilie Townes, *Womanist Ethics and the Cultural Production of Evil* (New York: Palgrave Macmillan, 2007), 119.

hegemonic imagination takes religious values and stereotypes about Black womanhood to engender punitive policies that cast individual blame without questioning structural inequities.[16] Sin is a religious value that marches in lockstep with negative societal appraisals to allocate burdensome policies and punish Black mothers without challenging the indignities of a deleterious carceral system.

In a 1962 speech delivered in California, Malcolm X once said, "the most disrespected person in America is the Black woman. The most unprotected person in America is the Black woman. The most neglected person in America is the Black woman."[17] Ophelia Williams, Rose McIntyre, Niko Quinn, and other Black women experienced firsthand the disrespect of a sinful system and diabolic white men who used unchecked power to make their lives a living hell. The legal system is an arbiter of innocence and guilt. The deciding factors of who receives the benefit of innocence or the burden of guilt depends on a hegemonic imagination and punitive gaze rooted in anti-Blackness and misogynoir. Society is vested in constructing Black and brown women as deviant, immoral, disrespectful, sinful, and criminal to preserve white goodness, innocence, purity, and superiority.

It is significant that the growth of the church and the rise of the Roman Empire corresponded with the emergence of the doctrine of original sin and theological justifications for punishment against the cosmic struggles between good and evil. It is even more revealing that sin is a human intervention that is not Christologically or religiously inspired. In his book, for instance, Matthew Fox asserts that Jesus never encountered the term "original sin." Additionally, Fox clarifies that "Islam rejects original sin (even though they keep the story of Adam and Eve); Judaism rejects it (even though they created the story of Adam and Eve, and Jesus was a Jew); Native Americans reject it ... Buddhism rejects it; Eastern Orthodox Christians do not emphasise original sin either."[18] Original sin belongs exclusively to Western Christianity for the preservation of the empire. Aware of

---

[16]Townes, *Womanist Ethics and the Cultural Production of Evil*, 120.
[17]Feminista Jones, "Malcolm X Stood Up for Black Women When Few Others Would," *ZORA* (blog), August 7, 2020, https://zora.medium.com/malcolm-x-stood-up-for-black-women-when-few-others-would-68e8b2ea2747 (accessed March 22, 2023).
[18]Fox, *Original Blessing*, 5.

the precarity of interpretations of sin, Fox concludes that sin is a product of "patriarchal control and pessimism, anthropocentrism, and original sin ideology is profoundly dangerous and deviant."[19]

Fox offers a redress to original sin and proposes a new paradigm that includes original blessings. Fox begins interpretations of human history with original blessings, which is the theological equivalent to "goodness" and synonymous with "original grace" and "original wisdom." Fox's rejection of original sin as a tool of the empire is an invitation to view Black women as original blessings—first as good and not bad or sinful. Also, with the complexity of human experience, there is room for Black women to carry both; however, it is critical to denounce the hegemonic claim that Black women are any more deviant or innately sinful than others because of their Blackness and womanhood.

Considered religion's worst ideology, the uncanny relationship between sin and punishment is a sacralized tool of social control. Sin is an extension of the empire used to discipline and control bodies into submission and conformity. The medieval, scholastic, and reformed periods offer interpretations of sin grounded in individual appraisals without social critique. These renderings of original sin do not represent America's social sins of policing that are rooted in racism, sexism, classism, and other interlocking oppressions. Thus, it is pivotal to contrast original sin, the notion that people are born sinful or inherit sin without choice or free will, and individual sin (the fact that people do knowingly and unknowingly commit harm as a part of their lived experiences) against social sin attributed to oppressive systems and structures that disproportionately targets the disinherited. In addition, it is critically important to look more closely at the manifestations of sin in connection to respectability politics as an ethical framework to problematize the policing of Black women who transgress normative boundaries.

Respectability Politics

Religious historian Evelyn Higginbotham coined the term "politics of respectability" in her 1993 landmark text, *Righteous Discontent:*

---

[19] Fox, *Original Blessing*, 6.

The Women's Movement in the Black Baptist Church, 1880–1920. This section places Higginbotham in conversation with Black feminist Brittney Cooper to uncover the original intentions of respectability politics and contemporary engagements that extend, or perhaps even improve, the term beyond its historical context. Cooper's shift from performance to inherent dignity provides a theoretical pathway to consider the applicability of respectability politics for the policing of Black womanhood in today's moment of mass incarceration. Importantly, respectability politics is a continuation of a discussion about sin. These two concepts are ethical and theological accomplices that sanction judgment to condemn and punish Black women.

It is critical to retrieve Higginbotham's original intentions of respectability as a protest while also troubling its assimilation politics for a contemporary age of mass incarceration. At its best, respectability politics is contingent upon performance and aesthetics rooted in protest that is oriented toward a telos of justice. At its worst, respectability politics engenders conservative elements that hinge upon assimilationist ideals of white middle-class values. Subsequently, a dialectical relationship arises. Generally understood, respectability is either protest or proper behavior. A closer and more nuanced reading, however, renders a fuller account that is the closest to Higginbotham's original intentions, whereby respectability is *both* protest *and* conformity to proper behavior, which work together to inform Black women's fight for equality.

Misinterpretations of respectability politics reduce the phenomenon merely to assimilationist tactics. However, respectability politics both encouraged conformity as a strategy of resistance to reform systems of racial oppression *and* promoted a fervor of protest to oppose white supremacist values. In a historical analysis of the Black church, Higginbotham posits, "Black women both *embraced and contested* the dominant values and norms of northern white Baptists, white women, and even Black men (italics mine).[20] Politics of respectability, in its earliest iteration, connoted both accommodation and protest as strategies that Black women used to uproot injustices and forge spaces of belonging in church and

---

[20] Evelyn Brooks Higginbotham, *Righteous Discontent: The Women's Movement in the Black Baptist Church, 1880–1920* (Cambridge, MA: Harvard University Press, 1993), 12.

society. Thus, one-sided readings of respectability do a disservice to the tradition of Black women whose embrace of white middle-class and patriarchal norms also contested hegemony. This clarification is important to aptly understand the ways in which some churches use respectability politics as an elitist high-brow tool to police Black women but not as a tool of resistance to overthrow the US carceral state.

For the period that Higginbotham is writing, law-breaking would have presumably played into the hands of the white supremacist state, which was all too ready to treat Black people as deviant, uncivilized, barbaric, wild, inferior, and subhuman. Law-breaking would seemingly counter the resistance strategies of a politic of respectability that used resistance but also conformity to proper behavior (including obeying rules, laws, and customs) as a means of upholding dominant values. Respectability requires individuals to be so morally upright, so respectable, so law-abiding, so righteous that it would make others who criticize feel ashamed themselves. However, contemporary contexts require us to ask the question: Is it possible to apply a historically situated respectability politics to the twenty-first-century context of mass incarceration?

Here, Black feminist Brittney Cooper's analysis of respectability politics is helpful. Cooper complicates Higginbotham's formulation of respectability. Cooper argues that respectability is socially contingent, but dignity is an undisputed and inherent quality that Black women secure on their own terms. Elucidating the distinction between respectability and dignity, Cooper states, "the call for dignity and the call for respectability are not the same, though they are frequently conflated. Demands for dignity are demands for a fundamental recognition of one's inherent humanity. Demands for respectability assume that unassailable social propriety will prove one's dignity. Dignity, unlike respectability, is not socially contingent. It is intrinsic and, therefore, not up for debate."[21] Importantly, Cooper's turn to dignity seemingly restores the moral integrity of Black women's practical wisdom by reclaiming its intrinsic worth apart from white middle-class values. Thus, the impetus for Black women's agency is not determined by external

---

[21] Brittney C. Cooper, *Beyond Respectability: The Intellectual Thought of Race, Women, Gender, and Sexuality in American History* (Urbana: University of Illinois Press, 2017), 5.

demands aligned with dominant social standards. Rather, Cooper emphasizes Black women's agency and the intrinsic value of an undisputed dignity.

Cooper's departure from Higginbotham's conceptualization of respectability is helpful to shift emphasis away from external judgments that encroach upon the humanity of Black women. Particularly resonant is Cooper's point that internal qualities of dignity are not socially contingent and, therefore, not determined by what others deem proper and acceptable but by what one decides is necessary for their own worth. For Black women, this internal quality of dignity is not attached to ecclesial or societal judgments but rather is self-defined.

Cooper provides a way forward that considers other strategies that Black women can use to navigate the public sphere beyond respectability. The internal value of dignity is grounded in an (Anna Julia) Cooperian approach to challenge respectability and dissemblance (a concept first introduced by historian Darlene Clark Hines to connote the ways in which Black women never made their private emotions public). In contrast to respectability and dissemblance, Black women can make their bodies and their feelings visible to the public by politicizing their interior lives.[22] Rather than conceal or control the body to protect external perceptions about Black women who do not conform to white middle-class values, Brittney Cooper advocates for Black women's autonomous agency that is internally driven.

Brittney Cooper draws from Anna Julia Cooper who challenged patriarchal limitations of Black women's possibilities and said, "Only the BLACK WOMAN can say 'when and where I enter in the quiet, undisputed dignity of my womanhood, without violence and without suing or special patronage, then and there the whole race enters with me."[23] This undisputed dignity signifies the autonomous agency that Black women have the power to exercise as agents of their own destiny and liberation. In this regard, Cooper's shift away from respectability marks a turn to the "material and embodied conditions of everyday Black people."[24] This emphasis on ordinary

---

[22]Cooper, *Beyond Respectability*, 39.
[23]Cooper, *Beyond Respectability*, 39.
[24]Cooper, *Beyond Respectability*, 39.

people is different than the elitism of respectability. Cooper's analysis is helpful in recognizing the value of undisputed dignity and internal worth that cannot be devalued by external systems of oppression and social control.

Thus, respectability politics is a lens some churches use to surveil Black women and cast judgments based on societal perceptions of deviance or failure to conform to middle-class values. These perceptions determine Black women's moral worthiness, which could mean either their damnation by doctrinal church teachings of sin or their destruction by policing in a corrupt and nefarious legal system. In this way, churches become complicit with the carceral state. In the spirit of Brittney Cooper, churches must go beyond respectability to see Black women's inherent dignity (not inherent sinfulness) that is not contingent upon societal perceptions of deviance but telling of their divine worth.

Hence, in the final section, I argue beyond Higginbotham and Cooper by redressing harmful church teachings of sin and practices of respectability to construct a womanist abolition ethic. Rather than dismissing Black women's experiences with state violence, a womanist abolition ethic centers their voices as a source of moral integrity that is instructive for dismantling the carceral state.

A Womanist Theological Ethic of Abolition

Against a fantastic hegemonic imagination that negatively constructs Black women as deviant and sinful, a womanist theological ethic changes the narrative and uses a different value system emerging from the goodness, moral integrity, and original blessings of Black womanhood. This value system upends negative societal perceptions in a radical reappraisal to reclaim the divinity and human dignity of Black women. Hence, a womanist theological ethic of abolition applies a restorative and transformative justice approach to create abolitionist sanctuaries that repair harm, restore relationships, and rebuild more just and equitable systems for communal flourishing.

The theological inquiries for a womanist theological ethic of abolition ask: How do we recognize the divine qualities of Black women? How do we work toward a world where Black women are not treated as sinful, accursed, disrespectful, and criminal but as good, blessed, worthy, and salvific? How do we reimagine alternative responses beyond punishment and create a world beyond policing and prisons?

Pushing beyond Higginbotham's dated respectability politics and drawing from Cooper's conception of undisputed dignity in relationship to Fox's construct of original blessings, a womanist ethic of abolition maintains the inherent worth and divinity of Black womanhood. However, to fully jettison the use of sin as a construct to target Black women as deviant and to justify punishment and policing, a new theological source is necessary. Ergo, I explore Eastern orthodoxy and African diasporic religious interpretations of deification and divination to reframe the existential realities of Black women as a site of cosmic and material goodness.

In the East, the early church fathers articulated models of redemption that emphasized restorative qualities of the divine within human activity. *Deification* is a concept central to Eastern orthodoxy's theology that emphasizes the divine restorative qualities of human nature to the *imago Dei*. In sharp contrast to Anselm's concept of sin to preserve the purity of Jesus and articulation of an atonement theology sanctioning violence to secure salvation, the Eastern Orthodox Church fathers of Alexandria expressed an alternative paradigm. Rather than the hegemonic hold of early Western church fathers such as Augustine and Anselm, or later reformists and thinkers such as Calvin and Niebuhr, a shift to deification is generative to construct Black women as divine.

Divinization is not exclusive to Christianity. In some practices of African diasporic traditions—Brazilian Candomblé, Cuban Lucumi (or Santeria), Haitian Voodoo, and Nigerian Yoruba—the experience of divination is a ritual reserved for women who are considered more susceptible to divine manifestations as mediums and portals to communicate to their communities. Namely, Mãe Stella, a prominent Candomblé priestess, states that "[W]omen make better leaders in Candomblé because of their natural "mothering" qualities, as well as their ability to be responsive to the demands of the *orixá*. The skills required to manage and sustain the *terreiro's* intricate dynamics of interpersonal relations, hierarchy, and spiritual powers are perhaps cultivated more consistently and effectively among female leaders."[25]

According to Stella's experience with the Candomblé spiritual tradition, women are viewed as more receptive to spiritual manifestations and divination than their male counterparts. This makes women, particularly mother figures, communicate to their village and conduct business on behalf of divine directives they encounter firsthand. In this sense, women are indispensable to village life and the preservation of communities. They are the carriers of not just progeny but also their people's stories, customs, and traditions. Women are conduits of the divine and caretakers of their village. This reverence of women leaders in Candomblé is very different than the demonization of womanhood by doctrines of sin in Christianity. Despite Augustine's roots in the Continent, his conception of original sin counters African religions' emphasis on the divine qualities of humanity and the fact that women are held closest to the divine. It makes sense that Christianity's alignment with the empire would maintain a dissonance with religions that predate colonialism and imperialism.

Though original sin is an imperial paradigm unfounded by other religions, divinization is a religious value that transcends Christianity, colonization, and carceral systems. Eastern orthodoxy and African spirituality provide theological alternatives to Western church teachings about sin and facilitate restorative religious understandings of human nature in relationship to the divine. Liberation theology and the social gospel are other routes to find emancipatory beliefs within Christianity.[26] However, non-Western traditions, such as Eastern orthodoxy and African diasporic religions, provide alternatives that are underutilized to redress Christianity.

In the salient endeavor to amplify sources breaking the relationship between sin and punishment sanctioning violence against Black women, a womanist theological ethic of abolition

---

[25] Rachel Elizabeth Harding, *Women and Religion in the African Diaspora: Knowledge, Power, and Performance* (Baltimore, MD: John Hopkins University Press, 2006), 12.
[26] For instance, James Cone's oeuvre in Black liberation theology; Gustavo Guitierrez and Jon Sobrino's research on liberation theologies in Latin America; womanist literature, particularly that of Delores Williams; and Gary Dorrien's work and primary sources on the Black social gospel.

draws from emancipatory theologies to reappraise Black women as divine, as original blessings, as good first, and as an invitation to create economies for Black women to thrive as valued leaders and members of communities who carry and nurture what society needs to generate equitable and just democratic ideals.

Hence, the implication for a womanist theological ethic of abolition is to extend the Black feminist and womanist canon to critically engage the doctrine of original sin and construct interventionist alternatives that center the experiences of Black women. In addition, a significant contribution is to provide a counter theology to harmful church teachings in Western Christianity that perpetuate degenerative policies upholding carceral systems deleterious to the safety and personhood of Black women. Rather, a womanist theological ethic of abolition creates an emancipatory theology that harnesses the deific origins of Black women like McIntyre, Quinn, and Williams. Over and against state terror that reinforces policing to preserve white privilege, Black women deserve safety in a world that affirms their inherent worth, believes their stories when they are harmed, and protects their civil and human rights in a just and equitable system. To live and abide by this theological ethic ensures that Black women and mothers are no longer the most disrespected in America but can flourish as the embodiment of the divine.

Conclusion

This chapter opened with the stories of Black women who were terrorized by Roger Golubski and disregarded by the Kansas City Kansas Police Department. I showed how the policing and devaluing of Black womanhood are rooted in the understandings of inherent worth that parallel theological concepts. Namely, I challenged the interpretations of original and individual sin that function to re-enforce social control and blame or punish Black women for their own misfortune. I showed the ways in which respectability politics function similarly to sin to construct Black women as deviant and undeserving of moral concern, public safety, and justice. In the final analysis, I propose a womanist theological ethic of abolition to redress the harmful teachings of sin with non-Western theologies in the Eastern Church and African diasporic religions that focus on deification and divination. The application of a womanist theological ethic in the world shifts the appraisals of Black women—not as deviant but as deserving and divine.

Bibliography

Cahill, Lisa Sowle. "Quaestio Disputata The Atonement Paradigm: Does It Still Have Explanatory Value?" *Theological Studies* 67 (2007): 418–32.

Calvin, Jean. *Institutes of the Christian Religion*. Peabody, MA: Hendrickson, 2008.

Cisneros, Juan, et al. "FBI Arrests Former KCKPD Detective Roger Golubski," *Fox News Kansas City*, September 15, 2022. https://fox4kc.com/news/fbi-arrest-former-kckpd-detective-roger-golubski/, accessed April 9, 2024.

Cooper, Brittney C. *Beyond Respectability: The Intellectual Thought of Race Women*. Urbana: University of Illinois Press, 2017.

Dorrien, Gary J. *The New Abolition: W. E. B. Du Bois and the Black Social Gospel*. New Haven, CT: Yale University Press, 2015.

Douglas, Kelly Brown. *Stand Your Ground: Black Bodies and the Justice of God*. Maryknoll, NY: Orbis Books, 2015.

Fox, Matthew. *Original Blessing: A Primer in Creation Spirituality: Presented in Four Paths, Twenty-Six Themes, and Two Questions*. New York: Jeremy P. Tarcher/Putnam, 2000.

Harriot, Michael. "A Criminal Injustice: How a City Ignored the Rape, Murder and Terrorism of Black Women for Four Decades." The Root, May 27, 2021. https://www.theroot.com/a-criminal-injustice-how-a-city-ignored-the-rape-murd-1846883970, accessed March 22, 2023.

Higginbotham, Evelyn Brooks. *Righteous Discontent: The Women's Movement in the Black Baptist Church, 1880–1920*. Cambridge, MA: Harvard University Press, 1993.

Jones, Feminista. "Malcolm X Stood Up for Black Women When Few Others Would." *ZORA* (blog), August 7, 2020. https://zora.medium.com/malcolm-x-stood-up-for-black-women-when-few-others-would-68e8b2ea2747, accessed March 22, 2023.

KCKPD Corruption. "KCKPD Corruption." https://kckcorruption.info, accessed March 22, 2023.

Lowe, Peggy. "Kansas Prosecutor Who Framed Innocent Man Surrenders Law License, Will Soon Be Disbarred." KCUR - Kansas City News and NPR, April 16, 2024. https://www.kcur.org/news/2024-04-16/

notorious-kansas-prosecutor-surrenders-law-license-will-soon-be-disbarred, accessed May 16, 2024.

Niebuhr, Reinhold. *Faith and History: A Comparison of Christian and Modern Views of History*. New York: Scribner, 1949. https://kinginstitute.stanford.edu/king-papers/documents/theology-reinhold-niebuhr#fn8, accessed April 9, 2024.

Niebuhr, Reinhold. *The Nature and Destiny of Men: A Christian Interpretation*. New York: Scribner's, 1943. Reprint. Louisville, KY: Westminster John Knox Press, 1996.

Ricono, Angie, and Cyndi Fahrlander. "KCK Woman Outraged That Disgraced Cop Golubski Allowed to Go Home." KCTV5 News, September 29, 2022. https://www.kctv5.com/2022/09/29/kck-woman-outraged-that-disgraced-cop-golubski-allowed-go-home/, accessed March 22, 2023.

Townes, Emilie. *Womanist Ethics and the Cultural Production of Evil*. New York: Palgrave Macmillan, 2007.

5

A Tale of "Two" Marys

Charlene Sinclair

I'm often asked why I chose to go to seminary. I had spent most of my professional life within justice-seeking movements and attended church sporadically, so many found the decision rather perplexing. I can't blame them for being perplexed. I was also perplexed! Who wouldn't be when a lack of church attendance was paired with the propensity for risqué language, impious behavior, a lack of academic inclination, and a twenty-year distance from a marginal-at-best college performance? Yet, what initially appeared to be an odd passing thought became an incessant, insistent, inescapable drumbeat. The Spirit will find you wherever you are and will demand a response, whether that response is yes or no.

The Spirit found me in the midst of my participation in the struggles for justice, and I said NO—HELL NO! I told myself it didn't make sense. I was forty years old; I didn't go to church; I liked vodka tonics; I swore like a sailor. But if I were to be really honest, the rationales for my no were created in the hopes of drowning the voices in my head that told me I had no right to follow this path. It didn't work. So I did what any self-respecting social justice activist would do—I told myself that the problems of the world were bigger than the problems in my head. I stepped out of the ring and let the voices fight it out while I attended to the larger problems of the world. But the problems in my head were the problems of the world, and I realized that I couldn't effectively find a pathway toward justice if I didn't attend to and understand the origins of this head battlefield.

I determined that I had to wrestle with ideas, but I had not come to terms with the fact that I needed to wrestle with myself: that the ideas had no depth, no clarity, and no fullness of meaning outside of myself. It was quite ironic that as a community organizer, I trained people to claim their own truths, but in the decision to go to seminary, I went in search of their truths and not my own. I had a lofty and, quite frankly, self-righteously sanctimonious goal. I had determined that white, particularly white male, social movement professionals didn't understand the role that faith played in fueling our visions and actions for justice. I was going to seminary to investigate how faith undergirded the struggle for rights and dignity even when the possibility of another world appeared to be no more than a utopian pipe dream. And I planned to return to my work as a grassroots community organizer, triumphant in my development of the theory and language to confront what I had determined was a gap in understanding, resulting in the degradation of the role of faith as a critical component of movement analysis and strategy. Whew! It was a mouthful and a headful.

However, the Spirit will find you wherever you try to hide. My plans took an unexpected turn when I was asked to curate a gathering for "God Behind Bars," a research project that studied women's spirituality while incarcerated. I began the work with a level of researcher detachment. You see, although the movements I participated in were dominated by the leadership of poor Black and brown women, I began developing the gathering believing I had no relationship to the women we were "studying." Growing up in Newark, New Jersey, in the 1970s meant that I knew young men from my community who were or had been incarcerated. I had spent many years ensuring that my younger brothers and my son did not become one of the incarcerated men I knew. This was not my issue, and I certainly had no relationship with women who were or had the experience of incarceration. Or so I thought.

As I reached out to women and began to engage them and their stories, I found myself catapulted back in time to the kitchens and the living rooms of the Black and brown women on welfare with whom I had lived, fought alongside of, and eventually became the community organizer for years before. The faces had changed, but the expressions of self-castigation and shame had not. I encountered women of extraordinary courage bound by the notions of sin, the wrath of God, and the inevitability of damnation and punishment. Women struggling with expressions of faith that told them that the problems in their lives were of their own making and redemption, although not assured, may be possible with the diligent rejection of personal sin, a commitment of time and money to the local church, and deep prayer to God. A faith that said poverty was inevitable and their individual situation meant that God's grace simply didn't shine upon them. One that entreated them to be more like Jesus than Jesus himself. A faith that told them that they and their bad decisions were the culprits and not the structures designed to be stacked up against them.

Pray more. Drink less. Run the bible study at church. Be virtuous. Be respectable. Strivings that held their lives hostage while the bills kept piling up every month. Strivings that often held a desperate mental grip on a belief in the miraculous even as it failed to deliver the job that could relieve their immiseration. But for many, the everyday struggle of a poverty-riddled life continued, and the abuse of the market was matched and sometimes exceeded by the abuse of their partners. And they died slow deaths—spiritually, mentally, physically—riddled with shame and self-blame.

During those conversations, I saw my sisters! I saw myself. I had wondered what happened to my community after Bill Clinton and Newt Gingrich entered their unholy alliance and colluded to "end welfare as we knew it." Now I knew. Ending welfare didn't end the grinding poverty, and many of my sisters had ended up incarcerated as they struggled to create strategies for their survival and the survival of their children. It was at that moment that I committed myself to understanding the relationship between the political economy of a racialized *and* gendered capitalism and the legitimation of the structures of social control of impoverished women, particularly that of poor Black women. More importantly, I committed myself to not only understanding the role theology plays in giving legitimacy to the systems of oppression and social control but also how a liberative theological framework may be designed and utilized to make those structures illegitimate and, hence, poised for dismantlement. But how might I actualize these commitments? The answer came to me quite unexpectedly in a workshop on poverty and the Bible.

The workshop was composed of folks working in movements for economic justice. During the discussion of the Jesus movement as a movement of the poor, Tara, a participant in the workshop, spoke of her tension with the Virgin Mary. Raised as a Roman Catholic, she had been encouraged to uphold the image of the Virgin Mary, humble, docile, quiet, and virginal, as the ideal. In addition, she was also introduced to the other Mary—Mary Magdalene, a pre- and post-penitent prostitute—to underscore and hold in place the idealized image of feminine perfection as virginal, docile, and white. These Marys were ever-present. The Virgin, prominent at the front of the church with a palpable stillness that can almost be felt. And Magdalene, never an image but an ever-present idea. The scepter doing double duty. A reminder of the whore who awaits capture if the fight to curb the sin of sexuality is lost while also symbolizing the pathway back to honor through the proper veneration and following of male authority and power.

Tara's life was not unique. Many women held the projections of both Marys in tenuous tension. However, after the birth of an out-of-wedlock child and a subsequent "fall from grace," she landed on the welfare rolls. The tension snapped; crisis ensued. As with so many of us, at the moment of crisis, Tara returned to her faith and began to reflect on her early Catholic teachings. This time, she did not center on God or the Virgin. Rather, it was Mary Magdalene who occupied her thoughts. She wanted to reclaim Mary Magdalene and challenged us to do so as well.

I responded to this challenge, but before reclaiming Mary Magdalene, I had to confront myself, for I had given both Marys no more than a passing glance. Like many Christians, my eyes had been trained on Jesus, and everyone else was merely supporting characters. Now here I stood, a former Black welfare mom, in the face of this challenge, realizing with deep embarrassment that as a feminist theo-ethicist I had paid scant attention to two of the most important women in Jesus' life. It was at that moment that I recognized myself and understood the urgency of Tara's challenge. I, too, had a child out of wedlock. I, too, had been a welfare mom. I, too, had been relegated to the land of the sinful castaways. Like Tara, I saw myself, as well as other welfare mothers, in Mary Magdalene: our true selves were completely distorted and imbued with notions of wanton sexuality. In this contradiction of image and reality, I saw the contradictions that poor mothers, whether on welfare, incarcerated, or formerly incarcerated, are forced to face. Seen not as hard-working moms but rather as lazy, welfare queens, criminals, and whores. So I set out to find them with a gusto fueled by contrition and a nascent awareness that this journey was placing me back into the ring to fight for the self and for the sisters I had created so much distance with!

When looking for Mary Magdalene, I found no docile, repentant prostitute. Instead, I encountered a strong and powerful woman with a very public persona, the antithesis of the roles usually ascribed to women. As far as we can tell, Mary Magdalene has no domestic domain—she is a follower of Jesus, a nomad. We hear of no husband, no father, no son: all markers of existence and security for women in antiquity. Her voice is not constrained to private spaces but is commissioned to be used in the proclamation of the Christian message. How do we account for the image of Mary Magdalene as a recovering prostitute or "the whore who loved and was forgiven by Jesus,"[1] despite historical facts that have indicated otherwise? How does this initial witness to what is arguably the critical Christian narrative become no longer a witness, interpreter, and extoller but a repentant harlot? Most importantly, how might reclaiming Mary Magdalene chart a path for the reclamation of me, Tara, and other welfare moms?

Jane Schaberg argues that the process of "whoring" Mary Magdalene "was a reaction against female power and authority of a major witness."[2] Schaberg tells us that

> gnostic materials present her as a leading intellectual and spiritual guide of the early, post-Easter community, as a visionary, the Savior's beloved companion, a conduit for and interpreter of his teachings. In spite of her importance in the Gospel narratives and noncanonical works, there is silence and confusion around this figure. In spite of the paucity of information about her, there is a great deal of tension or anxiety about her role.[3]

---

[1] Jane Schaberg, *The Resurrection of Mary Magdalene: Legends, Apocrypha, and the Christian Testament* (New York: Continuum, 2002), 68.
[2] Schaberg, *The Resurrection of Mary Magdalene*, 80.
[3] Schaberg, *The Resurrection of Mary Magdalene*, 66.

Therefore, to understand fully the reformulation of Mary Magdalene from apostle, prophet, and visionary to sinner and whore, we must first begin with the context in which the (re)formulation of Mary Magdalene occurs: amidst the complex and dynamic battle for the construction of Christianity's theo-political identity. In the ancient world, where multiple expressions of Christianity, as opposed to a singular Christianity, were developing, the question of who had the authority was as equally important as what that authority was. Gender, therefore, comes into focus as a tool for silencing the revolutionary theo-political participation and authority of women.

Given the gender battle for authority, we can assume that it was not only Mary Magdalene but rather the role of both Marys that might have been contested terrain. Mary Magdalene was distorted, ignored, or silenced through the process of "whoring" her image, and Mary, Mother of Jesus, receded in the background, made invisible save for the images of a docile embrace of a newborn son. Given this contestation, the journey to recapture the dignity, vision, and power of Mary Magdalene to enable women to shed the selves created by others and reclaim their personal truths must also entail a re-engagement with Mary, Mother of Jesus.

Today, many Christians read the story of the birth of Jesus, light the advent candles, and wait in anticipation of the marvelous day when his birth, his in-breaking into a tired and weary world, will be celebrated. Many forget to sit with Mary as she waited. Now, as I embark on this journey to reclaim the truths of both Marys, I sit with Mary, Mother of Jesus, not as the organizer, the activist, or the ethicist but as the pregnant teenager waiting for the birth of a child. I allow myself to come close to this Mary. To be transported back to the fear, the bewilderment, the ostracism—to the shame. Sitting with Mary was initially difficult. For me, Mary's story was like a heavy drop of dew falling from the tip of a leaf to explode into tiny fragments of itself. All emerging from the same source but different, disparate, and maybe desperate. Fragments can never be fully whole again, but they can be glued back into some semblance of wholeness. Can I glue back the pieces if I allow myself to be shattered? I was afraid. Until I encountered Mary of the Magnificat.

In the Gospel of Luke, we hear that when she found out that she was pregnant, Mary visited her cousin Elizabeth. When she arrived, Elizabeth greeted her and celebrated the coming of Mary's child. Mary's response to Elizabeth was a powerfully determined and liberationist hymn. Her response is not meek. It is angry and gives us a peek into the world in which she lived and is making an indictment against. In verses 52-53, the Magnificat/Mary's Song of Praise, she tells us that God "has brought down the powerful from their thrones and lifted up the lowly; he has filled the hungry with good things and sent the rich away empty."

Mary's pregnancy and the Magnificat are often separated, but in the Magnificat, Mary's strong indictment against the rich and powerful and call for a new life for the poor and the hungry is political, spiritual, and clearly highly personal. Were welfare moms not this Mary as well? The material reality of their impregnation made silent. The revolutionary act of living and raising their children in a world meant not for their life but rather for their death made invisible. The demand for docile respectability, the only path for legitimating their being.

In Hortense Spillers's "Mama's Baby, Papa's Maybe," we encounter Black women, enslaved and in current narratives, who are both refused the title of mother and whose children are seemingly created by them alone.[4] There is such a deep connectivity between the Virgin Mary, formerly enslaved Black women, and Black women deemed welfare queens. We have no idea of how this now-spiritualized birth was actually conceived. We don't know if the spiritualization of it was the way you could accept it. With God as progenitor and Mary now made virgin, the male child is, in effect, now severed from his mother, effectively silencing her active role in birthing and mothering, freezing her image through iconography and interpretation, and invisibilizing her revolutionary voice and actions.

The silences we encounter are the silences of interpretation. They are not biblical silences. We have Mary's Magnificat—where she is proclaiming revolutionary retribution. That is not a docile person. Traci West, in *Disruptive Christian Ethics*, shows us how Mary of the Magnificat is bringing forth a disruptive message that speaks of God's power, favor, grace, and justice for all that requires no apology from poor Black and brown welfare moms who have been vilified but does require justice from the society that has oppressed, vilified, and impoverished them.[5]

---

[4]Hortense Spillers, *Black White and in Color: Essays on American Literature and Culture* (Chicago, IL: University of Chicago Press, 2003), 203–29.
[5]Traci West, *Disruptive Christian Ethics: When Racism and Women's Lives Matter* (Louisville, KY: Westminster John Knox Press, 2006), 106.

Karen King identifies Mary Magdalene, stated within the Gospel account, as the disciple that Jesus loved "more than all other women" [6:1] and more than the disciples themselves [10:10].[6] Although the woman is assumed to be Mary Magdalene, nothing in the text identifies her as such. Interestingly, King, a church historian, places the text "around the time many now situate the Gospel of Luke."[7] Might the Mary of the Magnificat know the Mary of the Gospel of Mary? We have the documentation of Mary Magdalene leading disciples and no documentation to support the cultural interpretation that she must have been Jesus' lover. Might the Marys even be one and the same—two sides of the same gendered coin? Might we, along with King, be falling into the same trap we are fighting against? Can we imagine that a son could love his mother more than any other? Could she not be a revolutionary mother? Might she not have raised this revolutionary being? To imagine that would mean that she had a very present position within his life, his ministry, as his mother. Which would also mean that she informed that very ministry— because she raised him. How dare a woman just be a leader and not be sexualized? One woman made asexual—almost made a eunuch— and the other made highly sexual in order to dismantle her.

We do not come without politics or commitments. Our work is never merely an aesthetic, academic, or professional exercise; it is always also a sociopolitical one grounded in both our conscious and subconscious understanding of the world. To ignore the interpretive exploitation of theological narratives that invisibilize or foster women's beings as prone to personal pathology is to fail to contest for or counter the moral authority claimed by those with more conservative politics that would keep women marginalized, insecure, and primed for exploitation in low-waged, unhealthy, precarious working arrangements. Often, progressive politics engage faith-based conversations as conversations about personal or individual morality, rather than an engagement in the questions of who we, the collective, would like to be as a society and what policies and systems will guide us toward the actualization of vision. As a result, we invisibilize or make whore. Together, the historic structuring of

---

[6]Karen King, *The Gospel of Mary of Magdala: Jesus and the First Woman Apostle* (Santa Rosa, CA: Polebridge Press, 2003), 15–17.
[7]Hal Taussig, *A New New Testament: A Bible for the Twenty-First Century* (Boston, MA: Houghton Mifflin Harcourt, 2013), 217.

both Marys represents a component of the historical structuring of Black poor women's existence as both pathological and highly sexual. Can the recapturing and rearticulation of both Marys together, in conversation with and not isolated from each other, challenge us to question our often uninterrogated interpretation of the lives and choices of poor Black and brown women? Can we seek to recapture the dignity, vision, and power of both Marys and, through that journey, seek to assist poor women in shedding the distorted selves created by others and reclaiming their personal, political, and revolutionary truths?

Mary Magdalene and Mary of the Magnificat show us the courage and fierceness of women who, in spite of the world that attempts to foreclose their power, still dare to proclaim the world they want—and act toward bringing into being that world. There are no messages more needed today than those. As many come to terms with neighbors and possibly even family members who have embraced the cruelty of Donald Trump, his administration, and the depth of cruelty and othering he has unleashed, we are reminded by both Marys that a new way is yet possible. This new way is deeply spiritual and deeply political; it requires soul searching and possibly soul wrestling, but it is not sentimental or docile. It refuses shame and embraces the power of the leadership of women often cast in the role of outcast and outlaw to place us into action and help us navigate the terrain toward our true collective humanity, toward a just world.

Bibliography

King, Karen. *The Gospel of Mary of Magdala: Jesus and the First Woman Apostle*. Santa Rosa, CA: Polebridge Press, 2003.

Lorde, Audre. *Sister Outsider: Essays and Speeches*. Berkeley, CA: Crossing Press, 2007.

Schaberg, Jane. *The Resurrection of Mary Magdalene: Legends, Apocrypha, and the Christian Testament*. New York: Continuum, 2002.

Spillers, Hortense. *Black White and in Color: Essays on American Literature and Culture*. Chicago, IL: Chicago University Press, 2003.

Taussig, Hal. *A New New Testament: A Bible for the Twenty-First Century*. Boston, MA: Houghton Mifflin Harcourt, 2013.

West, Traci. *Disruptive Christian Ethics: When Racism and Women's Lives Matter*. Louisville, KY: Westminster John Knox Press, 2006.

6

Reclaiming Disabilities Theologically, Envisioning Just Flourishing

Heike Peckruhn

> *Liberatory theology of disability is the work of the bodily figuration of knowledge. As embodied theology, it is both the struggle of resistance and the revelation of our long-masked knowledge and images. It is ... grounded in the bodies and actions of people with disabilities and others who care.*[1]
> —NANCY EIESLAND

---

[1] Nancy L. Eiesland, *The Disabled God: Toward a Liberatory Theology of Disability* (Nashville, TN: Abingdon Press, 1994), 90.

*Disability is a central condition of our existence in the Anthropocene. [...] disability is a state of vitality, a way of being that matters in the world, a position from which critical knowledge unfolds.*²
—JULIA WATTS BELSER

We have what we always have had, and more.
We know how to mourn
to pray
to persist
to find resistance in the smallest of spaces
to find each other and make homes, alone and together
to lay down in the middle of the road and keen with grief and rage and block traffic
to crip innovate
to do some shit that no one says is possible
to do something wild and unexpected under the radar
*to keep going.*³
—LEAH LAKSHMI PIEPZNA-SAMARASINHA

Beginning with Disabilities

Disability theology as a field engages the notions of human difference and works toward envisioning and implementing greater inclusivity and flourishing of all embodied lives. Much of this theological work hinges on incorporating insights and frameworks emerging from the disability justice movements and disability theory/studies.⁴

---

²Julia Watts Belser, "Disability, Climate Change, and Environmental Violence: The Politics of Invisibility and the Horizon of Hope," *Disability Studies Quarterly* 40, no. 4 (2020), https://doi.org/10.18061/dsq.v40i4.6959 (accessed April 9, 2024).
³Leah Lakshmi Piepzna-Samarasinha, *The Future Is Disabled: Prophecies Love Notes and Mourning Songs* (Vancouver: Arsenal Pulp Press, 2022), 164.
⁴Disability studies/critical disability studies as an academic field is an inter- and multidisciplinary academic discipline in the humanities and social sciences,

A significant touchpoint, perhaps the most fundamental concept or presumption to begin theological construction that seeks to further disability justice, is to define disability as a human experience that is at once material, viscerally embodied, and socially constructed and shaped by culture. Disability is not self-evident—because of the vast diversity of people one might consider as disabled (from blind or deaf people to people living with mental illnesses or different intellectual functioning) and the diversity within specific disability experiences themselves (ranges of vision or mental capacities). And disability is but one of many markers of identity and social experience—race, gender, sexuality, geographic location, socioeconomic status, and the like all contribute to how "disability" manifests and how flourishing is envisioned and sought out.

In this chapter, I begin by providing a short overview of what it means to engage disabilities as lived experiences by introducing models of disability as conceptual frameworks. I then sketch disability theology as it emerged in collaborative conversation with feminist theological concerns. I not only trace where the call to begin with, engage from, and imagine with disability as lived experience has been heeded in theology, but also note that the urgency of this call has not waned but has become more important. Disability justice movements are leading the way in creating spaces for embodied flourishing, and theologians must tune in or miss critical interventions where prophetic imagination and action are lived and modeled today.

Engaging Disabilities

Disability studies provided theologians with a framework to recognize how language and imagination are guided to help us decode select human differences considered socially significant and how, in turn, we learn to feel, know, and act in certain ways when encountering such differences in ourselves and others. There are several basic models of disability: those most often constructively engaged in (disability) theology are the moral, medical, social,

---

concerned with the meaning and consequences of recognized differences in human embodiment, which is a significantly different approach than the study of disabilities in the medical fields.

and limits models.⁵ These models are theoretical tools (and as such each incomplete, with constructive potential and inherent flaws); they capture the way human differences are mapped, how they are coded and explained. And as such, they help us detect how everyday interactions imbue human differences, especially perceived limitations and impairments (physical, emotional, social, cognitive, and others) with meaning and value, by helping us notice how and what kind of model is used to decide what to "do about" this difference.

In the *moral* model of disability, specific, identified human differences are seen as a message—a punishment, reward, curse, blessing—from the divine or demonic. Physical or mental impairments are interpreted as having a moral value and require individual or communal action that might remedy a perceived sin or offense. A variation of this is the *tragedy* model of disability that frames impairments as suffering, thus deserving pity and charity. Disabled persons become the tools and means for abled people's virtue development. In the *medical* model, the language mapping human differences is overdetermined by diagnosis, identifying deficiencies from "normal" human functions and capacities and labeling disease and pathologies. Disability is diagnosed as the property of the individual who embodies lack, defectiveness, or abnormalities, and what is aimed for is treatment, repair, or cure—technologies that eradicate the undesirable difference from "normal." This perspective creates binaries of normal/abnormal, healthy/sick, patient/expert, pain/wellness. With the emergence

---

⁵There are other kinds of models or variations of models, many of which could be captured under a social model umbrella. Some differences can be linked to location and emergence. For example, whereas the North American social model is tightly linked to the disability rights movement (and therefore emphasizes civil rights concepts and language, such as minority group rights), the social model conceptualization emerged in the UK in disability alliance circles and tends to lean on social constructs and the power of labeling in social relations and emphasizes divisions between impairment/disability and focuses on equality in political and material participation. Or, the social relational model focuses on how oppression is a dynamic created in social interactions and relational dimensions. This model has much traction in fields such as education and childhood development. In theology, biblical studies, and other religious studies disciplines, the geographic location of the author and the academic discipline informing them often impacts which model might be utilized when discussing the social and cultural dimensions of the disability experiences.

of the disability rights movement and disability studies as a field, "disability" became a concept to deconstruct: the *social* model makes a distinction between impairment (human traits considered to be medically or biologically nonnormative) and disability (social and structural discrimination against persons with impairments, systemic barriers excluding persons who deviate from normative embodiment).[6] The social model enables investigating ableism in social, political, and cultural discourses and spaces and focusing on transforming communal practices toward liberation and inclusion. It allows for critical investigations into the shifting meanings and consequences of impairments—how universal human differences may or may not become disabling through socially enacted stigma. The *limits model* responds to some shortcomings of the social model, namely the inability to offer a more holistic approach to justice beyond access and the inattention to real experiences of pain and debility that can accompany impairment. This model (distinctly theological, developed by Deborah B. Creamer) presumes limits as a normal part of any lived existence, unsurprising, and even important to our being human (though not all good or necessary).[7] It seeks to move beyond the normal/abnormal framing of (dis)ability into a recognition of our complexly interwoven relatedness that often defies identity categories and labels. All human embodiment is limited, and disability is an unstable category that is nevertheless concrete, diverse, visceral, and complex.[8]

Beginning with disability is not tied to a specific field or method of inquiry, but inherently an inter- and multidisciplinary mode of critical inquiry. An awareness of the models of disability and

---

[6]The disability rights movement in the United States emerges on the heels of the civil rights movement, which aided the shaping of already mobilizing disability activist groups into a recognizable rights movement from the 1970s to the 1980s. Disability studies as an academic field emerged in the 1980s in the United States, UK, and Canada. Major scholarly figures include Lennard J. Davis, Rosemarie Garland-Thomson, Christopher M. Bell, Simi Linton, Douglas C. Baynton, David Mitchell, Sharon Snyder, and others situated in history, language, arts, and cultural studies.
[7]Deborah B. Creamer, *Disability and Christian Theology: Embodied Limits and Constructive Possibilities* (New York: Oxford University Press, 2009).
[8]For more on the models, and variations/different models, especially as they relate and/or frame theological concerns, see Marno Retief and Rantoa Letšosa, "Models of Disability: A Brief Overview," *HTS Teologiese Studies/Theological Studies* 74, no. 1 (2018), https://doi.org/10.4102/hts.v74i1.4738 (accessed April 7, 2024).

learning to detect their occurrence in everyday life and theologies reminds us to be cautious not to make disability a self-evident, fixed category. Disability emerges in individual, social, and structural dimensions within intersections of experience, representation, and communal meaning-making.

Connections to Feminist Theology

Recuperating the body, the female body, the at best undervalued and at worst slandered and discarded body of/in theology had been one of the ways in which feminist theology began grounding its work in lived experiences. Feminist theology deconstructed and reworked language, imagery, and metaphors based in what they revealed as oppressive sexist and patriarchal domination and committed to more inclusive ways of speaking and practicing community. Largely, the aim of feminist theology has been to uncover, critique, and reimagine human relational matrices grounded in ideologies that create hierarchies of power based in the codification of specific bodily traits as cultural and theological ideals. Disability theology as a field began in conversation with feminist theological concerns. Nancy Eiesland, whom many consider as the inaugural disability theologian, published *The Disabled God: Toward a Liberatory Theology of Disability* in 1994, drawing on embodied experiences and insights from disability studies and the disability rights movement to reimagine a Christian theology and practice that center disabled persons and their experiences. And in the same year, the *Journal of Feminist Studies in Religion* (JFSR), a roundtable of women with disabilities (including Eiesland), took feminist scholars to task for their literal and conceptual exclusions of disability as human experience in their analysis, politics, and theologies. Eiesland's monograph is more widely known, but it is the JFSR Roundtable conversation that clearly highlighted the commonalities and differences between feminist and disability theologies, and that offered up a variety of salient critiques. Those challenges presented to feminist theologians by other feminist theologians with disabilities were based in the common desire to image God and community in more inclusive and liberatory ways. Women with disabilities made plain the ableism in feminist works, especially the ways in which theologically, idealized "normal" female bodies were conceptualized in the pursuit of recognition of women as autonomous, independent, and whole human beings. What if our theologies assume difference and embodied limits, especially as they are lived in "disability," at the center of our lives and imaginations? What relational practices are intertwined with such theologies? These questions were taken up and developed in a variety of ways in theological conversations. Both Eiesland's work and the Roundtable conversation mark the beginning of disability theology as a collaborative project (between disability studies and disability movements and theologians, and between feminist and disability concerns).

The Disabled God—Emergence and Legacies

The basic premise emerging out of the disability rights movements and theorized through the disability studies in the social model made its way into theology with Nancy Eiesland's groundbreaking work *The Disabled God*. The social model points out that one is not born disabled, but one is disabled in/by a society that structures itself in ways that exclude "abnormal" or "deficient" bodies and therefore disable them. Additionally, language, symbols, and metaphors contribute to the material embodiment of human experience. In the social model, she shifted theological concerns *with* disability from pastoral and caring-for types of approaches to a liberation theology emerging *from* disability contexts. Eiesland held Christian communities to task for creating experiences for disabled persons that are at best patronizing accommodation and tolerance and at worst excluding and degrading, even hostile, to those with disabilities. She diagnosed the problem not in the practices themselves but in theologies that are fundamentally exclusive and deny justice. A disability theology, one that begins from within the disability context, builds from the radical notion that disabled embodiment is fully compatible with how we ought to imagine what is good and holy. Eiesland's constructive imagination reexamined the Christian story for openings toward justice for disabled people. The image of God as disabled, God in a sip-and-puff wheelchair, God as the scarred, broken, interdependent, disabled Christ who builds community with those who struggle to maintain bodily dignity and integrity has been an important contribution that continues to echo through theological discourses. The *imago Dei* is in the disabled bodies, and disability does not contradict the integrity of God, but is *as is* a model of beauty, wholeness in interdependence, mutuality, and solidarity.

Just like feminist theologies of the time reworked God-language and metaphors, one significant effect from Eiesland's work came in the form of reimagining God from a specific embodied experience.[9] And Eiesland's disabled God became a, if not the, symbolic prototype for the theological task of rethinking Christian images, rituals, and doctrines centering disabled experiences.[10] A major theological task was the re-symbolization and creation of new metaphors and language to give rise to subversive theologies and practices of mutuality and care, fostering identification with and centering of communities around the embodied experiences of disabled persons. With the emergence of disability theology, diverse metaphors and reconceptualizations of God, Christ, and Spirit developed, recognizing the diversity of the embodied disability experience itself and the need for variations in constructing theological symbols.[11] Notable feminist disability theologian Creamer made disability studies accessible as a methodology for theology and reconstructing theological anthropology centering disability justice (the limits model mentioned above); Sharon V. Betcher moved theological insights gained through disability methodologies into philosophy and cultural theory, critically linking environmental concerns and disability justice in her work.[12] The overall presumption that disabled embodiment in its variations and complexities is a preferred epistemological location continues to challenge and

---

[9] Not surprising and somewhat expected since Eiesland studied with Rebecca Chopp (whose feminist theological work focuses on language and its transformative power for embodied life and subject formation) and built on the methodologies and toolsets of early (feminist) liberation theologies.

[10] Eiesland, *The Disabled God*, 23. Eiesland grounds her work in experience and narratives, her own and, for example, that of disabled writer Nancy Mairs's writings.

[11] For example, a "Deaf God" in Hannah Lewis, *Deaf Liberation Theology* (New York: Routledge, 2016), or in Wayne Morris, *Theology without Words: Theology in the Deaf Community* (New York: Routledge, 2016). See also Lisa D. Powell, *The Disabled God Revisited: Trinity, Christology, and Liberation* (London: Bloomsbury, 2023).

[12] Sharon V. Betcher, *Spirit and the Politics of Disablement* (Minneapolis, MN: Fortress Press, 2007), and Sharon V. Betcher, *Spirit and the Obligation of Social Flesh: A Secular Theology for the Global City* (New York: Fordham University Press, 2013).

expand theological imaginations, including feminist theologies concerned with embodied justice.[13] Though staying with/in lived (disability) experiences as a site for doing theology also presents the challenge to not move to metaphor too quickly and constructing disability *metaphor* theologies, rather than *disability* theologies.[14]

Investigations into disability that use a social understanding of disability as a basic conceptual framework to approach topics of human difference have multiplied in diverse religious and theological subfields (biblical studies, systematic theology, theological ethics, practical theology, historical theology, etc.).[15] Disability studies methodologies inspired various inter- and multidisciplinary approaches in biblical and theological studies, such as analyzing disability as a literary trope, illuminating cultural constructions of disease and illness or forms of im/purity and deviance, or offering critical hermeneutical methods to counter ableist readings and theological constructions. Theological engagement centering disability that focused on the questions of being human, relationality, and communal life from specific locations such as autism, Down syndrome, mental illness, or profound intellectual disability have found traction, especially in practical theology and ethics.[16]

---

[13] Deborah B. Creamer, "Disability Theology," *Religion Compass* 6, no. 7 (2012): 339–46 (342). See also Talitha Cooreman-Guittin and Armand L. van Ommen, "Disability Theology: A Driving Force for Change?" *International Journal for the Study of the Christian Church* 22, no. 1 (2022): 1–4.

[14] Heike Peckruhn, *Meaning in Our Bodies: Sensory Experience as Constructive Theological Imagination* (New York: Oxford University Press, 2017), 21–2, 90.

[15] For example, in biblical studies: Rebecca Raphael, *Biblical Corpora: Representations of Disability in Hebrew Biblical Literature* (London: T&T Clark, 2008), Saul M. Olyan, *Disability in the Hebrew Bible: Interpreting Mental and Physical Differences* (New York: Cambridge University Press, 2008), or Candida R. Moss and Jeremy Schipper, eds., *Disability Studies and Biblical Literature* (New York: Palgrave Macmillan, 2011); in practical theology: John Swinton, *Dementia: Living in the Memories of God* (London: SCM Press, 2012); in moral theology and theological ethics: Mary Jo Iozzio, *Disability Ethics and Preferential Justice: A Catholic Perspective* (Washington, DC: Georgetown University Press, 2023), and Devan Stahl, *Disability's Challenge to Theology: Genes, Eugenics, and the Metaphysics of Modern Medicine* (Notre Dame, IN: University of Notre Dame Press, 2022).

[16] For example, Molly C. Haslam, *A Constructive Theology of Intellectual Disability: Human Being as Mutuality and Response* (New York: Fordham University Press, 2012); Hans S. Reinders, *Receiving the Gift of Friendship: Profound Disability, Theological Anthropology, and Ethics* (Grand Rapids, MI: Wm. B. Eerdmans, 2008); Amos Yong, *Theology and Down Syndrome: Reimagining Disability in*

Lived embodied experiences of disabled persons provide theological insights into the inadequacies and violences of theologies articulated from the center.[17] Most recently, beyond disability adjacent theological reflections, disability centered theologies begin again centered in lived multifaceted embodied experiences.[18] And a principal concern raised by Eiesland in *The Disabled God*, namely the exclusion of disabled people from religious communities and activities (or perhaps at best, marginal and "special" positionalities), especially from leadership and constructive contributions in communities and the academy, is getting renewed attention. Ableism is deeply embedded in the structures of the academy and religious institutions and communities and continues to impede disability inclusion, let alone disability justice.[19] More recently, disabled theologians and community leaders have emerged in public spaces as technology and social media enable public theological presence and conversations somewhat less confined by institutional barriers.[20] Mainstreaming acceptance and efforts to at least provide minimal access to communities and the academy certainly is part

---

Late Modernity (Waco, TX: Baylor University Press, 2007); Benjamin T. Conner, *Disabling Mission, Enabling Witness: Exploring Missiology through the Lens of Disability Studies* (Downers Grove, IL: InterVarsity Press, 2018); and Erin Raffety, *From Inclusion to Justice: Disability, Ministry, and Congregational Leadership* (Waco, TX: Baylor University Press, 2022).

[17]For example, Sarah Jean Barton, in *Becoming the Baptized Body*, investigates baptismal theologies and practices from disabled perspectives. She decidedly grounds her method in inclusive, partnered theological imaginations with persons with intellectual disabilities. See Sarah Jean Barton, *Becoming the Baptized Body: Disability and the Practice of Christian Community* (Waco, TX: Baylor University Press, 2022).

[18]For example, Rebecca Spurrier explores the practices of a Christian community in which more than half of the members identify as disabled and live in the intersections of mental illness, disability, and economic precarity. Here, theological visions of belonging, justice, access for all are illuminated for its messiness, complexity, and precarity. See Rebecca Spurrier, *The Disabled Church: Human Difference and the Art of Communal Worship* (New York: Fordham University Press, 2020).

[19]See also Margaret Price, *Mad at School: Rhetorics of Mental Disability and Academic Life* (Ann Arbor: University of Michigan Press, 2011), and Jay T. Dolmage, *Academic Ableism: Disability and Higher Education* (Ann Arbor: University of Michigan Press, 2017).

[20]See, for example, Rev. JJ Flag (revjjflag.com), Amy Kenny (amy-kenny.com), and Amy Kenny, *My Body Is Not a Prayer Request: Disability Justice in the Church* (Grand Rapids, MI: Baker Books, 2022), or Amy Panton and Miriam Spies, https://themadandcriptheologypodcast.buzzsprout.com (accessed April 7, 2024).

of this new recognition of disabled theologians' contributions, but barriers to leadership and/in organizational spaces continue to materially exclude persons with disabilities.

Disability theology urges feminist and other theologies to return again and again to theologizing as precarious, vulnerable, and decentered/ing work—one that makes vulnerable and questions the positioning of the theologian themselves, which renders theologies vulnerable to change and tensions. If being human is inherently being limited and is inseparable from embodied messiness, then theological work is inherently unfinished and complicated, with visions of justice always bearing impulses for violence and exclusions. The challenge is to pay attention to what happens and is expressed in multifaceted lived experience, not just in the spaces and places explicitly created and sanctioned as being of theological significance, but the peripheries, the entrances, unofficial gatherings, the bedrooms, the toilet stalls.[21]

Disability and Feminism—Other Initial Conversations and Continued Challenges for Theology

Though Eiesland's monograph is more widely known, the 1994 JFSR Roundtable conversation of women with disabilities (including Eiesland) clearly highlighted the commonalities and differences between feminist and disability theologies and offered a variety of additional critiques and challenges.[22] And a second JFSR roundtable in 2010, which honored the legacy of Eiesland

---

[21] See, for example, the essays by Darla Schumm, Judith Plaskow, Michelle M. Lelwica, and others in a forum on toilet justice, moderated in *Political Theology Network* by Julia Watts Belser, "Toilet Justice," *Political Theology Network*, published March 5, 2018, https://politicaltheology.com/symposium/toilet-justice/ (accessed April 7, 2024).

[22] The 1994 Roundtable reflected some "very 90's" feminist concerns (such as social and political liberation, economic access and equality, continued rights discussions) and urged to center disability in those areas as well to make women's liberation inclusive. Elly Elshout, Dorothee Wilhelm, Carole R. Fontaine, Nancy L. Eiesland, Valerie C. Stiteler, Adele B. McCollum, and Margaret Moers Wenig, "Roundtable Discussion: Women with Disabilities a Challenge to Feminist Theology," *Journal of Feminist Studies in Religion* 10, no. 2 (1994): 99–134.

in the wake of her passing, sought to continue the collaborative and critical conversations between feminist and feminist disability theologians and also to disrupt the noticeable whiteness and Christian domination of disability theologies.[23] These roundtables raised and critically expanded the concerns and resurging challenges posed by disability theories and theologies to feminist modes of analysis and imagination, with repeated and increased urgency.

Disability theologians appeal to recognize disabled experiences as fully embodied, meaning that they include sexual agency and complex desires, heightened risk for sexualized violence and other forms of abuse. Disability ought to be the preferential epistemological standpoint when thinking through issues of gendered and sexualized experiences, access to care, reproduction, caregiving, and medical technologies, more inclusively.[24] And when tapping disabled bodily experiences as epistemological foundation, theologians must hold together contextual complexities of pain, disappointment, failure AND joy, cooperation, hope—and the multiplicities of ways in which these experiences intermingle and transform each other in the varied embodied experiences shaped by colonialism and capitalist imperialism.[25]

Disability theologians began by, and continue, critiquing the feminist desire to be seen as equally fit, whole, capable, and in control of one's body, which is only a thinly veiled desire to not be disabled. Using concepts of "normal" explicitly or implicitly to overcome social constructions of woman/female/feminine as "deviance" maintains ableism (disability as a mark for undesirable embodied deficits and as a trope for the felt oppressions of sexism). A disability perspective includes noticing where "normalcy" is at work, creating delusions of unobtainable wholeness and naturalized generic bodies to maintain binaries and dualisms that uphold the

---

[23] A dynamic that mirrored the field of disability studies, which was/is still white, Western, cishetero dominated.
[24] Elshout, "Roundtable Discussion," 103. This challenge is taken up for example in Iozzio, *Disability Ethics*, and in Stahl, *Disability's Challenge to Theology*.
[25] Elshout, "Roundtable Discussion," 121–2; Mayra R. Rivera, "Unsettling Bodies," *Journal of Feminist Studies in Religion* 26, no. 2 (2010): 119–23 (121). Some of this is taken up in Armand L. Van Ommen, "JDR Special Issue: Joy and Disability," *Journal of Disability and Religion* 24, no. 3 (2020): 249–51, and Julia Watts Belser, "Vital Wheels: Disability, Relationality, and the Queer Animacy of Vibrant things," *Hypatia* 31, no. 1 (2016): 5–21.

sociocultural and economic value of ability and result in material harm.[26] Ableism must be excised in/from colonial, neoliberal, AND progressive justice ideologies, such as discourses on health, work, immigration, economics, racial justice, and theological conversations on salvation, sin, suffering, and redemption.[27] Ableism also informs and constructs Christian superiority and supremacies, all the while disability experiences can be a shared entry point for entering interreligious conversations and justice collaborations.[28]

Notably, the 1994 Roundtable already placed theological roots of ableism as central to any analysis of environmental abuses and the climate crisis. This appeal is elaborated on in the 2010 JFSR follow-up conversation, naming the devaluation of body and matter, the conceptualization of nature in fixed and unchanging ways, as idolatry—one that belies the embodied realities of flux and change, of living with uncertainty, of creation and reality as contingent on precarious bodies, realities that disability experiences embody and from which flourishing can be imagined constructively.[29]

Disability Justice—Intersectional Visions for Theologies Today

Disability studies as a field, especially as it takes up intersectional and transnational analyses, continues to provide resources for feminist justice work. One of the crucial insights coming out of intersectional investigations in disability studies is that the

---

[26] Deborah B. Creamer, "Embracing Limits, Queering Embodiment: Creating/Creative Possibilities for Disability Theology," *Journal of Feminist Studies in Religion* 26, no. 2 (2010): 123–7.

[27] Heike Peckruhn, "Debilitating Trauma, Techniques of Violence, Creative Madness," *Political Theology Network* (2019), https://politicaltheology.com/tracing-debility-and-webbing-resistance-to-state-violence-through-crip-epistemologies/ (accessed April 7, 2024).

[28] Wilhelm, "Roundtable Discussion," 105; Darla Y. Schumm, "Reimaging Disability," *Journal of Feminist Studies in Religion* 26, no. 2 (2010): 132–7.

[29] Elshout, "Roundtable Discussion," 128; Sharon V. Betcher, "Becoming Flesh of My Flesh: Feminist and Disability Theologies on the Edge of Posthumanist Discourse," *Journal of Feminist Studies in Religion* 26, no. 2 (2010): 107–18 (109–10). Betcher notably moved disability concerns as central forward in eco-theologies and eco-philosophies.

concept of disability and its associations often function as a trope to justify discrimination and exclusion from full rights and citizenship of people groups based on race, gender, ethnicity, sexual orientation, and other markers cast as "unfit." And importantly, efforts toward liberation, groups marked as "disabled" via their gender or race sought inclusion by disassociating with disability, thereby maintaining the legitimacy of disability as a rationale for exclusion.[30] This does not diminish the importance of accounting for disability. On the contrary, a critical disability lens is essential in any intersectional theological investigation to counteract the continued utilization of normal/abnormal categories and their conceptual equivalents in the analysis of multiple dynamics of oppression.

As an academic field, disability studies faced its own crucial challenges and transformations, such as confronting the entrenchment of whiteness in its own constitutive canon and producing disability scholarship that is always intentionally intersectional (a concern first raised by Christopher Bell), and centering a material conception of disability that focuses on actual lived experiences rather than fetishizing disability as a universal category for poststructural analysis (argued by Nirmala Erevelles).[31] Multiple and multifaceted oppressions are always inextricably linked. No doubt, the whiteness and Western imperial domination of disability studies contributed to the distance between, for example, Black and/or Global South intellectual and activist work and disability scholarship, a dynamic that maintains a mainstreaming of disability politics as shaped by and in white hegemonic discourses, leaving disability justice work from other locations underexplored.[32] But strategies and

---

[30] See Douglas C. Baynton, "Disability and the Justification of Inequality in American History," in *The Disability Studies Reader*, 5th ed., ed. Lennard J. Davis (New York: Routledge, 2017), 17–34, and Douglas C. Baynton, "Slaves, Immigrants, and Suffragists: The Uses of Disability in Citizenship Debates," *PMLA* 120, no. 2 (2005): 562–8.

[31] Chris Bell, "Is Disability Studies Actually White Disability Studies," in *The Disability Studies Reader*, 5th ed., ed. Lennard J. Davis (New York: Routledge, 2017), 406–16, and Christopher M. Bell, ed., *Blackness and Disability: Critical Examinations and Cultural Interventions*, vol. 21 (Münster, Germany: LIT Verlag, 2011); see also Nirmala Erevelles, *Disability and Difference in Global Contexts: Enabling a Transformative Body Politic* (New York: Palgrave Macmillan, 2011).

[32] Sami Schalk, *Black Disability Politics* (Durham, NC: Duke University Press, 2022), 6.

methods to transform ableism, racism, sexism, nationalism, and other oppressions cannot and must not favor one positionality over the other, but explore, for example, how Blackness and disability, global militarism and disability, gendered citizenship and disability, and other interwoven experiences dynamically manifest together.[33]

Yet today, it is the *disability justice movement*—which is, in some ways, an heir to the disability rights movement and, in some ways, a new, decidedly intersectional, activist practice—that leads the way in imagining and embodying justice for all. It not only builds on the more readily available concerns of access and inclusion made visible and political with the disability rights movement, but also critiques the latter for their rights-based language and activism (e.g., disability pride movement), which functions on socially sanctioned identity categories but struggles to employ deeply intersectional analysis and action. Disability justice as a varied and cross-solidarity movement was developed by disabled queer people, disabled queer people of color, and disabled people of color such as Patty Berne, Leah Lakshmi Piepzna-Samarasinha, Mia Mingus, Alice Wong, Lydia X. Brown, Stacey Park Milburn, who frame white supremacy and ableism as entwined in and enabled by the practices and ideologies of colonialism, capitalism, and Christian supremacy. It centers sick and disabled people of color, queer, and trans-disabled people in leadership and knowledge creation.[34] Disability justice investigates the materiality of political and governing bodies, interspecies relations and formations, ecojustice, transnational labor, and more. It invites us to begin with and continuously loop through *real*

---

[33] For example, one useful entry point for analysis is provided in the concept of debility. Debility can nuance our understanding of how bodies are impaired, disabled, maimed but kept alive in order to be malleable subjects in the service of neoliberal racialized capitalism. Debilitated bodies are a necessary byproduct of global capitalist labor structures and become profitable as well in health management systems and the racist prison industrial complex. Cultural and theological analysis requires nuanced tools and recognize the affinity and overlap of debility and disability in their interrelated function to socially and materially create conditions of exclusion and precarity. See Julie Livingston, *Debility and the Moral Imagination in Botswana* (Bloomington: Indiana University Press, 2005), Jasbir K. Puar, *The Right to Maim: Debility, Capacity, Disability* (Durham, NC: Duke University Press, 2017), and Margrit Shildrick, "Neoliberalism and Embodied Precarity: Some Crip Responses," *South Atlantic Quarterly* 118, no. 3 (2019): 595–613.

[34] Patty Berne, "Disability Justice: A Working Draft," https://www.sinsinvalid.org/blog/disability-justice-a-working-draft-by-patty-berne (accessed April 9, 2024).

and diverse experiences and reminds us to keep closely together the political *and* the personal. Disability justice as intersectional movement envisions radical and creative webs of mutual care, which embody reciprocal relationships that do not follow progressive success models (which are built on the growth and sustainability of a system), but center on the sustainability of life. It recognizes that to imagine a future that is crip, sick, disabled, Black, brown, neurodivergent, deaf … disabled experience must be central and *alive*—meaning, disabled *persons* must be centered and *living*. The knowledge in *living* disabled experience, an epistemological gift for envisioning creation and flourishing, depends on Black, trans, Indigenous, queer disabled people to be and stay alive, to be present. Only then can a future in which no one is left behind be imagined and created from a present where lived and living experiences of surviving and creative caring can forge visions of flourishing.[35]

Grounding Theological Work in Intersectional Disability Justice

The importance of the appeal to keep disability at the center of theological projects has not waned; if anything, it has become more urgent. Embracing bodily limits to enter the multitude of identity discourses presents an invitation into questioning, subverting, and playing with complex embodiments, to claim liberation for specific lived complexities while naming all that is at stake. Beauty, dignity, and creative knowledges of flourishing, of keeping each other and everyone alive dwells in multiplying marginalized disabled lives. An intersectional disability justice approach can produce a politics that can do significant work in imagining and creating liberation. Disability theologians insist on staying with vulnerability, precarity, pain, decay, failure, hope in lived embodiments, our "flesh—where dread and disgust and humiliation get played out, in economic, cultural, and political, if also deeply

---

[35] Leah Lakshmi Piepzna-Samarasinha, *Care Work: Dreaming Disability Justice* (Vancouver: Arsenal Pulp Press, 2018), and Mia Mingus, "Access Intimacy: The Missing Link," https://leavingevidence.wordpress.com/2011/05/05/access-intimacy-the-missing-link/ (accessed April 9, 2024).

personal registers."³⁶ The embodied experience of "disability" in its multiplicity and intersections is the locus where the complex and contradictory experiences of pain, pleasure, and joy are metabolized and capaciously transformed. Disability justice is an important conversation partner and center for theologies seeking wisdom for liberation and transformation toward more just futures, such as postcolonial, queer, and/or ecojustice theologies.³⁷ The challenge is to hold together a critique of the production of normalized body AND find new ways to articulate corporeality, for example, in postcolonial tracing and working through the embodied trauma of greed and violence that incarnates in the flesh.³⁸

Today, the most critical feminist disability conversations take place in intersectional disability justice movements, and again, feminist and feminist disability theologians are urged to pay attention. Disability justice activists are doing the work of creating communities of life where no one is left behind. For example, already in the early unfolding of the multiple and multifaceted COVID pandemic crises, intersectional disability justice analyses connected the experiences of loss, disposability, grief, debility, racialized colonial capitalism, and disruption of this global health crisis with the lived experiences of climate catastrophes and disruptions, and offered examples of ingenuity and creative adaptions, building interdependent networks of adaptation, support, and care.³⁹ And some, though not all, of their work is public/published. Befittingly, much of what is publicly available is shared in non-academic formats/presses: art, zines, performances, social media, essay collections, science fiction stories,

---

³⁶Sharon V. Betcher, "Becoming Flesh of My Flesh," 110. See also Nancy Mairs, "Growing into God," *Journal of Feminist Studies in Religion* 26, no. 2 (2010): 137–9; and Alison Kafer, *Feminist, Queer, Crip* (Bloomington: Indiana University Press, 2013).
³⁷Some examples of connecting disability justice and intersectional theological work have been in sexuality and queer studies, for instance, Max Thornton, "Trans/Criptions: Gender, Disability, and Liturgical Experience," *Transgender Studies Quarterly* 6, no. 3 (2019): 358–67, and Susannah Cornwall, "Theologies of Resistance: Intersex/DSD, Disability and Queering the 'Real World,'" in *Critical Intersex*, ed. Morgan Holms (New York: Routledge, 2016), 215–43.
³⁸Rivera, "Unsettling Bodies," 122.
³⁹Examples can be found, for instance, in the "Public Archive Project: Disability and Climate Change," curated by Julia Watts Belser, http://disabilityclimatechange.geo rgetown.domains/ (accessed April 9, 2024).

and other forms of creative imagination emerging from activism and local movements.⁴⁰ To pay attention to disability justice where it is created and lived today is to venture into the living experiences of disabled, queer, Black, brown, trans, Indigenous communities and to witness (again) how vulnerability, precarity, intersectional care work are embodied and shared. There is much to learn and know in the humor, irreverence, self-depreciating analysis that is also deadly serious about the dignity and worth of all life, sometimes shared and passed on in street performances, protests, poetry, TikTok, science fiction, podcasts, and the like.

One of the most poignant, prophetic voices currently in theological discourse modeling what this might look like is Julia Watts Belser's, a rabbi and scholar who writes with clarity, urgency, sharp insight at the edge of climate crisis pains, disabled vulnerabilities, queer liberation, and Jewish joy. Her scholarly work is deeply informed by and embedded in intersectional disability justice movement work and the direction it points toward. Watts Belser insists that the lived experience of disability incorporates honed skills for living with precarity: it is a state of vitality and political and affective epistemological unfolding from which to move into actions that recognize the brutality and exacerbations in the intersectional manifestations of racism, classism, colonialism, environmental harm, and disablement.⁴¹ She illustrates how the embrace of multiple and complex experiences of intertwined painful grief and vibrant joy in the intersectional and diverse living disability experience, and how critical intersectional disability knowledge has implications for theological imaginations that can answer to the multiple crises in the world today.⁴²

---

⁴⁰For example, the Disability Visibility Project (disabilityvisibilityproject.com), Sins Invalid (sinsinvalid.org), or Toronto-based artists such as Syrus Marcus Ware (syrusmarcusware.com). Academic publications that incorporate disability justice insights are more often found in journals such as the *Disability Studies Quarterly* and others; most academic journals and book publications on disability and theology focus on the kinds of works already mentioned above.

⁴¹Belser, "Disability, Climate Change, and Environmental Violence." In too moral deliberations on the effects of multiple climate crises and environmental injustices, disability functions as the scare tactic, the warning, the marker, the harbinger of the to-be avoided danger of damage and debilitation.

⁴²See Julia Watts Belser, *Loving in Our Bones: Disability Wisdom and the Spiritual Subversiveness of Knowing Ourselves Whole* (Boston, MA: Beacon Press, 2023), and the public archive project curated by her "Disability and Climate Change."

Feminist theologians need better tools to analyze the structures of othering and can do so by resisting the insulation of disability as a specialty and centering critical reflection on ableism as a feminist concern.[43] This means to resist framing disability as an individual pathology and look deeply into the cultural fears of weakness, vulnerability, and precariousness. And centering disability as a shared global human experience[44] also offers avenues to break out of religious/theological boundaries and to join interreligious and comparative conversations that can move us toward greater flourishing.[45] Disability justice movement activism and analysis provides the necessary conceptual frameworks and living examples to uncover the ways in which bodies are shaped into recognition and control, and to stay with (not remedy) the gritty realities and multiplicities of corporeal existence that include loss, grief, exposure to violence, and joy, desire, pleasure in relationships to self, others, and nonhuman life.[46] Perhaps feminist theologians might even learn to embrace the delightful playfulness with various genres, forms, and content, creating engagement with disruptive, unruly, and messy sites of embodiment that may help us navigate environmental and economic crisis. Critical disability knowledge and innovative embodied justice are here, and they are vital for mutual survival and flourishing.

---

[43] Julia Watts Belser, "Returning to Flesh: A Jewish Reflection on Feminist Disability Theology," *Journal of Feminist Studies in Religion* 26, no. 2 (2010): 127–32.

[44] While it is easy to recognize that, at best, all humans are only temporarily able-bodied, recognizing disability as a global experience must also differentiate between the complex causes and experiences of disability and link capitalist racist dynamics to the various ways in which disability is caused/created in global dynamics.

[45] See Darla Y. Schumm, "Reimaging Disability," *Journal of Feminist Studies in Religion* 26, no. 2 (2010): 132–7, Darla Y. Schumm and Michael Stoltzfus, "Chronic Illness and Disability: Narratives of Suffering and Healing in Buddhism and Christianity," *Journal of Religion, Disability and Health* 11, no. 3 (2007): 5–21, and Julia Watts Belser, *Rabbinic Tales of Destruction: Gender, Sex, and Disability in the Ruins of Jerusalem* (New York: Oxford University Press, 2017) on how disability reflections out of Buddhist or Jewish contexts can enrich and further theological and ethical projects.

[46] See, for example, Favianna Rodriguez and Leah Lakshmi Piepzna-Samarasinha, *Pleasure Activism: The Politics of Feeling Good*, vol. 1 (Chico, CA: AK Press, 2019), or Sonya Renee Taylor, *The Body Is Not an Apology: The Power of Radical Self-love* (Oakland, CA: Berrett-Koehler, 2021).

Bibliography

Barton, Sarah Jean. *Becoming the Baptized Body: Disability and the Practice of Christian Community*. Waco, TX: Baylor University Press, 2022.

Baynton, Douglas C. "Disability and the Justification of Inequality in American History." In *The Disability Studies Reader*, 5th ed., edited by Lennard J. Davis, 17–34. New York: Routledge, 2017.

Baynton, Douglas C., "Slaves, Immigrants, and Suffragists: The Uses of Disability in Citizenship Debates." *PMLA* 120, no. 2 (2005): 562–8.

Bell, Chris. "Is Disability Studies Actually White Disability Studies." In *The Disability Studies Reader*, edited by Lennard J. Davis, 406–15. New York: Routledge, 2017.

Bell, Christopher M., ed. *Blackness and Disability: Critical Examinations and Cultural Interventions*. Münster, Germany: LIT Verlag, 2011.

Belser, Julia Watts. "Disability, Climate Change, and Environmental Violence: The Politics of Invisibility and the Horizon of Hope." *Disability Studies Quarterly* 40, no. 4 (2020). https://doi.org/10.18061/dsq.v40i4.6959, accessed April 9, 2024.

Belser, Julia Watts. *Loving in Our Bones: Disability Wisdom and the Spiritual Subversiveness of Knowing Ourselves Whole*. Boston, MA: Beacon Press, 2023.

Belser, Julia Watts. *Rabbinic Tales of Destruction: Gender, Sex, and Disability in the Ruins of Jerusalem*. New York: Oxford University Press, 2017.

Belser, Julia Watts. "Returning to Flesh: A Jewish Reflection on Feminist Disability Theology." *Journal of Feminist Studies in Religion* 26, no. 2 (2010): 127–32.

Belser, Julia Watts. "Toilet Justice," *Political Theology Network*, March 5, 2018. https://politicaltheology.com/symposium/toilet-justice/, accessed April 7, 2024.

Belser, Julia Watts. "Vital Wheels: Disability, Relationality, and the Queer Animacy of Vibrant Things." *Hypatia* 31, no. 1 (2016): 5–21.

Berne, Patty. "Disability Justice: A Working Draft," www.sinsinvalid.org/blog/disability-justice-a-working-draft-by-patty-berne, accessed April 9, 2024.

Betcher, Sharon V. "Becoming Flesh of My Flesh: Feminist and Disability Theologies on the Edge of Posthumanist Discourse." *Journal of Feminist Studies in Religion* 26, no. 2 (2010): 107–18.

Betcher, Sharon V. *Spirit and the Obligation of Social Flesh: A Secular Theology for the Global City*. New York: Fordham University Press, 2013.

Betcher, Sharon V. *Spirit and the Politics of Disablement*. Minneapolis, MN: Fortress Press, 2007.

Conner, Benjamin T. *Disabling Mission, Enabling Witness: Exploring Missiology through the Lens of Disability Studies*. Downers Grove, IL: InterVarsity Press, 2018.

Cooreman-Guittin, Talitha, and Armand L. van Ommen. "Disability Theology: A Driving Force for Change?" *International Journal for the Study of the Christian Church* 22, no. 1 (2022): 1–4.

Cornwall, Susannah. "Theologies of Resistance: Intersex/DSD, Disability and Queering the 'Real World.'" In *Critical Intersex*, edited by Morgan Holmes, 215–43. New York: Routledge, 2016.

Creamer, Deborah B. *Disability and Christian Theology: Embodied Limits and Constructive Possibilities*. New York: Oxford University Press, 2009.

Creamer, Deborah B. "Disability Theology." *Religion Compass* 6, no. 7 (2012): 339–46.

Creamer, Deborah B. "Embracing Limits, Queering Embodiment: Creating/Creative Possibilities for Disability Theology." *Journal of Feminist Studies in Religion* 26, no. 2 (2010): 123–7.

Davis, Lennard J., ed. *The Disability Studies Reader*, 5th ed. New York: Routledge, 2017.

"Disability and Climate Change," Public Archive. http://disabilityclimatechange.georgetown.domains/, accessed April 9, 2024.

Disability Visibility Project. disabilityvisibilityproject.com, accessed April 9, 2024.

Dolmage, Jay T. *Academic Ableism: Disability and Higher Education*. Ann Arbor: University of Michigan Press, 2017.

Eiesland, Nancy L. *The Disabled God toward a Liberatory Theology of Disability*. Nashville, TN: Abingdon Press, 2022.

Elshout, Elly, Dorothee Wilhelm, Carole R. Fontaine, Nancy L. Eiesland, Valerie C. Stiteler, Adele B. McCollum, and Margaret Moers Wenig. "Roundtable Discussion: Women with Disabilities a Challenge to Feminist Theology." *Journal of Feminist Studies in Religion* 10, no. 2 (1994): 99–134.

Erevelles, Nirmala. *Disability and Difference in Global Contexts: Enabling a Transformative Body Politic*. New York: Palgrave Macmillan, 2011.

Hasla, Molly C. *A Constructive Theology of Intellectual Disability: Human Being as Mutuality and Response*. New York: Fordham University Press, 2012.

Iozzio, Mary Jo. *Disability Ethics and Preferential Justice: A Catholic Perspective*. Washington, DC: Georgetown University Press, 2023.

Kafer, Alison. *Feminist, Queer, Crip*. Bloomington: Indiana University Press, 2013.
Kenny, Amy. Amy-kenny.com, accessed April 7, 2024.
Kenny, Amy. *My Body Is Not a Prayer Request: Disability Justice in the Church*. Grand Rapids, MI: Baker Books, 2022.
Lelwica, Michelle Mary. "The Politics of Peeing and Pooping and the Saving Power of Interdependence." *Political Theology Network*, March 27, 2018. https://politicaltheology.com/the-politics-of-peeing-and-pooping-and-the-saving-power-of-interdependence/.
Lewis, Hannah. *Deaf Liberation Theology*. New York: Routledge, 2016.
Livingston, Julie. *Debility and the Moral Imagination in Botswana*. Bloomington: Indiana University Press, 2005.
Mairs, Nancy. "Growing into God." *Journal of Feminist Studies in Religion* 26, no. 2 (2010): 137–9.
Mia Mingus, "Access Intimacy: The Missing Link." leavingevidence.wordpress.com/2011/05/05/access-intimacy-the-missing-link/, accessed April 9, 2024.
Morris, Wayne. *Theology without Words: Theology in the Deaf Community*. New York: Routledge, 2016.
Moss, Candida R., and Jeremy Schipper, eds. *Disability Studies and Biblical Literature*. New York: Palgrave Macmillan, 2011.
Olyan, Saul M. *Disability in the Hebrew Bible: Interpreting Mental and Physical Differences*. New York: Cambridge University Press, 2008.
Panton, Amy, and Miriam Spies. themadandcriptheologypodcast.buzzsprout.com, accessed April 7, 2024.
Peckruhn, Heike. "Debilitating Trauma, Techniques of Violence, Creative Madness." *Political Theology Network*, 2019. https://politicaltheology.com/tracing-debility-and-webbing-resistance-to-state-violence-through-crip-epistemologies/, accessed April 7, 2024.
Peckruhn, Heike. *Meaning in Our Bodies: Sensory Experience as Constructive Theological Imagination*. New York: Oxford University Press, 2017.
Piepzna-Samarasinha, Leah Lakshmi. *Care Work: Dreaming Disability Justice*. Vancouver: Arsenal Pulp Press, 2018.
Piepzna-Samarasinha, Leah Lakshmi. *The Future Is Disabled: Prophecies Love Notes and Mourning Songs*. Vancouver: Arsenal Pulp Press, 2022.
Plaskow, Judith. "Breaking a Powerful Silence." *Political Theology Network*, March 18, 2018. https://politicaltheology.com/breaking-a-powerful-silence/, accessed April 7, 2024.
Powell Lisa D. *The Disabled God Revisited: Trinity, Christology, and Liberation*. London: Bloomsbury, 2023.

Price, Margaret. *Mad at School: Rhetorics of Mental Disability and Academic Life*. Ann Arbor: University of Michigan Press, 2011.

Puar, Jasbir K. *The Right to Maim: Debility, Capacity, Disability*. Durham, NC: Duke University Press, 2017.

Raffety, Erin. *From Inclusion to Justice: Disability, Ministry, and Congregational Leadership*. Waco, TX: Baylor University Press, 2022.

Raphael, Rebecca. *Biblical Corpora: Representations of Disability in Hebrew Biblical Literature*. London: T&T Clark, 2008.

Reinders, Hans S. *Receiving the Gift of Friendship: Profound Disability, Theological Anthropology, and Ethics*. Grand Rapids, MI: Wm. B. Eerdmans, 2008.

Retief, Marno, and Rantoa Letšosa. "Models of Disability: A Brief Overview." *HTS Teologiese Studies/Theological Studies* 74, no. 1 (2018). https://doi.org/10.4102/hts.v74i1.4738, accessed April 7, 2024.

Rivera, Mayra R. "Unsettling Bodies." *Journal of Feminist Studies in Religion* 26, no. 2 (2010): 119–23.

Rodriguez, Favianna, and Leah Lakshmi Piepzna-Samarasinha. *Pleasure Activism: The Politics of Feeling Good*. Chico, CA: AK Press, 2019.

Schalk, Sami. *Black Disability Politics*. Durham, NC: Duke University Press, 2022.

Schumm, Darla. "Do Your Business." *Political Theology Network*, March 7, 2018. https://politicaltheology.com/do-your-business/, accessed April 7, 2024.

Schumm, Darla Y. "Reimaging Disability." *Journal of Feminist Studies in Religion* 26, no. 2 (2010): 132–7.

Schumm, Darla Y., and Michael Stoltzfus. "Chronic Illness and Disability: Narratives of Suffering and Healing in Buddhism and Christianity." *Journal of Religion, Disability and Health* 11, no. 3 (2007): 5–21.

Shildrick, Margrit. "Neoliberalism and Embodied Precarity: Some Crip Responses." *South Atlantic Quarterly* 118, no. 3 (2019): 595–613.

Sins Invalid. sinsinvalid.org

Spurrier, Rebecca. *The Disabled Church: Human Difference and the Art of Communal Worship*. New York: Fordham University Press, 2020.

Stahl, Devan. *Disability's Challenge to Theology: Genes, Eugenics, and the Metaphysics of Modern Medicine*. Notre Dame, IN: University of Notre Dame Press, 2022.

Swinton, John. *Dementia: Living in the Memories of God*. London: SCM Press, 2012.

Taylor, Sonya Renee. *The Body Is Not an Apology: The Power of Radical Self-love*. Oakland, CA: Berrett-Koehler, 2021.

Thornton, Max. "Trans/Criptions: Gender, Disability, and Liturgical Experience." *Transgender Studies Quarterly* 6, no. 3 (2019): 358–67.
Van Ommen, Armand L. "JDR Special Issue: Joy and Disability." *Journal of Disability and Religion* 24, no. 3 (2020): 249–51.
Yong, Amos. *Theology and Down Syndrome: Reimagining Disability in Late Modernity*. Waco, TX: Baylor University Press, 2007.

PART TWO

The Praxis of Living Relationally

7

Traveling between Mountains and White Doves: Spiritual Rhythms of *Runa* Feminisms

Mónica A. Maher with Samay Cañamar M.

> Ritual bath.
> Seasonal ceremony. Sacred space-time.
> Fresh spring at dawn.
> Surrender to the spirit of the Apu Imbabura,
> as water comes—quickly and cold—calling, cleansing,
> healing, awakening.
> First, we ask for permission.
>
> ~~~
>
> *Mother nature/allpa mama is constituted by several bodies and time-spaces or pachas, sacred territories or wakas with their own powers, where we cannot*

enter without first asking permission, through prayers, greetings, chants, whistles.
Minkachiway is the beginning of an entering ritual to a space. The grandfathers say minkachiway when they start walking at the foot of a mountain. The grandmothers ask permission for announcing the arrival at a chakra/crop. The nights before a purification bath ritual, one reaches the water spring by saying minkachiway, just as one announces her own arrival to someone else's house.
This is how we now enter a waka or a sacred place such as our apus, spirits of the mountain with diverse powers beyond the feminine and masculine, personified in names, actions, and stories.

Minkachiway (Kallari willkay) Initiation
I ask for your permission
to enter into your realm
while I gently gather my desires, acts and words
with clear dreams.
I wish to talk about your time
in these paths,
arrive to your lake's edge
get closer to your house's entrance and start my path
at the foot of the mountains.
I ask for your permission, dear Apu.
Give me permission, dear Mother Earth.
My body has been getting ready
and my soul wants some rest.
Welcome me,
sacred place that gives breath to good ways of living.
I am arriving to your house and your river to touch you,
blessed land, with this heart.

Let the deepest dreams come blessing me with your powers.
Let me go beyond all my tears
and wake up in this conversation full of colorful and breathing words.
With the rain coming down I will hear your words talking to me.[1]

~~~

This chapter invites the reader into the spiritual rhythms of *Runa*[2] feminisms, into ways of being and knowing based on ancestral cosmovisions, reflected in the poetic opening words, translated from the original Kichwa,[3] of Tsaywa Samay Cañamar Maldonado. The intersectional, intergenerational, intercultural, and transnational lens allows for an exploration of the theoretical and practical implications for Christian theology of Andean ancestral spirituality as lived out and expressed by women writers of the original peoples of the Plurinational States of Bolivia and Ecuador.

Traveling between mountains and white doves entails a voyage in search of a feminist theological ethic that takes seriously the visions and claims of Andean feminist scholar-activists, an ethic grounded in ancestral views and values based on the principles of mutual respect and reciprocity with all beings. The social setting of political praxis is the variety of indigenous feminist struggles for territorial and bodily sovereignty in the region. Sources include community feminist discourses on reclaiming body-land territories in Abya-Yala. This broader feminist movement for territorial sovereignty serves as the contextual and conceptual reference.

---

[1] Tsaywa Samay Cañamar Maldonado, *Shunku-yay/Mirarse en la eternidad del corazón*, translation from Kichwa by Fredy A. Roncalla (Ecuador: Siwar Mayu, 2022). This English translation is digital: http://siwarmayu.com/shunku-yay-looking-at-each-other-through-the-infinite-of-the-heart-tsaywa-samay-canamar-m/ (accessed April 7, 2024). "Wakas" are also transliterated from the Kichwa into English as "wacas" or "huacas" as evidenced in the rest of this chapter.
[2] *Runa* is the Kichwa word for "human being."
[3] Kichwa, along with Spanish, is the official language of the Plurinational State of Ecuador.

The methodology interweaves Latin American feminist theological reflections based on the foundational work of María Pilar Aquino and Ivone Gebara with the deep insights of the Aymara theologian Sofía Nicolasa Chipana Quispe of Bolivia and the young Kichwa psychologist and poet Tsaywa Samay Cañamar Maldonado, a member of the *Runa* Feminists collective of Ecuador. This tapestry serves to challenge and shift basic Christian theological categories of being, knowing, and power toward new ontological, epistemological, and political frameworks.

Reweaving the Tapestry: Feminist Ecumenism and Religious Biodiversity

In her classic essay on Latin American feminist theology twenty-five years ago,[4] systematic theologian María Pilar Aquino described alternative ecumenism as one of its key principles. She asserted the increasing importance of ecumenism in the face of the deepening social, racial, sexual, religious, and cultural divisions that accompany the predatory logic of modern civilization.[5] In the face of patriarchal ecclesial censorship of feminist theology, Aquino proposed "feminist ecumenism" as a process in need of strengthening and a challenge in need of living.[6] This prophetic call rings as true as ever. Aquino has worked to carry out this vision through advancing intercultural feminist theology,[7] discussed further below.

Ecofeminist and Brazilian theologian Ivone Gebara also, twenty-five years ago, affirmed the importance of "religious biodiversity" in the urgent task to transform the death-dealing anthropocentric and androcentric dimensions of patriarchal theology.[8] Drawing

---

[4] María Pilar Aquino, "Teología Feminista Latinoamericana," in *Teología Feminista Latinoamericana*, ed. María Pilar Aquino and Elsa Támez (Quito, Ecuador: Ediciones Abya-Yala, 1998), 9–73.
[5] Aquino, "Teología Feminista Latinoamericana," 65.
[6] Aquino, "Teología Feminista Latinoamericana," 66.
[7] María Pilar Aquino and María José Rosado-Nunes, eds., *Feminist Intercultural Theology: Latina Explorations for a Just World* (Maryknoll, NY: Orbis Books, 2007).
[8] Ivone Gebara, *Longing for Running Water: Ecofeminism and Liberation*, translated from Portuguese by David Molineaux (Minneapolis, MN: Augsburg Fortress, 1999), 205–11.

on poetic metaphors,[9] she asserted: "Religious biodiversity gives a heartfelt welcome to the diversity of tapestries. It is an exercise of going beyond our striving to make one single group the herald of a one-and-only truth, the self-appointed bearer of salvific formulas for everybody."[10] Tapestries must be reworked, renewed, recreated. "A tapestry cannot be eternal, atemporal, or valid forever. It will lose its beauty and its aesthetic qualities. Ephemeral things enjoy the eternity of the present moment, and in this resides their evocative and inspirational task."[11]

How can we rediscover and revive the Christian religious tradition, recovering renewable moral resources[12] and engaging new elements? "Often the tapestry has to be rewoven, even if some of the old designs are copies—or even though we manage to reuse some threads that have not decayed," claims Gebara. "This is recreation, religious biodiversity, respect for new moments, creative inspiration, and the welcoming of new hands prepared to weave marvelous designs."[13] This "process" reflects the ongoing evolution of the whole planet and cosmos, and all beings;[14] nothing is static.

This organic unfolding and redesigning apply to the feminist theological tradition. Indeed, this creative, demanding, and joy-filled task is the aspiration motivating this collective writing. By opening the windows and allowing new air to enter, fresh winds clear away mental confusion and create space for new intuitions and insights.

Gebara asserts: "This challenge will open us up to a new understanding not only of the Christian experience but of others as well, based on a frame of reference that incorporates a broader understanding of universal brotherhood/sisterhood and a devotion

---

[9] "Religion Is the Tapestry Hope Weaves with Words," Rubem Alves, *O Suspiro dos Oprimidos* (São Paulo, Brazil: Paulinas, 1984); poem quoted in Gebara, *Longing for Running Water*, 208.
[10] Gebara, *Longing for Running Water*, 209.
[11] Gebara, *Longing for Running Water*, 209.
[12] In his interreligious work, Daniel Maguire spoke of mining the "renewable moral energies" of religions, which are "at root life-enhancing responses to the sacred." Daniel C. Maguire, *Sacred Choices: The Right to Contraception and Abortion in Ten World Religions* (Minneapolis, MN: Augsburg Fortress Press, 2001), 25.
[13] Gebara, *Longing for Running Water*, 209.
[14] Gebara, *Longing for Running Water*, 208.

to all the manifestations of this one and multiform Sacred Body."[15] It implies embracing "alternative languages, meanings, and friendships."[16]

In the Kichwa poem of friend and colleague Samay Cañamar, with which this chapter began, the apu/mountain grants permission. The mountain is a mutual moral agent with the capacity to communicate. This is a different ontology from the Judeo-Christian tradition, one that recognizes agency on the part of nature within the reality of a range of interconnected living beings. According to Ecuadorean anthropologist Patricio Guerrero Arias, the Andean cosmovision affirms that "in the biosphere all has spirit, all has heart, all is alive and all is sacred."[17] The mountain is a living being, a deity in constant communication with humans, animals, and all other nature spirits.

~~~

Imbabura Woman Mountain Deity

Covered by grasslands
—deep eyes and working hands— you are the great mother
*   of children, animals and rivers.*
Your summit is Lake Illull, Lake Chakishka, Lake Hatun.
Their waterfalls and the rain come down valleys and crevices.
Great woman,
you come from inside the sacred spaces, play with the
*   shepherd girls,*
live talking with a black puma,
teach the foxes certain powers,
and keep the magic in your wakas.
The sun is at the middle of his path
and you sing with august winds.
The hummingbirds bring us your message and the valleys
*   open up to receive us.*

---

[15]Gebara, *Longing for Running Water*, 211.
[16]Gebara, *Longing for Running Water*, 209.
[17]Patricio Guerrero Arias, *La Chakana del Corazonar: Desde las Espiritualidades y las Sabidurías Insurgentes de Abya-Yala* (Quito, Ecuador: Abya-Yala/Universidad Politécnica Salesiana, 2018), 462.

This day all the apus celebrate.
You hold a well balanced basket and wait for us.[18]

~~~

Toward an Intercultural, Interreligious, and Decolonial Dialogue with Ancestral Spiritualities

Chipana describes the need for the decolonization of being in order "to recognize all the inner wells which flow in each being" and the decolonization of power "to recognize that there are other forms of circular power that come not only from the human community but from other communities and beings who co-habitat with us":[19] "The mountain plays, protects, talks, teaches, sings, waits."

According to Eugen Drewermann, "We need a fundamental new religious reflection that is able to break with Judeo-Christian anthropocentrism in order to recover a sense of unity and a shared religious experience of the world—notions that in the history of Western ideas have always been combated as anti-Christian, pantheist or even atheist."[20]

Embracing the Andean cosmovision with its broader ontology, which recognizes the life and agency in all of nature, allows for this break, this shift to recognize the unity with all creatures. And yet, to fully embrace such a notion, it is necessary to go beyond dualistic concepts into a new kind of interreligious, inter-spiritual dialogue. In writing about the current challenges to Latin American liberation theologies to recognize fully the ancestral spiritualities of Abya-Yala, Chipana stresses the need to go beyond the categorizations of religions as monotheist, polytheist, animist, or pantheist. Rather, she invites Christian churches to grow in a "sincere, intercultural,

---

[18] Cañamar, *Shunku-yay. Wakas* and *apus* refer to sacred spaces, especially mountains.
[19] Sofía Nicolasa Chipana, "De la Sanación a la Liberación," in *Re-encantos y Re-encuentros: Caminos y Desafíos Actuales de las Teologías de la Liberación*, ed. Dalíns Rufín Pardo and Luis Carlos Marrero (Buenos Aires, Argentina: Juanuno1 Ediciones, 2018), 164–5. Translation from Spanish by Mónica A Maher.
[20] Eugen Drewermann, *Le Progrés Meurtrier* (Paris: Stock 1993), 86; quoted in Gebara, *Longing for Running Water*, 211.

interreligious and decolonial dialogue with the ancestral spiritualities of indigenous and afro-descendent communities."[21]

Needed is "an attitude of humility,"[22] according to Gebara and also, according to Chipana, of *ch´uju*. "Those of us who were touched in our being by Christianity, find ourselves in the challenge of entering into the dynamic mystery of *ch´uju* (silence of reason) in order to feel and welcome our ancestors again into our heart as the roots which sustain our existence."[23] Silence of reason is required in order to reconnect with the ever-living ancestral roots. As in the Mayan sacred teachings of the Popul Vuh, "they pulled off our fruit, they cut our branches, they burned our trunk, but they could not kill our roots."[24]

Chipana emphasizes that decolonizing knowledge, in addition to being and power, is necessary not only for colonized peoples in Abya-Yala but for the whole human community. This process to disrupt "the absolute truth of only one way of thinking, feeling and living" implies "breaking all the hegemonic pretenses in order to incite spaces of *aphtapis*, knowledge, from which we can weave other forms of wisdom."[25] It is a process of *corazonar*, of thinking from the heart, "which is the very space of the healing spirituality which touches life and transfigures bodies."[26] *Corazonar* refers to a way of knowing not based on sole analytical understanding but on a more holistic process and source, a broader and deeper intuitive wisdom, distinguishing it from traditional Western rational epistemology.[27]

Gebara, decades ago, called for a new Christian epistemology to replace the Aristotelian-Thomistic paradigm, unquestioned by traditional liberation theology, of absolute, eternal, and immutable truths.[28] She proposed an ecofeminist epistemology in order to replace and transform the dualistic categories underlying the androcentrism and anthropomorphism of Christian theology. Her

---

[21] Chipana, "De la Sanación a la Liberación," 165.
[22] Gebara, *Longing for Running Water*, 209.
[23] Chipana, "De la Sanación a la Liberación," 160.
[24] Chipana, "De la Sanación a la Liberación," 160. This is a direct reference of Chipana to the sacred book of the Maya, *Popul Vuh*.
[25] Chipana, "De la Sanación a la Liberación," 164.
[26] Chipana, "De la Sanación a la Liberación," 164.
[27] *Corazonar* is a term coined by Particio Guerrero Arias, *La Chakana del Corazonar*.
[28] Gebara, *Longing for Running Water*, 42–8.

ecofeminist theological epistemology expressed interdependence in knowing, a "sacred interdependence that is vibrant and visceral," and "knowing as process."[29] In addition, it affirmed the bond between spirit and matter and was gender-based, ecological, contextual, holistic, affective, and inclusive.[30]

The work of Aquino on intercultural feminist theologies also emphasizes an approach to knowing as an ongoing process, moving away from oppressive patriarchal epistemological patterns. "The feminist practice of interculturality seeks to transform the supposedly universal character of kyriarchical-monocultural knowledge and to offer emancipatory models." An intercultural framework for feminist theology implies "the renunciation of conceptual absolutisms and doctrinal dogmatisms" in order to make "collaborative communication and open deliberation possible" with the plurality of voices.[31] The purpose is global justice-making, for intercultural feminist theology is most basically "an alternative ethical-political project for advancing toward a new world of justice."[32]

Indeed, an alternative episteme to the traditional Western patriarchal framework emerges and is sustained and expanded in the struggles for justice in the face of the systemic violence of neocolonialism, capitalism, racism, and patriarchy. According to Latin American development experts, the movements of "territorial resistance are the epistemic sphere from which we anticipate transcending modernity and radicalizing democracy."[33] The philosophical starting point is the recognition of human interdependence with all living beings "in relations of respect,

---

[29]Gebara, *Longing for Running Water*, 54.
[30]Gebara, *Longing for Running Water*, 56–65.
[31]María Pilar Aquino, "Feminist Intercultural Theology: Toward a Shared Future of Justice," in *Feminist Intercultural Theology: Latina Explorations for a Just World*, ed. María Pilar Aquino and María José Rosado-Nunes (Maryknoll, NY: Orbis Books, 2007), 18.
[32]Aquino, "Feminist Intercultural Theology," 9.
[33]Miriam Lang, Horacio Machado Aráoz, and Mario Rodríguez Ibáñez, "Transcender la Modernidad Capitalista para Re-existir. Reflexiones Sobre Derechos, Democracia y Bienestar en el Contexto de las Nuevas Derechas," in *¿Cómo Se Sostiene la Vida en América Latina? Feminismos y Re-existencias en Tiempos de Oscuridad*, ed. Karin Gabbert and Miriam Lang (Quito, Ecuador: Edición Fundación Rosa Luxemburg and Ediciones Abya Yala, 2019), 372.

reciprocity and care," and of justice as intercultural, interspecies and intergenerational.[34]

For Chipana, cultural identity is inseparable from spirituality;[35] what marks the difference between the original women of Abya-Yala and the ecofeminists is "spirituality linked to the women ancestors," which accompanies and motivates their justice struggles.[36] Resistance movements are grounded in ancestral knowing, historical remembrance, and deep wisdom. Memories of carefully creating and cultivating life over the centuries in the face of the violence of colonization motivate, empower, inspire, and compel "many people […] to struggle for the land and inhabited territory," a struggle carried out for the ancestors themselves as well as all other living beings,[37] a struggle to care for life "with tenderness, feeding, loving and protecting it."[38]

Cañamar expresses the deep pain of what has been destroyed, the deep desire to rediscover what was and still is, and writing as a valiant action to reclaim ancestral wisdom and heal memory.

~~~

To Write

They have asked me: what is writing?
A heartfelt confusion spread across time, memory and my hands.
After a few seconds I answered:
Writing liberates me.
But there was a splinter silently bothering me.
I was swamped by nostalgia
and emptiness.
Growing in the mist of memories an ambiguous voice
   screamed inside

---

[34]Lang et al., "Transcender la Modernidad Capitalista para Re-existir," 374.
[35]Sofía Chipana Quispe, *Sosteniendo la Vida: Ante las Violencias Extractivas y el Neoliberalismo Verde Colonial*, online Forum of FLACSO-Ecuador and CLACSO-Argentina, lecture delivered October 4, 2021.
[36]Chipana, "De la Sanación a la Liberación," 162.
[37]Chipana, "De la Sanación a la Liberación," 162.
[38]Chipana, "De la Sanación a la Liberación," 162, footnote 9. Explanation by Chipana of the meaning of the Aymara word *uywaña*.

Bringing rain drops to my face.
I know that at one point in time
the alphabet was forced upon us punch by punch. With a
    God, lord,
King, and language,
that would mutilate knowledge and sweep my gardens killing
    diversity.
Thinking about the origins of this alphabet
I can feel how they emptied my fields, weavings and hands.
I feel the threads and their designs are no longer there.
It's a loss that my eyes did not see but was felt by my people.
I ask myself: where is our writing?
And hanging from the roof
there are weavings appearing in front of me: figures drawn
    with wool thread,
the band that holds grandmothers hair,
the manta that my grandfather (made) with his life, the zigzag
    I carry in my skirt.
If they were to ask me again why I write
I would repeat: to heal memory and remembrance. Now
    I am healed with what at one point tied our bones. I now
    write with their letters.[39]

~~~

Vital Forces for the Healing of Body/Land Territories

Boaventura de Sousa Santos has highlighted the killing of systems of knowledge of original peoples by the Eurocentric, racist, capitalist processes of colonization and neocolonization, which have resulted not only in genocide, feminicide, and ecocide but also "epistemicide."[40] As Chipana writes, "Christian religious colonization set out to extinguish the supposed idolatries of our peoples, burying our Divinities in forgetfulness and with them, our

---

[39] Cañamar, *Shunku-yay.*
[40] Boaventura de Sousa Santos, *Epistemologies of the South: Justice against Epistemicide* (London: Routledge, 2014).

wisdom, leaving without a doubt an inner emptiness."[41] Yet, as she and Cañamar affirm, the wisdom was not completely destroyed. Connecting to those memories and sources of knowledge is an everyday spiritual practice.

Chipana asserts: "I also cultivate a profound and daily connection with the spiritualities of resistance of many peoples who refused to die. This is a great inheritance, because over the course of more than five centuries, the memory remained alive in many peoples who in an attitude of vigil conserved the fire among the ashes so it would not go out."[42] Power for justice and healing lies in remembering these "forces connected to the female and male ancestors, wise ones, guardians, warriors, in complete contact with the *Huacas*" (sacred/vital forces).[43]

From 1560 to 1572 in the Quechua territories of Ayacucho and Arequipa, Peru, the *Taqui Onkoy* movement of resistance emerged "from the connection with the heart of the Great Web or Community of Life," in order to "heal the territories wounded because of the disharmony produced by the profane presence of Inquisition of the invaders." Through song and dance, they entered "into communion with the destroyed sacred sites, called *Wacas*, where they located the vital forces that acquired life in their bodies." The socioreligious movement involved a "search for the recreation of life" and "Andean unification through common ties that came from the ancestral spiritualities linked to the mountains, lagoons, lakes, seas, forests, and *paquarinas*—places where the memory and force of the men and women ancestors lived—that referred to the origins of life."[44]

The ancestors invoked protector spirits to heal both the invaded peoples as well as their lands, for "bodies and territories are one integrated reality."[45] Indeed, "ancestral spiritualities have the force of healing or restoration not only for the human body and spirit but also

---

[41] Chipana, "De la Sanación a la Liberación," 160.
[42] Chipana, "De la Sanación a la Liberación," 160.
[43] Chipana, "De la Sanación a la Liberación," 162.
[44] Sofía Chipana Quispe, "*Íbamos a Triunfar, Me lo Dijo el Río*," Espiritualidades en Resistencia, Blog en Movimiento de Acción Noviolenta de las Américas, 2022, https://accionnoviolenta.org/ibamos-a-triunfar-me-lo-dijo-el-rio/ (accessed January 26, 2023).
[45] Chipana, "De la Sanación a la Liberación," 161.

for the whole *Pacha* (inhabited cosmos)."[46] The ancestral, relational spiritualities still serve "as a healing force that recreates life in the face of the oppressions of patriarchy, capitalism, racism and sexism."[47] This wisdom "inconveniences extractive capitalism which tries at all costs to recolonize the land territories and the body territories, with the complicity of State armed forces." Capitalist violence destroys land territories, body territories "of communities of living beings of our space time" and beyond. Contaminated and expropriated are "communities of mountains, lagoons, rivers, streams, forests, volcanoes."[48] This process of destroying territories also means "the destruction of the symbolic world," and therefore, "the loss of our identities and the disappearance of many peoples, given that their cosmovisions and spiritualities have their origins and their wise nutrients in their millennial territories."[49]

Chipana underlines the importance of "the epistemological, spiritual and political contribution" of *body territory* and *land territory*, "developed in spaces of indigenous women who self-identify as feminists" whose ancestral spirituality "nurtures and accompanies their struggles for the *land territories* in full connection with their bodies."[50] The nondualistic epistemic interface, *body land territory*, is the conceptual articulation of Xinca community feminist and ancestral healer of Guatemala Lorena Cabnal, who considers "healing as a political cosmic path in the dynamics and relationships of daily life, where to resist is also to recreate life."[51] According to Cabnal,

> In view of the historic recovery and defense of my body land territory, I assume the recovery of my expropriated body in order to generate within it, life, happiness, vitality, pleasure and the construction of liberating knowledge for making decisions, and to this power, I add the defense of my land territory because I cannot conceive of this woman's body without a space on the land that dignifies my existence and promotes my life in fullness. Historic and oppressive violence exist as much for my first body

---

[46] Chipana, "De la Sanación a la Liberación," 161.
[47] Chipana, "*Íbamos a Triunfar.*"
[48] Chipana, "De la Sanación a la Liberación," 162.
[49] Chipana, "De la Sanación a la Liberación," 161–2.
[50] Chipana, "De la Sanación a la Liberación," 162.
[51] Chipana, "*Íbamos a Triunfar.*"

territory as also for my historic territory, the land. In this sense, all forms of violence against women attack that existence which should be complete.⁵²

Chipana, with Cabnal, recognizes the exclusion of and violence against women within Indigenous communities, which result in a lack of communal balance and harmony, taking away vital energy for transformation and *Sumak Kawsay*—living well. Women must be included for *Sumak Kawsay* to be possible, with the plenitude of vital forces, *Ajayu*, and courage, *Qamasa*.⁵³ According to Cañamar, "Ritual, spiritual and ancestral practice is part of a way of life of healing, of resistance, much more present in women adults, women midwives, women healers of the community" in the highlands of Ecuador.⁵⁴

In fact, the original women of Abya-Yala are guardians of the vital forces. From their continental sisterhood, they are in a continual process of announcing the reality of the pluriverse, challenging the epistemological, political, economic, and religious "hegemony of the one" and promoting the "flourishing of the pluridiversity."⁵⁵ As weavers of the ancestral spiritualities, they honor the vital principles of life: everything is alive, everything has its time and place, and life exists in mutual creation. Aymara grandmothers, for example, practice relationships of profound tenderness with other living beings—seeds, plants, animals—in an inter-nurturing of life.⁵⁶

These spiritual practices, in harmony with vital forces and with the protector spirits of each space, are forms of resistance, which is also re-existence.⁵⁷ Spirituality grounded in vital energy that pervades bodies, lands, and all life has echoes in feminist theology. From her

---

⁵²Lorena Cabnal, "Acercamiento a la Construcción de la Propuesta de Pensamiento Epistémico de las Mujeres indígenas Feministas Comunitarias de Abya Yala," in *Feminista Siempre. Feminismos Diversos: El Feminismo Comunitario* (Madrid: Asociación para la Cooperación con el Sur, Acsur-Las Segovias, 2010), 10–25. Quoted in Chipana, "De la Sanación a la Liberación," 162. Translation from Spanish by Mónica A. Maher.
⁵³Chipana, "De la Sanación a la Liberación," 162.
⁵⁴Samay Cañamar, "Convivir con la espiritualidad ancestral/Ñukanchik usaykunawan kawsashpa", Espiritualidades en Resistencia, Blog en Movimiento de Acción Noviolenta de las Américas, 2022, https://accionnoviolenta.org/convivir-con-la-espiritualidad-ancestral-nukanchik-ushaykunawan-kawsashpa/ (accessed April 7, 2024).
⁵⁵Chipana, *Sosteniendo la Vida*.
⁵⁶Chipana, *Sosteniendo la Vida*.
⁵⁷Chipana, *Sosteniendo la Vida*.

ecofeminist framework, Gebara describes God as "sacred energy," an energy that pervades the cosmos and all living matter.[58] God is "the sap of human life, but also the sap of the life in trees, flowers, animals, and all that exists."[59] Gebara asserts that the experience and name of the mysterious reality of God is "relatedness," which is *"attraction, flux, energy* and *passion."*[60] She describes Jesus as obedient to "the generative source of life within himself and his fellow human beings" and a "center of loving energy among us."[61] From their intercultural feminist perspective, theologians Maricel Mena-López and Aquino "give thanks for the transforming action of the divine Wisdom in our lives, who is present as *aché*, as fount of energy, liberating goodness."[62]

Fount of energy.
Infinite source.
Sacred sap.
Vital force.
Spiral of liberation.
Attraction, passion.
Power. In flux.
Motivating. Mutating.

~~~

We are also spirit that mutates within air, fire, wind, water, mother earth. An infinite force that very few of us manage to experience fully.

I am vital energy

I am vital energy.
One that grows moving.
I am strength and confluence. A renewed energy
standing up
and exploding.

---

[58] Gebara, *Longing for Running Water*, 117.
[59] Gebara, *Longing for Running Water*, 116.
[60] Gebara, *Longing for Running Water*, 103–4.
[61] Gebara, *Longing for Running Water*, 181–2.
[62] Maricel Mena-López and María Pilar Aquino, "Feminist Intercultural Theology: Religion, Culture, Feminism and Power," in *Feminist Intercultural Theology: Latina Explorations for a Just World*, ed. María Pilar Aquino and María José Rosado-Nunes (Maryknoll, NY: Orbis Books, 2007), xxvii.

*My life is the spiral of the past
and what comes ahead
tied up by the wisdom of a Condor.
I am the heart of the wind
that nurtures your vital energy
and makes the tremors of fear
sound gently.
I am like a spiritual song
touching all the memories of the universe.*

*I have the beauty of a fresh water spring of quiet mountains
vast and exalted lands
and silence.*

*I am young and beautiful.
I go on clothed by the land. Moving on and on.*[63]

~~~

Moving On: Radical Polypraxis

New directions for feminist theology emerge when taking seriously the spiritual paradigms that underlie *Runa* feminisms of the Andes and Indigenous feminisms of Abya-Yala more generally.

These new directions echo calls made by feminist theologians of Latin America in the past, particularly in the pioneering visions of Aquino and Gebara. They broke ground decades ago in systemizing feminist Latin American theology, proposing ecofeminist models, and incorporating intercultural frameworks. A new tapestry emerges when interweaving their theological threads of collective intuitions with the wise words and Andean worldviews of Aymara and Kichwa women leaders, Chipana and Cañamar.

Ancestral spiritualities of Latin America, inseparable from cultural identities, communal histories, and political struggles, challenge Christian theology's frameworks of being, knowing, and power. An intercultural, interreligious, and decolonial dialogue with the

---

[63] Cañamar, *Shunku-yay*.

original spiritualities of Abya-Yala has clear theoretical and practical implications for Christian theological paradigms. Engaging in a process of decolonizing Christianity leads to shifting ontological, epistemological, and socio-ethical constructs. The ontology of Indigenous spiritualities expresses the inseparability of the human community with all living beings and with the cosmos, interrogating the assumed ontological difference between humans and other species. The epistemology embraces a mind-heart knowing of *corazonar*, which is holistic and inclusive. These perspectives on being and knowing have commonalities with the ecofeminist and intercultural theological approaches introduced by Gebara and Aquino.

What are the consequences for action? Ancestral spirituality gives momentum and strength for the struggle, as well as assurance and guidance. In resistance/re-existence movements for body-land territories, spirituality motivates and helps persevere. "I knew we were going to succeed, the River told me."[64] These words of Berta Cáceres, the Indigenous feminist ecological activist, reflect the relationship between ancestral ontology, epistemology, and political power. Cáceres now an ancestral guiding spirit, lives in the sacred spaces (*wacas*) in the River Gualquarque, sacred to the Lenca people, which she defended.[65] The ancestors speak through and in nature to give strength to and encourage the community. The river renovates, renews, refreshes, and returns us to the infinite force we are, mutating throughout space and time.

The clear political implications of taking seriously ancestral spiritualities are multiple. They include an urgent call to live in harmony with all of nature, to keep close historical memories of the recreation of life, to listen to the guiding voices of the ancestors, to persevere for justice through connection to the vital forces, and to struggle for all living species, past as well as future generations.

---

[64] Quoted by Chipana, "*Íbamos a Triunfar, Me lo Dijo el Río.*" For sayings of Berta Cáceres, see Nancy Arévalo, "Once frases por las que Berta Cáceres no se murió, se multiplicó," *Once Noticias*, March 2, 2018, http://www.oncenoticias.hn/once-frases-ambientalista-berta-caceres/ (accessed April 7, 2024).

[65] For more on the role of ancestral spirituality in the indigenous territorial struggles of feminist rights defender, Berta Cáceres, see Mónica A. Maher, "A Rebellion of Spirituality: On the Power of Indigenous Civil Resistance in Honduras," in *Civil Resistance and Violent Conflict in Latin America: Mobilizing for Rights*, ed. Cécile Mouly and Esperanza Hernandez Delgado (New York: Palgrave Macmillan, 2019), 41–63.

The epistemic interfaces of Indigenous feminisms also demand recognition of the interconnected forms of violence against original women of Abya-Yala, the inseparability between humans and other species, and the continuum between spirited matter of body territories and land territories.

The task of decolonizing power leads to ethical-political projects of global solidarity that represent an inter-spiritual radical polypraxis. In defending their body land territories, Indigenous women continue to struggle not just for the survival of their own communities but for the thriving of all of life. As Nemonte Nenquimo of the Waorani Nation of the Ecuadorean Amazon, and winner of the 2020 Goldman Environmental Prize, states:

> Our spirituality is based on our interconnectedness with all living beings and the most profound principle of respect: reciprocity. That is why until today, despite centuries of displacement and violence against our peoples, we are protectors of 80% of our planet's biodiversity. We are only 5% of the world's population, and yet in our territories, we have been able to keep our planet Earth's ecosystems alive and flourishing.[66]

All life is implicated. All must participate. A radical polypraxis, based on new frameworks of knowing and being, demands spiritually grounded sociopolitical action on many fronts: multidimensional, transnational, transgenerational.

In sum, a feminist theological ethic arises in decolonizing epistemology, ontology, and power that reveals an inclusive radical polypraxis of resistance, healing, and liberation based in a continuous intercultural, interreligious dialogue with ancestral worldviews. This active dialogue is an interweaving of poetic words, theological languages, heart-mind explorations, and spiritual practices and actions in solidarity for all of life: humans, ancestors, the natural world, the spirit world, and the cosmos. The invitation is to live in harmony and balance with the vital forces in order to

---

[66]Nemonte Nenquimo, "Protecting Indigenous Territory and Life in the Amazon," The Goldman Environmental Prize, December 15, 2020, https://www.goldmanprize.org/blog/nemonte-nenquimo-protecting-indigenous-territory-and-life-in-the-amazon/ (accessed April 7, 2024).

co-create, cultivate, and recreate life with exquisite awe, quiet joy, deep respect, and profound tenderness so that all might flourish.

Returning in spiral space time,
Ritualizing, remembering, resisting, re-existing.
Traveling between mountains and doves...
Moving to spiritual rhythms, *Runa* feminisms,
Circle dancing, singing, invoking the ancestors,
Reconnecting to the wakas.

~~~

Ritual, spiritual and ancestral practice is part of a way of life of healing, of resistance. This demands a return to ourselves, a call to youth for their survival, a dialogue and resistance with our actions in the face of hegemonic power, of capitalism which sees our bodies as products and our persons as instant—and that hardly gives room for the spiritual body which is the heart of matter.[67]

~~~

Knock at my door and let us travel between mountains and white doves.

On the way, the black jaguar of the rocks will greet you, you will tell her of the mountain woman you carry inside, the wool cloths of grandmother mountain will cover you, you will come down with the rain, you will run in the eyes of the water, you will love each scent, texture and color of the wakas.

You will embrace yourself with each woman of the Earth and of spiraled time, with sweet and bitter tastes, you will love and value yourself in every conversation. The shouting from outside will fall into the sacred water, it will go away with the flowers which flow with the river. You will walk with the wisdom of the moon, you will sit around an altar together with your own, your shadows, your desires, your fears. You samay, will return to yourself, to your rhythm, to your time.[68]

~~

---

[67] Cañamar, "Convivir con la Espiritualidad Ancestral."
[68] Tsaywa Samay Cañamar Maldonado, *Shunku-yay/Mirarse en la Eternidad del Corazón* (Ecuador: Siwar Mayu, 2022). Translation from Spanish by Mónica A. Maher.

Bibliography

Aquino, María Pilar. "Teología Feminista Latinoamericana." In *Teología Feminista Latinoamericana*, edited by María Pilar Aquino and Elsa Támez, 9–73. Quito, Ecuador: Ediciones Abya-Yala, 1998.

Aquino, María Pilar and María José Rosado-Nunes, eds. *Feminist Intercultural Theology: Latina Explorations for a Just World*. Maryknoll, NY: Orbis Books, 2007.

Cabnal, Lorena. "Acercamiento a la Construcción de la Propuesta de Pensamiento Epistémico de las Mujeres Indígenas Feministas Comunitarias de Abya Yala." In *Feminista Siempre. Feminismos Diversos: El Feminismo Comunitario*, 11–25. Madrid: Asociación para la Cooperación con el Sur, Acsur-Las Segovias, 2010.

Cañamar, Samay. "Convivir con la Espiritualidad ancestral/Ñukanchik Usaykunawan Kawsashpa." Espiritualidades en Resistencia. Blog en Movimiento de Acción Noviolenta de las Américas, 2022. https://accionnoviolenta.org/convivir-con-la-espiritualidad-ancestral-nukanchik-ushaykunawan-kawsashpa/, accessed April 7, 2024.

Cañamar Maldonado, Tsaywa Samay. *Shunku-yay/Mirarse en la Eternidad del Corazón*. Translated from Kichwa by Fredy A. Roncalla. Ecuador: Siwar Mayu, 2022. Kichwa to English translations: http://siwarmayu.com/shunku-yay-looking-at-each-other-through-the-infinite-of-the-heart-tsaywa-samay-canamar-m/, accessed April 7, 2024.

Chipana, Sofia Nicolasa. "De la Sanación a la Liberación." In *Re-encantos y Re-encuentros: caminos y desafíos actuales de las teologías de la liberación*, edited by Dalíns Rufín Pardo and Luis Carlos Marrero, 157–66. Buenos Aires, Argentina: Juanuno1 Ediciones, 2018.

Chipana Quispe, Sofía. "*Íbamos a Triunfar, Me lo Dijo el Río*." Espiritualidades en Resistencia. Blog en Movimiento de Acción Noviolenta de las Américas, 2022. https://accionnoviolenta.org/ibamos-a-triunfar-me-lo-dijo-el-rio/, accessed January 26, 2023.

Chipana Quispe, Sofía. *Sosteniendo la Vida: Ante las Violencias Extractivas y el Neoliberalismo Verde Colonial*. Online Forum of FLACSO-Ecuador and CLACSO-Argentina. Lecture delivered October 4, 2021.

De Sousa Santos, Boaventura. *Epistemologies of the South: Justice against Epistemicide*. London: Routledge, 2014.

Gebara, Ivone. *Longing for Running Water: Ecofeminism and Liberation*. Translated from Portuguese by David Molineaux. Minneapolis, MN: Augsberg Fortress, 1999.

Guerrero Arias, Patricio. *La Chakana del Corazonar: Desde las Espiritualidades y las Sabidurías Insurgentes de Abya-Yala*. Quito, Ecuador: Abya-Yala/Universidad Politécnica Salesiana, 2018.

Lang, Miriam, Horacio Machado Aráoz, and Mario Rodríguez Ibáñez. "Transcender la Modernidad Capitalista para Re-existir. Reflexiones Sobre Derechos, Democracia y Bienestar en el Contexto de las Nuevas Derechas." In ¿Cómo Se Sostiene la Vida en América Latina? Feminismos y re-Existencias en Tiempos de Oscuridad, edited by Karin Gabbert and Miriam Lang, 343–85. Quito, Ecuador: Edición Fundación Rosa Luxemburg and Ediciones Abya Yala, 2019.

Maguire, Daniel C. *Sacred Choices: The Right to Contraception and Abortion in Ten World Religions*. Minneapolis, MN: Augsburg Fortress Press, 2001.

Maher, Mónica A. "A Rebellion of Spirituality: On the Power of Indigenous Civil Resistance in Honduras." In *Civil Resistance and Violent Conflict in Latin America: Mobilizing for Rights*, edited by Cécile Mouly and Esperanza Hernandez Delgado, 41–63. New York: Palgrave Macmillan, 2019.

Nenquimo, Nemonte. "Protecting Indigenous Territory and Life in the Amazon." The Goldman Environmental Prize Acceptance Speech, December 15, 2020. https://www.goldmanprize.org/blog/nemonte-nenquimo-protecting-indigenous-territory-and-life-in-the-amazon/, accessed April 7, 2024.

8

An Embodied Feminist Theology of Peace as Radical Praxis

Keun-joo Christine Pae

Writing about peace from a feminist theological perspective is a challenging task. For, as Kwok Pui-lan argues, "widespread myths" about religion create barriers to thinking theologically about peacebuilding. These myths portray religion as a source of conflict (i.e., the clash of civilizations) and as irrational, absolutist, divisive, and, thus, incompatible with modernity.[1] Religion is given limited space in international politics marked by armed conflict, treaties, international law, and tribunals. Religious women's spaces are even more limited. Women's voices are rarely heard in male-dominated political and religious spaces, especially in war zones in Asia, Africa, and Latin America. The words of 2011 Nobel Peace Prize laureate Leymah Gbowee prove this: "In the traditional telling of war stories, women are always in the background ... You have not heard it [my/our story] before ... [because] African women's stories

---

[1] Kwok Pui-lan, *Postcolonial Politics and Theology: Unraveling Empire for a Global World* (Louisville, KY: Westminster John Knox, 2021), 170–1.

were rarely heard."[2] Yet, Gbowee clearly wants the world to know how Liberian Christian and Muslim women raised their voices and organized their bodies against war and gender-based violence. Hence, she reclaims Liberian women's agency of choosing the stories they want to tell, as the Western media, with their pornographic interests in wars in Africa, perpetuate the stereotypical images of raped and mutilated African women.

In a world where no one knows peace free from war, how can we feminist theologians reconstruct theology by empathetically engaging the lived experiences of women like Gbowee who witness and resist war? With a keen awareness of barriers to Christian women's peacebuilding, my chapter proposes *a feminist theology of peace as radical praxis*. Radical praxis is rooted in the feminist theological tradition for justice. As radical praxis, feminist theology of peace collects and recollects women's wisdom of peacebuilding. Simultaneously, feminist theologians critically analyze military labor through gender and sexuality, disabusing Christianity of justifying war and making myths about self-sacrificial soldiers (or just warriors), myths scaffolded onto ideas about the crucified Jesus. Such radical praxis challenges us to *see* the physical realities of war by interrogating how state military operations exploit ordinary people's gendered and sexualized labor. Based on conversations with various feminist theologians and woman peacemakers, I argue that *seeing* entails the concerted work of the physical, the spiritual, and the intellectual. Together, such work may not only *arouse* our passion for global peace with justice but may also spur us to take concrete actions to demilitarize our lives and liberate us from fear, and so to imagine radical peace.

What Is Radical Praxis?

As many feminist theologians argue, theology is praxis, not merely a God-talk. Gender and sexual politics visibly or invisibly shape, affect, or taint any theological discourses, practices, and imaginations. Furthermore, feminist theology has never been

---

[2]Leymah Gbowee with Carol Mithers, *Mighty Be Our Powers: How Sisterhood, Prayer, and Sex Changed a Nation in War* (New York: Beast Books, 2011), preface, Kindle.

value-neutral but justice-oriented, with a goal of transforming white supremacist heteropatriarchal theology and social structures into more just forms. As seen in various liberation theologies developed particularly by Black, Indigenous, and People of Color (BIPOC) in the United States and across the globe, many feminist theologians reflect critically on how theologies can bring about actual material changes, not mere changes into religious languages, symbols, and metaphors.³ For such scholars, feminist theology is always about "doing," namely, praxis.

I ground praxis in Argentinian feminist, queer theologian Marcella Althaus-Reid's idea of "passion-arousing" articulated in her *Indecent Theology*. Emphasizing the necessity of incorporating sexuality analysis into Liberation Theology, Althaus-Reid articulates "a passion-arousing style" developed from the "see-judge-act" or "see-discern-act" method.⁴ Althaus-Reid reconstructs the method of liberation theology through sexual metaphors, arguing, "Learning to see ... is in itself a sexual challenge for Christianity."⁵ As a sexual act, the method for Indecent Theology challenges viewers (i.e., feminist theologians) to interrogate critically the sexual desires and stereotypes in Christian rituals, prayers, and images. This critical interrogation is connected to viewers' capacities to "see" women and gender queer persons' suffering as entangled with complex social structures (e.g., war, violence, global capitalism, and patriarchy).⁶ A "passion-arousing" method emphasizes the body, the real flesh and blood of race, gender, sexuality, class, and religious and cultural meaning or what Susan Thistlethwaite calls "critical physicality"— in theological analysis and imagining.⁷ Simultaneously, the method

---

³For example, according to womanist ethicist Rima Vesely-Flad, state-sanctioned police violence against Blacks and their mass incarceration are the materialization of "the symbolic constructs of racialized and polluted bodies." Christianity has aided in constructing Black bodies as symbolically polluted bodies. See Rima Vesely-Flad, *Racial Purity and Dangerous Bodies: Moral Pollution, Black Lives and the Struggle for Justice* (Minneapolis, MN: Fortress Press, 2017), xvi–xvii.
⁴Marcella Althaus-Reid, *Indecent Theology: Theological Perversions in Sex, Gender, and Politics* (London: Routledge, 2000), 126.
⁵Althaus-Reid, *Indecent Theology*, 127.
⁶Althaus-Reid, *Indecent Theology*, 136–44.
⁷The term "critical physicality" comes from Susan Thistlethwaite's use of gender and sexuality in critically analyzing militarized violence against women and just war theory. Although Althaus-Reid does not use precisely this term, her method does emphasize the body in the center of theological thinking, which is congruent with

highlights the inseparability between the body and the spirit and spirituality and sensuality.

Here, I reinterpret Althaus-Reid's "passion-arousing" in order to delineate a feminist theology of peace with attention to the body and the physicality of peacebuilding. Passion refers to both suffering and desire. Suffering and desire are intimately and complicatedly connected, evoking physical, emotional, spiritual, and sensual reactions among people who experience or see unjust violence. "Arousing" points out all these entangled feelings and reactions that peace activists experience when engaging with victims-survivors of militarized violence, or overcoming their own victimhood and trauma, or intentionally remembering and witnessing (her)stories of violence against women and nongender conforming people. Peace activists may simultaneously experience suffering, excitement, and ecstasy because they are passionate about demilitarizing the world, peace and justice, and the cessation of the suffering of all living beings. Hence, praxis is not simply a theory-action-reflection model like that presented by many liberation theologians. Instead, praxis requires *the wholeness of the body and the spirit* working together intellectually, sensually, physically, and emotionally.

"The radical" in radical praxis only adds to how to revitalize praxis in feminist theology. Just as the Latin origin of the term *radical* is *the root* or *the ground*, radical praxis means going back to the root of feminist theology but in a renewed way. To conceptualize "the radical," I borrow the term "radical resurgence" from Nishnaabeg poet, scholar, and activist Leanne Betasamosake Simpson from the First Nation, Canada. Adding radical to a resurgence movement, Simpson emphasizes the importance of taking back resurgence from neoliberalism and simultaneously confirming the "body sovereignty of Indigenous people," which Canada's white settler colonial government has severely destroyed, raped, exploited, and killed.[8] Resurgence is not about celebrating cultures dismantled

---

Thistlethwaite's critical physicality. See Susan Thistlethwaite, *Women's Bodies as Battlefield: Christian Theology and the Global War on Women* (New York: Palgrave Macmillan, 2015), 4–5.

[8]Leanne Betasamosake Simpson, *As We Have Always Done: Indigenous Freedom through Radical Resurgence* (Minneapolis: University of Minnesota Press, 2017), 47–8. Indeed, Indigenous peoples in the United States, Australia, and New Zealand share similar experiences with those in Canada and the confirmation of their body sovereignty, as political scientists and criminologists Marianne Nielsen and Linda

by settler colonialism or merely retrieving what has been lost in history. Instead, radical resurgence engages "visioning, thinking, acting, and mobilizing around Indigenous systemic alternatives that respect ancestors, Two-spirit people, non-binary gender hierarchy, nature, and non-human nations."[9] Gender and sexuality must be centered in resurgence because gender and sexual violence have been the deadly tool of white settler colonialism.

Indigenous knowledge for a radical resurgence movement reveals interrelationality or interconnectedness among all beings—ancestors, sovereign nations of the natural world (e.g., trees, animals, air, water, and Earth), tribal nations, people in revolutionary movements against neo/colonialism, heteronormative patriarchy, and neoliberal capitalism. In this understanding of interconnectedness, Indigenous activists in radical resurgence pursue solidarity with those in other resurgence movements, such as the Black Lives Matter movement, the Black feminist movement, the antiwar feminist movement, and many other decolonizing movements across the globe.[10] For this reason, activists of radical resurgence are internationalists who *see* the interconnectedness of all forms of oppression due to the interconnected nature of all living beings. Although different groups of diverse radical resurgence movements have different roots for their wisdom, these roots are interconnected.[11]

Simpson's radical resurgence and Althaus-Reid's passion-arousing actions resonate with Palestinian Quaker peace activist Jean Zaru's life. Palestinian women's resilience, survival wisdom, and popular resistance against the Israeli Occupation of their land, water, and agricultural resources radicalize Zaru's understanding of peace in an ongoing way. Interweaving her multiple social identities of being Arab, Palestinian, Quaker, and woman, Zaru grounds her theological understanding of nonviolence in Quaker

---

Robyn's comparative studies of white settler colonialism shows. See Marianne Nielsen and Linda Robyn, *Colonialism Is Crime* (New Brunswick, NJ: Rutgers University Press, 2019).
[9]Simpson, *As We Have Always Done*, 49.
[10]Simpson, *As We Have Always Done*, 50.
[11]These roots should not be considered to be individual taproots, but to be pluralistic. I have previously reflected on Althaus-Reid's indecent theology in light of Simpson's radical resurgence in my essay, "Indecent Resurgence: God's Solidarity against the Gendered War on COVID," in *Doing Theology in the New Normal*, ed. Jione Havea (London: SCM, 2021), 179–95.

teachings that "war is ... contrary to the teachings of Christ."[12] Yet, her spirituality is rooted in "the human dignity and human rights of all people, and the sacredness of Mother Earth."[13] Hence, she reconstructs the meanings of Christian conversion as to be empathetically, spiritually, and physically connected to the struggle of the downtrodden everywhere.[14] For Zaru, all forms of oppression are interconnected. So are all human struggles for justice, peace, and liberation. Nonviolence is a "practical" way to achieve justice and peace for all without losing the practitioner's integrity.[15]

Zaru resists the self-righteousness and moral superiority often implicitly or explicitly presented by pacifists. Her family tragedy influences Zaru's understanding of nonviolence as a practice that is inseparable from one's faith and life and *not a moral teaching*. In the early 1950s, Hanna Mikhail, Zaru's only brother, left for the United States to study. After earning a doctoral degree at Harvard University, Hanna taught at different colleges across the United States. Although Hanna wanted to come home after the Arab-Israeli War of 1967 to be with his people, his entry to Palestine was denied. Israel did not allow any Palestinians who were absent from the census data collected right after the 1967 War to return to their homeland or have residency rights.[16] Hanna lived in Jordan and Lebanon near his family in Ramallah and was involved in the Palestinian Liberation Organization (PLO). During the Lebanese Civil War in 1976, Hanna went missing. He is still missing. Agonized about the uncertainty of her brother's life, Zaru asked her house guest at that time, a notable American pacifist, to help her apply to Amnesty International to seek information about the brother. This pacifist refused because Hanna worked with the PLO, a terrorist organization, and helping people who took the path of violence would be against his "moral principle."[17] Zaru

---

[12] Jean Zaru, *Occupied with Nonviolence: A Palestinian Woman Speaks* (Minneapolis, MN: Fortress Press, 2008), chapter 6, Kindle.
[13] Zaru, *Occupied with Nonviolence*, chapter 1.
[14] Zaru, *Occupied with Nonviolence*, chapter 6.
[15] Zaru, *Occupied with Nonviolence*, chapter 6.
[16] Zaru, *Occupied with Nonviolence*, chapter 1.
[17] Zaru, *Occupied with Nonviolence*, chapter 1.

was disheartened by the pacifist's judgments on Hanna without knowing his character or worrying about his fundamental right to life, liberty, and security.[18] Nonetheless, Zaru did not give up nonviolence but proposed "practical nonviolence." Nonviolence is a *practice* and an effective way to resist injustice and violence. This practice requires hope, faith, and steadfastness. One can teach nonviolence by courageously embodying nonviolent resistance in the face of violence and certainly not by moral judgment.[19] Zaru's practical nonviolence is a Christian example of radical praxis.

Just as Althaus-Reid's passion-arousing style suggests new perspectives on liberation and methods of *seeing* by consciously incorporating gender and sexuality in theological thinking of liberation, so too Simpson underscores the necessity of gender and queer analysis for an Indigenous radical resurgence. Zaru's gender identity and Palestinian women's experiences of living under heteropatriarchal culture and masculinized Israeli military occupation cannot be separated from her interrogation of religious, cultural, economic, and military violence. Gender and sexuality are critical tools in analyzing and articulating a feminist theology for peace as radical praxis.

Resignifying Gender and Sexuality for a Feminist Theology of Peace

A gender and sexuality analysis brings *the human body to the center of the theological inquiry about war*. Any war projects mobilize human bodies for killing, fighting, prostituting, and more. Hence, we must *see* what gender and sexual ideologies the military promotes, how military operations (re)align human bodies with these ideologies, what bodies are mobilized, and how the church participates in strengthening or disrupting war-gender-sexuality ideologies. Seen through the frames of gender and sexuality, every military project is about nothing but killing and death.

---

[18]Zaru, *Occupied with Nonviolence*, chapter 1.
[19]Zaru, *Occupied with Nonviolence*, chapter 6.

Gender and Sexuality in Soldiering and Prostitution

Elsewhere, through scholar Jin-kyung Lee's concept of "necropolitical labor," I analyzed prostitution and soldiering in the context of US bases in South Korea. Both prostitution and soldiering have been significant parts of US overseas military operations. Both recruit or force particular bodies to carry out gendered and sexualized labor. The two bodies, however, have been treated very differently. The prostituted body is condemned as dirty, polluted, and decadent, while the soldiering body is glorified and even compared to the self-sacrificial Christ. As an analytical concept, necropolitical labor shows the interlocking forces of gender, sexuality, race, and class in war capitalism and it highlights military labor's proximity to death.

Lee explains that

> The notion of necropolitical labor highlights an *intermediate stage where the extraction of labor is related to and premised on the possibility of death*, rather than the ultimate event of death itself ... necropolitical labor as *the most disposable labor* ... [is] the ultimate labor commodity or worker, something or be thrown out, replaced, and/or (both literally and figuratively) killed after or as the labor is performed.[20] (Emphasis added.)

If war is understood to be "as much a means of achieving sovereignty as exercising its right to kill," then soldiers physically carry out sovereignty's right to kill.[21] Simultaneously, they are constantly exposed to being killed while participating in killing enemies. Soldiering is necropolitical labor, not because they kill but because their job always pushes them to the verge of death—their own and others'.

---

[20] Jin-kyung Lee, *Service Economies: Militarism, Sex Work, and Migrant Labor in South Korea* (Minneapolis: University of Minnesota Press, 2010), 6, also cited in Keun-joo Christine Pae, "Proletarianized Sexuality of Soldiering and Prostitution: Making a Christian Ethic of Peace Countering Necropolitics of War," in *Faith, Class, and Labor: Intersectional Approaches in a Global Context*, ed. Jin Young Choi and Joerg Rieger (Eugene, OR: Pickwick, 2020), 144.
[21] Achilles Mbembe, *Necropolitics*, trans. Steven Corcoran (Durham, NC: Duke University Press, 2019), 66.

To be certain, the US military recruits both men and women of all racial, ethnic backgrounds and sexual orientations. However, this recruitment practice does not mean that the underlying white hypermasculine culture of the US military has changed fundamentally. As a former marine officer, Anuradha Bhagwati states, institutionalized language, such as calling Black marines dark green (dark refers to their skin color and green, to the color of the uniform) and women marines W.M.s, suggests that real marines mean only white males.[22] Moreover, feminist scholar Zillah Eisenstein argues that by featuring female soldiers' faces in its advertising, the US military intends to deliver a gendered message to the public that military service is ordinary, safe, and easy (i.e., if a woman can do it, anyone can do it).[23] If Eisenstein's argument were convincing, the US military's gendered message would accelerate militarizing ordinary Americans' lives, unbeknownst to many Americans. Women's presence in the US military or participation in necropolitical labor has received critical attention from many feminist scholars. Still, they disagree on whether female soldering is considered gender equality in what is the most masculinized bastion—the military.

In the 1990s, when the American public debated whether to allow female soldiers to be active combatants on the frontline, Christian feminist, ethicist Mary Hunt urged the public to contemplate why American society would ever want anyone to kill others or be killed in a highly perilous situation.[24] Hunt reminded the public of the necropolitical labor of soldiering as the normal part of any war. Rather than debating whether women are physically, psychologically, and intellectually capable of killing enemies and dealing with complex military technology, the American public should ask why certain people are asked to kill other human beings

---

[22]Setsu Shigematsu with Anuradha Kristina Bhagwati, and Eli Paintedcrow, "Women-of-Color Veterans on War, Militarism, and Feminism," in *Feminism and War: Confronting US Imperialism*, ed. Robin Riley, Chandra Mohanty, and Minnie Pratt (New York: Zed Books, 2008), 96.

[23]Zillah Eisenstein, "Resexing Militarism for the Globe," in *Feminism and War: Confronting US Imperialism*, ed. Robin Riley, Chandra Mohanty, and Minnie Pratt (New York: Zed Books, 2008), 39.

[24]Mary Hunt, "Medals on Our Blouses? A Feminist Theological Look at Women in Combat," in *Feminist Theological Ethics*, ed. Lois K. Daly (Louisville, KY: Westminster John Knox Press, 1994), 318.

and what moral, physical, spiritual, and psychological consequences these people experience after killing.[25]

Gender-based violence, including sexual assault against female soldiers, in the military has motivated feminist scholars and activists to scrutinize and criticize toxic masculinity normalized in the US military. The groundbreaking documentary film *The Invisible War* (2012) shows the alarming rate of sexual violence against servicewomen in the military and the military authorities' repeated failures to punish sexual violators because some consider sexual violence a job hazard of serving in the military. In response to the film, feminist theologians Rita Nakashima Brock and Gabriella Lettini, in their study of moral injury, detailed the trauma of survivors of military sexual violence. Wartime moral injury, which can debilitate soldiers' souls and psyches, occurs after they have had to act against their moral principles or will, witness unjust acts done by their superiors or organizations, or fail to protect the weak and the vulnerable, including their fellow soldiers.[26] Killing, torturing, assaulting, and raping people—whether they are armed enemies or unarmed civilians—are actions not permitted in civil society, but are expected of soldiers during wartime. Indeed, soldiers, as human beings of conscience, are not immune to intentionally harming others. As a result, many soldiers experience a severe moral injury that disables them from trusting themselves and others, or put differently, from trusting their moral capability. The degree of moral injury can be more severe if soldiers think they are fighting an unjust war or feel empathy toward their enemies.[27] Suppose that moral capacity is one of the crucial elements that make humans human and give meaning to human life. In that case, those who live with a moral injury cannot live the everyday life, for it is filled with

---

[25] Many scholars in various disciplines, including psychology, philosophy, and theology, have produced prolific resources on how killing in war changes human beings. See Dave Grossman, *On Killing: The Psychological Cost of Learning to Kill in War and Society* (New York: Back Bay Books, 2009), Nancy Sherman, *Afterwar: Healing the Moral Wounds of Our Soldiers* (New York: Oxford University Press, 2015), and Jonathan Shay, *Achilles in Vietnam: Combat Trauma and the Undoing of Character* (New York: Simon & Schuster, 1995). Shay is the first person who introduced the term "moral injury" in the psychological study of war.

[26] Rita Nakashima Brock and Gabriella Lettini, *Soul Repair: Recovering from Moral Injury after War* (Boston, MA: Beacon Press, 2012), xi–xviii.

[27] Brock and Lettini, *Soul Repair*, 76–9.

various decision-making moments. Brock and Lettini argue that female victim-survivors of military rape experience post-traumatic stress disorder that is as severe as that of combat veterans. They do not experience it as moral injury, for they did nothing immoral![28] By contrast, those who witness military rape or participate in the act against their will may experience moral injury.

The other side of the spectrum of necropolitical labor is military prostitution. Killing, military rape, and prostitution are intimately connected if they are all seen through what many feminist scholars call "militarized masculinity"—feelings of "power and superiority over women and willingness to inflict violence on anyone deemed inferior."[29] Much as militarized masculinity has justified the intimate connection between the US military and prostitution industries in Asian countries and the United States, so too Christianity has condemned prostitutes as sinners responsible for morally corrupting societies.[30] In reality, the US military has routinely used commercialized prostitution to maintain military morale and to appease soldiers' anxiety, fear, and stress. Systemic prostitution has been the staple of US bases in Okinawa, Japan, South Korea, the Philippines, Thailand, and so on. During the Vietnam War, prostitution industries around the US bases in these countries were systemized.[31] As Cynthia Enloe argues, military prostitution is not separate from military rape.[32] Since US military sexual assault against local women can cause diplomatic conflicts with the countries that host US bases, the US military authorities and politicians have secretly found safe, commercialized sex for their soldiers. Military prostitutes perform gendered and sexualized

---

[28]Brock and Lettini, *Soul Repair*, 51–2.
[29]Cynthia Enloe, "Beyond 'Rambo': Women and the Varieties of Militarized Masculinity," in *Women and the Military System*, ed. Eva Isskson (New York: St. Martin's Press, 1988), 71–93; quoted in David Vine, *Base Nation: How U.S. Military Bases Abroad Harm America and the World* (New York: Metropolitan Books, 2017), chapter 10, Kindle.
[30]Rita Nakashima Brock and Susan Thistlethwaite, *Casting Stones: Prostitution and Liberation in Asia and the United States* (Minneapolis, MN: Fortress Press, 1996), 235–7.
[31]Sheila Jeffreys, *The Industrial Vagina: The Political Economy of the Global Sex Trade* (New York: Routledge, 2009), 116–20.
[32]Cynthia Enloe, *The Curious Feminist: Searching for Women in a New Age of Empire* (Berkeley: University of California Press, 2004), 121.

necropolitical labor that constantly exposes them to death and violence while working.

Militarized labor as necropolitical labor should be considered a spectrum, ranging from killing on the battlefield to sexual violence in the military and military prostitution. This form of labor is gendered and sexualized and has detrimental consequences, such as spiritual and physical death, moral injury, and post-traumatic stress disorder. Hence, feminist theologians must see gender and sexuality as factors embedded in the necropolitical labor of war.

Hero-Mythmaking

Susan Thistlethwaite argues that misogynistic violence is deeply ingrained in Western culture, and that institutionalized Christianity is in part responsible for that.[33] The Christian teachings of hierarchical duality between God and humans, humans and nature, the spirit and the body, and men and women have offered a moral ground to justify violence to discipline women and children. In the Christian moral traditions of war, every form of violence should be judged in the court of nonviolence. Thus, theologically speaking, only "just" violence has been approved by the church and Western society. The image of a "just warrior," which has dominated how the American public views its soldiers, is a clever way for the US government to justify and execute military projects abroad and militarize violence in the domestic context. Yet, Thistlethwaite debunks the cruelty behind just violence professed by the just warrior, typically represented by a muscular, heterosexual white man. Just violence is not intrinsically just: instead, it is "justified" by the heteropatriarchal church—in secular language, "militarized masculinity" living inside the church, or (in Althaus-Reid's words) in the church "closeted" in heteropatriarchal-military-capitalism.[34]

A just warrior can be analogous to early Christian martyrs. Some of them were soldiers who, in fact, refused to participate in the killing because it was against Jesus' teachings of nonviolence. Unfortunately, the institutionalized church has lost Christian martyrs' staunch belief in nonviolence and no-killing. Instead,

---

[33]Thistlethwaite, *Woman's Bodies as Battlefield*, 3–4.
[34]Thistlethwaite, *Women's Bodies as Battlefield*, 130–1 and 135.

the church's apparitions of warrior martyrs have been resurrected through the bodies of soldiers in many wars that have evoked the name of a Christian God until recently. One such example is Pat Tillman, a former football player for the Arizona Cardinals, who was killed by so-called friendly fire in Afghanistan in April 2004. In his patriotic response to terrorist attacks on September 11, 2001, Tillman joined the US Army Rangers, leaving behind his promising future as a professional football player and his newly formed family.[35] During his tours in Iraq and Afghanistan, Tillman had not been involved in any active combat. In the mountainous Afghan areas, his ranger unit was divided into two groups or serials in order to tow a disabled vehicle in the canyon. When the two serials were positioned on top and at the bottom of the canyon, Serial Two mistook the other party as Taliban fighters and started shooting them. After a cease-fire, two people, including Tillman, were found dead.[36]

Historian Jonathan Ebel critically analyzes heroic mythmaking and scapegoating through Tillman's case. At first, the US government hid the factual context behind Tillman's death. To boost the American public's support for the unpopular wars in the Middle East, the Bush administration, along with the conservative news media, portrayed Tillman as a true, patriotic American who sacrificed his career and even his life to save his country from the Taliban.[37] For a while, it portrayed Tillman as an all-American hero and scapegoat who could be compared to a scapegoat given to God in the Book of Leviticus and even Jesus, the scapegoat of redeeming human beings (i.e., Americans) from sins.[38] Furthermore, if American civil religion were understood through the narratives, rituals, and symbols produced by the United States' nationalistic understanding of its place in the world and in human history, the soldier would be the living symbol of American civil religion.[39]

---

[35] Jonathan Ebel, *G.I. Messiahs: Soldiering, War, and American Civil Religion* (Oxford: Oxford University Press, 2015), 166.
[36] Ebel, *G.I. Messiahs*, 173.
[37] Ebel, *G.I. Messiahs*, 174–5.
[38] Ebel, *G.I. Messiahs*, 176–7, 187.
[39] Ebel, *G.I. Messiahs*, 2–4; Robert Bellah, who first coined the term "American civil religion" that shapes and molds American spirit through rituals, symbols, and narratives, argues that American civil religion is not associated with any particular traditions. However, many scholars have criticized Bellah and the scholars of American

Tillman's death was appropriated for American nationalism as a symbol of civil religion, which always needs rituals and symbols. When Tillman's family discovered the US government's fabrication of his death, they felt understandably betrayed by the government.[40]

Thistlethwaite points out, "Christian theology has often been bought into heroic myth to lend support for violent retribution in a presumed battle between good and evil."[41] This version of Christian theology generates Christian triumphalism—the ultimate victory of Christ who was crucified but resurrected to bring victory over death and evil. A triumphant theology justifies Jesus' crucifixion not as state-sanctioned violence but as a necessary sacrifice for greater victory. The just warrior–hero myth influenced by the triumphant narratives of Jesus Christ necessitates the constant invocations of Jesus through soldiers' bodies like Tillman's in order to justify America's wars morally and theologically. Tillman's background and muscular body were an ideal symbol of a muscular Christ who would judge evil. When combined with American nationalism, as happened with Tillman, Christian triumphalism becomes a dangerous ideology that fosters American exceptionalism as the divine will and turns anyone who criticizes America for its imperialistic expansion into the enemy of the country. Yet, fallen soldiers cannot be resurrected. They are just "dead."[42]

Redoing Theology

So far, I have attempted both to redefine a feminist theology of peace as radical praxis grounded in feminist theological wisdom and women's peacebuilding activism and to resignify gender and sexuality in analyzing militarism—both military labor and its ideologies. With all this knowledge and all these critical methods of

---

civil religion for ignoring white masculine Christianity embedded in American civil religion; see Grace Yukish and Penny Edgell, eds., *Religion Is Raced: Understanding American Religion in the Twenty-First Century* (New York: New York University Press, 2020).
[40] Ebel, *G.I. Messiahs*, 188.
[41] Thistlethwaite, *Woman's Bodies as Battlefield*, 101.
[42] Thistlethwaite, *Women's Bodies as Battlefield*, 101.

doing theology, how can we "redo" theology? In bringing this chapter to a close, I contemplate this question with two peacebuilders.

"What does peace mean to you?" I asked executive director Soon Duk Woo of the Sunlit Center when I first visited there. The center is located near a US military garrison, Camp Humphreys, in Anjeongri of Pyeongtaek, a southern satellite city of Seoul. For more than twenty years, the Sunlit Center has advocated for now elderly Korean women who used to work in prostitution industries around the US bases in South Korea. These women catered to the sexual needs of American soldiers until they could no longer conduct sexual labor. Without adequate resources for living, these women, like hovering ghosts, continue to live around the Anjeongri camp town, embodying traumatic histories and memories of the active Korean War (1950–3), followed by the division of the Korean peninsula and the US military's presence for an indefinite period.[43] Executive Woo's answer was surprisingly mundane, "Peace means that every woman at the Sunlit Center can have a bowl of warm steamed rice every day. She is not worried about dying alone anymore. She is also respected as an elder in our society."

I still reflect on her words when thinking about peace, free from the fear of violence. Just as hot steamed rice in a shiny stainless steel bowl is analogous to "daily bread" in the Lord's Prayer, peace is tangible, material, and inseparable from everyday life. In the Korean context, a bowl of rice signifies the strength of life. It signifies that no matter how hard your life is and how harshly society (in this case, specifically militarized violence) treats you, you can overcome life's difficulties at least while eating a warm bowl of steamy rice particularly with others in the community. You can rise again and again with that power of rice. Although G.I.s pejoratively called Asian prostitutes "little brown fucking machines fueled with rice," that rice indeed sustained Asian women amid militarized violence.[44] To redo theology, we should pay attention to the everyday material needs of those whose lives were violated by military campaigns—how they experience God, the Sacred, and the

---

[43]The Korean War broke out on June 25, 1950, and ended as a truce between the North Korea-China ally and the United Nations on July 27, 1953. The war is still ongoing.
[44]Katherine Moon, *Sex among Allies: Military Prostitution in U.S.–Korea Relations* (New York: Columbia University Press, 1997), 34.

Divine in their everyday life. By *passionately seeing* their everyday lives and "my" connection to their lives, we, feminist theologians, can empathetically understand the suffering inflicted by war and women's deep yearnings for peace in a bowl of rice. Peacebuilding is not simply about creating a just global order but, more importantly, it is also about rebuilding ordinary people's everyday lives, which have been shattered by war and military operations.

When the documentary film *Living Along the Fenceline* was released in 2012, I interviewed Reverend Debbie Lee, the narrator of the film. On behalf of the Women for Genuine Security, a grassroots organization based in the San Francisco Bay Area, Lee guided viewers through the stories of women whose lives had been shattered by US bases and their anti-military activism, from San Antonio, Texas, and Vieques, Puerto Rico, to Hawaiʻi, Guam, Okinawa, South Korea, and the Philippines.[45] When I asked her how her theology and Christian faith influenced her peace activism, Lee was silent for a minute. She then said, "I have not "theologized" our work for peace. However, religion is an important part of peace activism, depending on how you define religion. For example, peace is spirituality for Hawaiians. Protecting nature from militarization is an active spiritual practice. As a Christian, I see militarism go against every Christian teaching—it destroys life, the sacred."[46]

Lee's words are the old wisdom of feminist peacebuilding, which Zaru already articulated. We cannot theologize peace; we can only embody it. Peacebuilding is embodied theology that must liberate people from gendered and sexualized necropolitical labor and fear of death and in its place, bring healing, compassion, and reconciliation into war-trodden society.

Finally, peacebuilding requires the concerted efforts of diverse people's physical, spiritual, and intellectual work. Scholars, activists,

---

[45]Women for Genuine Security is a member organization of the International Women's Network against Militarism, an umbrella organization networking among women's antiwar grassroots organizations in the mainland United States, Hawaiʻi, Puerto Rico, Guam, Okinawa, Philippines, and South Korea. *Living Along the Fenceline* was the collective product of the International Women's Network against Militarism organization.

[46]Elsewhere, I have reflected on interviews with Soon Duk Woo and Debbie Lee. See Keun-joo Christine Pae, "A Politics of Empathy: Christianity and Women's Peace Activism in U.S. Military Prostitution in South Korea," in *Women and Asian Religions*, ed. Zayn Kassam (Santa Barbara, CA: ABC-CLIO, 2017), 223–39.

soldiers, prostitutes, and pastors have roles to play in building peace, both from where they stand individually and by working together for peace and healing on an individual, communal, social, and global level. For instance, if soldiers and military prostitutes produce bodily knowledge of militarized necropolitical labor, then theologians and pastors can choose to *see* critically the militarized Christian theology, ritual, and symbols that might well have increased the military laborers' suffering. Together, they create a new theology of peace free from war and violence. This theology emerges when they empathetically embrace one another and courageously and creatively resist war and militarism. In addition, working together means empowering diverse peacebuilding groups, such as antiwar feminists, activists, theologians, veterans, pastors, military prostitutes, and so forth. A feminist theology of peace can be a platform on which to connect these groups and to speak about our interconnected activism and lives.

Bibliography

Althaus-Reid, Marcella. *Indecent Theology: Theological Perversions in Sex, Gender, and Politics*. London: Routledge, 2000.
Brock, Rita Nakashima, and Gebriella Lettini. *Soul Repair: Recovering from Moral Injury after War*. Boston, MA: Beacon Press, 2012.
Brock, Rita Nakashima, and Susan Thistlethwaite. *Casting Stones: Prostitution and Liberation in Asia and the United States*. Minneapolis, MN: Fortress Press, 1996.
Dick, Kirby, director. *The Invisible War*. Chain Camera Pictures, 2012.
Ebel, Jonathan. *G.I. Messiahs: Soldering, War, and American Civil Religion*. Oxford: Oxford University Press, 2015.
Eisenstein, Zillah. "Resexing Militarism for the Globe." In *Feminism and War: Confronting US Imperialism*, edited by Robin Riley, Chandra Mohanty, and Minnie Pratt, 27–45. New York: Zed Books, 2008.
Enloe, Cynthia. *The Curious Feminist: Searching for Women in a New Age of Empire*. Berkeley: University of California Press, 2004.
Enloe, Cynthia. "Beyond 'Rambo': Women and the Varieties of Militarized Masculinity." In *Women and the Military System*, edited by Eva Isskson, 71–93. New York: St. Martin's Press, 1988.
Gbowee, Leymah with Carol Mithers. *Mighty Be Our Powers: How Sisterhood, Prayer, and Sex Changed a Nation in War*. New York: Beast Books, 2011. Kindle.

Grossman, Dave. *On Killing: The Psychological Cost of Learning to Kill in War and Society*. New York: Back Bay Books, 2009.
Hosino, Lina and Gwyn Kirk, directors. *Living Along the Fenceline*. Women for Genuine Security, 2012.
Hunt, Mary. "Medals on Our Blouses? A Feminist Theological Look at Women in Combat." In *Feminist Theological Ethics: A Reader*, edited by Lois K. Daly, 315–25. Louisville, KY: Westminster John Knox Press, 1994.
Jeffreys, Sheila. *The Industrial Vagina: The Political Economy of the Global Sex Trade*. New York: Routledge, 2009.
Kwok, Pui-lan. *Postcolonial Politics and Theology: Unraveling Empire for a Global World*. Louisville, KY: Westminster John Knox, 2021.
Lee, Jean-kyung. *Service Economies: Militarism, Sex Work, and Migrant Labor in South Korea*. Minneapolis: University of Minnesota Press, 2010.
Mbembe, Achilles. *Necropolitics*, translated by Steven Corcoran. Durham: Duke University Press, 2019.
Moon, Katherine. *Sex among Allies: Military Prostitution in U.S.–Korea Relations*. New York: Columbia University Press, 1997.
Nielsen, Marianne, and Linda Robyn. *Colonialism Is Crime*. New Brunswick, NJ: Rutgers University Press, 2019.
Pae, Keun-joo Christine. "Indecent Resurgence: God's Solidarity against the Gendered War on COVID." In *Doing Theology in the New Normal*, edited by Jione Havea, 179–95. London: SCM, 2021.
Pae, Keun-joo Christine. "A Politics of Empathy: Christianity and Women's Peace Activism in U.S. Military Prostitution in South Korea." In *Women and Asian Religions*, edited by Zayn Kassam, 223–39. Santa Barbara, CA: ABC-CLIO, 2017.
Pae, Keun-joo Christine. "Proletarianized Sexuality of Soldiering and Prostitution: Making a Christian Ethic of Peace Countering Necropolitics of War." In *Faith, Class, and Labor: Intersectional Approaches in a Global Context*, edited by Jin Young Choi and Joerg Rieger, 143–63. Eugene, OR: Pickwick, 2020.
Shay, Jonathan. *Achilles in Vietnam: Combat Trauma and the Undoing of Character*. New York: Simon & Schuster, 1995.
Sherman, Nancy. *Afterwar: Healing the Moral Wounds of Our Soldiers*. New York: Oxford University Press, 2015.
Shigematsu, Setsu, with Anuradha Kristina Bhagwati and Eli Paintedcrow. "Women-of-color Veterans on War, Militarism, and Feminism." In *Feminism and War: Confronting US Imperialism*, edited by Robin Riley, Chandra Mohanty, and Minnie Pratt, 93–102. New York: Zed Books, 2008.

Simpson, Leanne Betasamosake. *As We Have Always Done: Indigenous Freedom through Radical Resurgence.* Minneapolis: University of Minnesota Press, 2017.

Thistlethwaite, Susan. *Women's Bodies as Battlefield: Christian Theology and the Global War on Women.* New York: Palgrave Macmillan, 2015.

Vesely-Flad, Rima. *Racial Purity and Dangerous Bodies: Moral Pollution, Black Lives and the Struggle for Justice.* Minneapolis, MN: Fortress Press, 2017.

Vine, David. *Base Nation: How U.S. Military Bases Abroad Harm America and the World.* New York: Metropolitan Books, 2017.

Yukish, Grace, and Penny Edgell, eds. *Religion Is Raced: Understanding American Religion in the Twenty-First Century.* New York: New York University Press, 2020.

Zaru, Jean. *Occupied with Nonviolence: A Palestinian Woman Speaks.* Minneapolis, MN: Fortress Press, 2008.

9

Decolonizing Dialogues: Bridging Ecofeminism, Religion, and the Decological Path Forward

Elaine Nogueira-Godsey

Introduction

This chapter[1] argues that ecofeminism remains a vital framework for addressing intertwined systems of oppression. Studying the women-nature nexus today is also important because it foregrounds the dominator-subordinated dynamics in modern survival and relationship models. I present the dominator-subordinated dynamic as a modern and poststructuralist reiteration of reason-nature dualism, which has been a dominant influence in Western philosophy and theology, traditionally placing humans as superior to the Earth and to each other. To effectively challenge the prevailing

---

[1] Portions of this chapter are reprinted with permission from Taylor & Francis Ltd, UK. Originally published in 2022 as "A Decological Way to Dialogue: Rethinking Ecofeminism and Religion," in *The Routledge Handbook of Religions, Gender, and Society*, ed. Emma Tomalin and Caroline Starkey, 365–84 (London: Routledge).

model characterizing the unfolding global climate crisis—which disproportionately impacts rural women and children in the Global South[2]—I contend that Western feminist and ecofeminist scholars, whether or not engaged in religious or theological studies, must move beyond the Western imperialism of knowledge. Accordingly, I propose an alternative way of dialogue: a decological way.

Part I of this chapter's four sections defines dominator-subordinated dynamics and outlines the context informing the development of this decological dialogue. Part II draws a parallel between the resistance of early Latin American male liberation theologians and Western feminists to include gender and religion as a category of analysis crucial to the liberation of the oppressed. Part III applies a decolonial lens to the intersection of gender and religion, revealing insights into the failure of these two distinct political movements to sustain a more constructive dialogue during the 1990s. Part IV outlines the principles guiding my development of this decological way of dialog and learning. I conclude by proposing that in a world with many conflicting political visions, feminist and ecofeminist discourses need a shared moral commitment to decolonial ways of dialogue.

My Own Ecofeminist Journey

I grew up in rapidly changing postcolonial Brazil; became a scholar in a post-apartheid/colonial South Africa; and then accepted a position in the American context of theological education.[3] My traditional Christian community in Brazil taught me that to please God, I had to be an obedient daughter and submissive wife. My maternal grandfather was probably Kaiowá, an Indigenous man, a fact seldom discussed in my family. This silence may stem from the marginalization of Indigenous peoples in Brazil, who are often viewed through colonial lenses that relegate them to the natural world,

---

[2]The Intergovernmental Panel on Climate Change (IPCC), *Climate Change 2007: Impacts, Adaptation and Vulnerability. Contribution of Working Group II to the Fourth Assessment Report of the Intergovernmental Panel on Climate Change* (Cambridge: Cambridge University Press, 2007),
[3]On the necessity of methodological self-declarations in feminist work, see Rita Gross, *Feminism and Religion: An Introduction* (Boston, MA: Beacon Press, 1996), 6.

to be dominated for economic progress. In the Religious Studies Department at the University of Cape Town, I discovered the social scientific study of religion. This academic framework helped clarify my personal experience of the intersection of Christian theology, colonialism, racism, patriarchy, and environmental destruction. Rethinking my own gender role, identity, and theological paradigms have coalesced to inform my ecofeminist and decolonial perspective. This view recognizes gendered oppression, racial discrimination, and natural resource rapacity as overlapping products of a colonial legacy, itself perpetuated by a neoliberal insistence on capital building at any cost. Through this lens, untangling these oppressions from their colonialist roots is clearly a deeply feminist, ecological, and decolonial task.

My PhD investigated the intellectual trajectory and ecofeminist praxis of Brazilian feminist liberation theologian Ivone Gebara; specifically, her progression from pure liberation theology to feminist, and later, ecofeminist perspectives. Gebara's on-the-move methodology reflects her own history of resistance and the experiences of the impoverished women around her. The political aspect of ecofeminist theological praxis and cooperation between Southern and Northern ecofeminist theologians coincide in this methodology.[4] I was inspired by Gebara's willingness to learn from others' experiences, her humility in questioning her own views, and her courage in breaking academic barriers by entering into dialogue with Western feminist philosophy and theology.

I realized how strongly Gebara's openness and adaptability contrasted with early male liberation theologians' resistance to including gender as a critical analytical category for engaging the liberation of the oppressed. This realization brought into focus what I have called the *dominator-subordinated dynamic*: the colonial model of relationships characterizing modern organizational structures of thought and practice. The term "subordinated" better conveys the notion of enforced inferiority than does the more forceful "subjugated." The oppression of marginalized groups does often involve violent subjugation; however, more indirect and subtle forms of forced subordination are at least as

---

[4]Elaine Nogueira-Godsey, "A History of Resistance: Ivone Gebara's Transformative Ecofeminist Liberation Theology," *Journal for the Study of Religion* 26, no. 2 (2013): 89–106.

instrumental today. Such forms animate an often unconscious bias toward modern and poststructuralist reiterations of the reason-nature dualism.

Liberation Theology and Feminist Liberation Theology

Liberation theologians in 1960s Latin America, inspired by Marxist thought, pioneered a unique theology as political resistance to oppressive militarist regimes. This approach emphasized the lived experiences of the poor and applied social science methods to interpret Christian scriptures and history. Liberation theologians aimed to dismantle the spirit-matter dualism, advocating for Christian responsibility that extends beyond spiritual guidance to include aiding the poor's material needs through political action.[5]

By the mid-1970s, women liberation theologians identified the distinct challenges of impoverished women, leading to the emergence, in the late 1980s, of feminist liberation theology. They urged the inclusion of a gender-cultural analysis into liberation theology's socioeconomic methodologies.[6] Ivone Gebara pointed out that gender dualism was replicated at every juncture of human relationships.[7] Male theologians resisted, however, fearing that focusing on gender and sexuality would distract from the primary struggle against political oppression in Latin America.[8]

I was unsatisfied with the explanation that liberation theologians neglected gender and sexuality as a domain of domination in capitalist societies simply because they were mostly men. As Althaus-Reid pointed out, those were celibate priests "who as a group are

---

[5]Nogueira-Godsey, "A History of Resistance."
[6]Rosângela S. De Oliveira, "Feminist Theology in Brazil," in *Women's Visions: Theological Reflection, Celebration, Action*, ed. Orfelia Ortega (Geneva, Switzerland: World Council of Churches, 1995).
[7]Ivone Gebara, "A mulher faz Teologia: Um ensaio para reflexão," *Revista Eclesiástica Brasileira* 46, no. 181 (March 31, 1986).
[8]Marcella Althaus-Reid, "'Let Them Talk ...!' Doing Theology from Latin American Closets," in *Liberation Theology and Sexuality*, ed. Marcella Althaus-Reid (Burlington, VT: Ashgate, 2009).

notorious for their sexual conflicts."⁹ I was, however, curious about how such praxis-oriented theologians could continue to ignore the extent of women's domination in Latin America even after being made aware of them. Why could they not apply their own methods to rethink their political praxis, and develop sustainable alliances? I discovered the answer in the intersection of ecofeminism and decolonial theory. Certainly, the identification of dualist thinking and the resulting hierarchies in human relations has been key in the rising of liberation movements in modern Western societies; however, this identification alone is insufficient to challenge the colonial models of relationships entrenched in modern models of survival.

Ecofeminism, Essentialism, Spirituality, Religion, and the Antifeminist Backlash

In the 1970s, grassroots exposures of environmental injustice affecting women and children prompted ecofeminist responses in Europe and North America. Ecofeminist scholars pointed to the link between the oppression of women, sexuality, and the Earth's degradation—a connection conceptualized as the "women-nature nexus."[10] Ecofeminist scholars have since explored the specific vulnerabilities of women and children to environmental harm, examined the reasons for such disparities, and proposed challenges to the patriarchal, androcentric, and anthropocentric systems perpetuating these differences. Their research has aimed to inform policy-making, enhance ecological consciousness, empower women, and promote positive social change.

Western philosophical dualism has been pivotal to the development of both feminist and ecofeminist analyses of women's repression. Second-wave feminists have critiqued the nature-culture dualism and its negative influence on male-female relationships, and identified the privileging of purported male culture/reason over

---

[9] Althaus-Reid, "'Let Them Talk ...!'" 7.
[10] Nina Hoel and Elaine Nogueira-Godsey, "Transforming Feminisms: Religion, Women, and Ecology," *Journal for the Study of Religion* 24, no. 2 (2001).

purported female nature/emotion.[11] Building upon this, ecofeminist analyses recognize gender and sexual oppression as interconnected to the exploitation of the Earth. Over time, this understanding has come to include all subordinated groups and aspects of life once seen as closer to nature.

As ecofeminism spread to the Global South, an expanded ecofeminist framework emerged, allowing feminist theologians from these regions to highlight the interconnection between the colonization of women's bodies and environmental destruction, and how this dynamic persists in contemporary lifeways. The resulting focus on interconnected forms of oppression and domination became ecofeminism's analytical nexus, generating a rich tapestry of global initiatives over the past four decades.[12] Nonetheless, Western ecofeminism in the mid-1990s was discredited by poststructuralists and other third-wave feminisms on charges of essentialism (biological determinism) and for its connection with spirituality/religion.[13]

Greta Gaard argues that these critics, "[f]ocusing on the celebration of goddess spirituality and the critique of patriarchy advanced in cultural ecofeminism,"[14] misrepresented the movement as exclusively essentialist, thereby discrediting ecofeminism's diversity of arguments and standpoints. This misrepresentation prevented ecofeminism from becoming what many had hoped would be feminism's "third wave," an integration of ecological perspectives into the (anthropocentric) critiques of first- and second-wave feminisms.[15]

---

[11] Sherry B. Ortner, "Is Female to Male as Nature Is to Culture?" *Feminist Studies* 1, no. 2 (1972).
[12] Rita M. Gross, "Buddhism and Ecofeminism: Untangling the Threads of Buddhist Ecology and Western Thought," *Journal for the Study of Religion* 24, no. 2 (2011): 17–32.
[13] Greta Gaard, "Ecofeminism Revisited: Rejecting Essentialism and Re-Placing Species in a Material Feminist Environmentalism," *Feminist Formations* 23, no. 2 (2011): 26–53; Chaone Mallory, "What's in a Name? In Defense of Ecofeminism (Not Ecological Feminisms, Feminist Ecology, or Gender and the Environment): Or 'Why Ecofeminism Need Not Be Ecofeminine—But so What If It Is?'" *Ethics and the Environment* 23, no. 2 (2018): 11–35.
[14] Gaard, "Ecofeminism Revisited," 31.
[15] Gaard, "Ecofeminism Revisited," 31.

In short, in ecofeminism's infancy, some cultural feminists linked with the women's spirituality movement sought new spiritual practices celebrating women's corporeality and relationship with nature. By stressing the organic relationship between humans and nature, they hoped that such spiritualities might foster social harmony and care for the Earth.[16] Inspired by archeologist Marija Gimbutas's interpretations of Neolithic female imagery,[17] they assumed the existence of an ancient matricentric tradition, invoking a time when Goddess-worshipping societies revered both the Earth and female deities; when women were valued as highly as men and controlled their own bodies and lives.[18]

Based on feminist scholarship that had connected the Abrahamic "God the Father" to the patriarchal domination of women,[19] spiritual ecofeminists, as they became known, proposed that projecting attributes associated with motherhood, such as caring and nurturing, onto the divine could reduce male tendencies toward violence and militarism and potentially foster a more equitable and life-affirming world. Some claimed women's unique physical experiences, like menstruation, pregnancy, and childbirth, as "an epistemological privilege,"[20] using this to defy patriarchal stigmas against women's bodies and affirm women's natural connection to nature, countering the detachment from the Earth that patriarchal monotheistic religions often promote.[21]

---

[16]Charlene Spretnak, *The Politics of Women's Spirituality: Essays on the Rise of Spiritual Power within the Feminist Movement* (Garden City, NY: Anchor Press, 1982).
[17]Marija Gimbutas, "Women and Culture in Goddess-Oriented Old Europe," in *Weaving the Visions: New Patterns in Feminist Spirituality*, ed. Judith Plaskow and Carol P. Christ (San Francisco, CA: HarperCollins, 1989).
[18]Riane Eisler, *The Chalice and the Blade: Our History, Our Future* (San Francisco, CA: HarperCollins, 1987); Kathryn Roundtree, "The New Witch of the West: Feminist Reclaim the Crone," *Journal of Popular Culture* 30, no. 4 (2007).
[19]Mary Daly, *Beyond God the Father* (Boston, MA: Beacon Press, 1985) and *Gyn/ecology: The Metaethics of Radical Feminism* (Boston, MA: Beacon Press, 1978).
[20]Heather Eaton, "Women, Nature, Earth," in *Religion, Ecology, and Gender: East-West Perspectives*, ed. Sigurd Bergmann and Yong-Bock Kim (Berlin, Germany: LIT, 2009), 9, and Catriona Sandilands, *The Good-Natured Feminist* (Minneapolis: University of Minnesota Press, 1999).
[21]Carol P. Christ, "Rethinking Theology and Nature," in *Weaving the Visions: New Patterns in Feminist Spirituality*, ed. Judith Plaskow and Carol P. Christ (San Francisco, CA: HarperCollins, 1989), 314–25, and Ynestra King, "Healing the Wounds: Feminism, Ecology, and the Nature/Culture Dualism," in *Reweaving the*

Second-wave feminists rejected this view, arguing that gender equality depended on severing any association between women and nature to overcome the culture/men versus nature/women dualism in all spheres. The call for "healing Earth," they argued, reinforced the stereotype of women as caretakers.[22] The harshest critique of ecofeminism, however, came from feminists who struggled to integrate religious perspectives into Western ecofeminist thought. Former ecofeminist Janet Biehl acknowledged the need for nurturing traits to address the ecological crisis, but associated religion and spirituality with a lack of "consciousness, reason, and above all freedom."[23] She concluded that ecofeminism could no longer be seen as a viable project for "serious feminists."[24]

Adopting the academic posture of exposing essentialism and preserving academic integrity, Biehl's views were echoed by other feminists who agreed that ecofeminism would effectively extend the domestic caretaking role into the public sphere.[25] Early ecofeminists, such as Carolyn Merchant[26] and Mary Mellor,[27] who themselves did not subscribe to spiritual ecofeminism, often explained that ecofeminism's political impact was overshadowed by early writings connecting essentialism with a return to matricentric social arrangements. This focus, they argued, detracted from the critical ecofeminist political project of dismantling economic and social hierarchies. Consequently, ecofeminism's political efficacy was trivialized as mere "political naïvety"[28] that undercut "women's hopes for a liberatory, ecologically-sane society."[29] I believe that these critiques only partially addressed the issue. In my view, resistance to ecofeminism also stemmed from the inability, first,

---

World: The Emergence of Ecofeminism, ed. Irene Diamond and Gloria F. Orenstein (San Francisco, CA: Sierra Club Books, 1990).
[22]Ariel Salleh, *Ecofeminism as Politics: Nature, Marx and the Postmodern* (London: Zed Books, [1997] 2017).
[23]Janet Biehl, *Rethinking Ecofeminist Politics* (Boston, MA: South End Press, 1991), 26.
[24]Biehl, *Rethinking Ecofeminist Politics*, 5.
[25]Salleh, *Ecofeminism as Politics*.
[26]Carolyn Merchant, *Earthcare: Women and the Environment* (New York: Routledge, 1996).
[27]Mary Mellor, *Feminism and Ecology* (New York: New York University Press, 1997).
[28]Mellor, *Feminism and Ecology*, 45.
[29]Merchant, *Earthcare*, 14.

to move beyond Enlightenment assertions of a singular, objective, effable "Truth," and second, to incorporate religion and nature as analytical categories crucial for Western feminist thought.

Rethinking Ecofeminism and Religion

During the 1990s, while ecofeminism was being heavily criticized in North America, Latin American feminist liberation theologians found a dialogue partner in Western ecofeminists. Ann Hidalgo showed how the myth of an ancient matriarchal, Goddess-worshipping society empowered women of Indigenous and African descent in Latin America to confront the patriarchal Christian orthodoxy imposed upon them by European colonization.[30] Judith Ress explains that women saw the myth as endorsing their long-held desire to reclaim their semi-lost Indigenous cultures.[31] Initially, this project involved validating the legitimacy of diverse Indigenous heritages, female symbols, and experiences.[32] In the Global South, movements for social and environmental justice are already keenly aware of "the uneven power dynamics associated with the materiality of the global economy."[33] By entering into dialogue with ecofeminism, feminist liberation theologians reimagined denigrated cultural practices such as *mãe-de-santo* and *curanderas*, which Laura Pulido described as "valuable assets in our collective struggle to create more ecologically and culturally sustainable lifeways."[34]

As many ecofeminists in the Global North and South have shown, the bifurcation between spirituality/religion and political action is

---

[30] Ann Hidalgo, "Weaving Ecofeminisms and Spiritualities Reflections from Latin American Women," in *Ecofeminism in Dialogue*, ed. Douglas A. Vackoch and Sam Mickey (Lanham, MD: Lexington Books, 2018).
[31] Mary Judith Ress, "The Con-Spirando Women's Collective: Globalization from Below?" in *Ecofeminism and Globalization: Exploring Culture, Context, and Religion*, ed. Heather Eaton and Lois A. Lorentzen (Lanham, MD: Rowman & Littlefield, 2003).
[32] Mary Judith Ress, *Ecofeminism in Latin America* (Maryknoll, NY: Orbis Books, 2006).
[33] Laura Pulido, "Foreword," in *Latinx Environmentalism: Place, Justice, and the Decolonial*, ed. Sarah D. Wald, David Vazquez, Prischilla Solis Ybarra, Sarah Jaquette Ray, and Stacy Alaimo (Philadelphia, PA: Temple University Press, 2019), xiv.
[34] Pulido, "Foreword," xiv.

unfounded,[35] making resistance to integrating gender and religion into feminist discourse questionable. If feminists' main problem was, in fact, ecofeminists' essentialist claims, what explains their reluctance to address the intersection of gender and religion[36]—even after diverse ecofeminists voiced multiple nonessentialist views on spirituality and political action? These ecofeminists have investigated the women-nature nexus within their own Abrahamic, Eastern, and Indigenous religious contexts. They explored religion's role in both enabling and alleviating the environmental crisis, and refuted inherited female epistemological privilege. Moreover, widespread evidence confirms that movements opposing oppressive regimes were often led by faith-based movements. To dismiss religion as the antithesis of reason, and fail to recognize how religious movements, such as liberation theology, have contributed to democracy and freedom,[37] exposes scholars' historical ignorance—and, I daresay, arrogance.

The intersection of ecofeminism with religion is dynamic, continually embracing new insights and fostering cross-cultural dialogues. In the Global South, ecofeminism dialogues across religious contexts, generating innovative and interconnected decolonial approaches. Yet, many Northern feminist scholars, including ecofeminists outside of religious studies, remain largely unaware of the critical ecofeminist work developed by theologians in the Global South.

Heather Eaton argued that the coalescence of ecofeminism and spirituality has been a stumbling block for feminists. She observed that those rejecting the relationship between ecofeminism and essentialism uncritically dismissed religion altogether.[38]

---

[35]Ecofeminist spirituality and political activism against war, nuclear power, and racism in Europe and North America. Starhawk, "20 Years Later How We Really Shut Down the WTO," https://starhawk.org/20-years-later-how-we-really-shut-down-the-wto/ (accessed April 3, 2024); Charlene Spretnak, "Ecofeminism: Our Roots and Flowering," in *Reweaving the World: The Emergence of Ecofeminism*, ed. Irene Diamond and Gloria Orenstein (San Francisco, CA: Sierra Club Books, 1990); Sarah-Louise Ruder and Sophia Rose Sanniti, "Transcending the Learned Ignorance of Predatory Ontologies: A Research Agenda for an Ecofeminist-Informed Ecological Economics," *Sustainability* 11, no. 5 (2019).
[36]Gaard, "Ecofeminism Revisited," 31–5.
[37]David Chidester, *Religions of South Africa* (New York: Taylor & Francis, [1992] 2014).
[38]Eaton, "Women, Nature, Earth."

Mallory and Gaard demonstrated that although the resistance to ecofeminist religious perspectives within feminist discourse was part of a broader effort to discredit ecofeminism, it also stemmed from a deeper fear of spirituality[39] as apolitical or backward, and inherently essentialist. This position, I argue, has inadvertently marginalized the knowledge of women from the Global South, whose contributions often weave together religion, environmental concerns, and gender discrimination.

At this juncture, it seems pertinent to ask: to what extent has the notion of religion as irrational hindered meaningful dialogue between Northern ecofeminists and feminists, fueling their shared lack of engagement with Southern ecofeminist theologians? Perhaps the defensive stance against essentialism, and the resulting antagonism toward ecofeminism, may signal a deeper, unacknowledged issue: one that reflects a historical bias that has portrayed people of color either "as agents of environmental destruction [and/or] devoid of a larger structural analysis."[40]

Such bias echoes imperialist justifications of colonial projects through positioning reason against religion, thereby dismissing non-Western peoples' cultures as primitive, and hence unreasoning.[41] What counts as feminist political strategy seems to be clouded by such biases. Biehl's critique, for instance, claimed the secular as the sphere of reason, dismissing the entire body of ecofeminist scholarship and its political significance to the feminist movement. She argued that ecofeminism, like all religions, focuses on developing the nonrational, denigrating the Enlightenment's rationalist legacy.[42]

The antifeminist backlash against ecofeminism in the Global North paralleled the conflict between male and female liberation theologians in Latin America. Although those were different discourses, notably, both used the same argument to reject the inclusion of gender and religion: a frivolous category of analysis to the liberation of the oppressed. Despite their differing starting

---

[39]Mallory, "What's in a Name?"; Gaard, "Ecofeminism Revisited."
[40]Pulido, "Foreword," xiii.
[41]Tyler M. Tully, "Native Futurities in an Age of 'Permanent Settler War': Conceptualizing Settler Coloniality as an Ongoing Ecological Structure," paper presented at *2020 Virtual Annual Meetings of the American Academy of Religion*, 2020.
[42]Biehl, "Rethinking Ecofeminist Politics," 94.

points and geographic location, liberation theologians and Western feminists exhibited the dominator-subordinated model of dialogue. Although these feminists and male liberation theologians proclaimed different reasons for rejecting feminist and ecofeminist theologies, both evidenced the dominator-subordinated model of dialogue.

Just as male liberation theologians were aware of sexual oppression, feminists such as Biehl, an active contributor to social ecology, clearly understood the disproportionate effects of the ecological crisis on women and children. Yet, ecologically concerned Western feminists have distanced themselves from ecofeminism to maintain credibility within a male-dominated ecological movement. "[A]re serious feminists," Biehl demanded, "to accept images of women as 'emotional,' 'caring,' and 'mediating,' in contradistinction to men in a presumably shared ecology movement or in building a new society?"[43]

According to Greta Gaard, in their efforts to protect Western feminism from an essentialist revival, feminists adopted a stance that excluded species and nature "as analytical categories crucial for feminist thought."[44] This position was so pervasive that by 2010, it became exceedingly rare to encounter any published work "devoted to issues of feminism and ecology (and certainly not ecofeminism), species, or nature in most introductory anthologies used in women's studies, gender studies, or queer studies."[45]

I wonder if feminist scholars overlooked the intersection of gender, religion, and ecology because they saw the domination of the Earth as a secondary form of oppression; or perhaps because they viewed ecofeminist theologians as lacking a larger structural analysis. Val Plumwood points out that many feminists expected environmental issues and their impact on poor women to "'wither away' once the 'fundamental' form" of oppression, patriarchy, is overcome. By trivializing ecofeminist engagement with religion, feminists echoed the dismissive attitudes of male liberation theologians. This tendency to devalue certain human experiences and environmental issues as lesser forms of oppression reflects the paternalistic, hierarchical logic that colonial powers used to justify the subjugation of Indigenous and African peoples. This

---

[43] Biehl, "Rethinking Ecofeminist Politics," 12.
[44] Gaard, "Ecofeminism Revisited," 35.
[45] Gaard, "Ecofeminism Revisited," 31.

kind of domination is especially difficult to apprehend when the perpetrators have themselves been active in liberation movements.

The Dominator-Subordinated Dynamic

In 1993, Val Plumwood urged feminists to come to terms with the reason-nature dualism so that we do not "remain trapped within it [and] settle for one of its new versions."[46] She contended that the "dominator identity" of the *master*, rather than purely a masculine identity, is the overlooked motif underlying Western cultural ideals. She identified a "master model": the Western dualist, hierarchical organizational system that places human reason over nature, men over women, white over Black, freedom over necessity, rationality over animality (emotion), and self over other. Plumwood argued that the dualism between reason and nature continues to shape Western perceptions of rationality and the resulting dynamics of control inherent in the self-other relationship models.

In general, Western philosophy has assumed that humans are superior to the Earth in their capacity to "focus on rational thought."[47] This view has generated an understanding of nature "as passive, as non-agent and non-subject, as the 'environment,' or the background condition for human survival."[48] Ecofeminist scholars explain the oppression of women and other marginalized groups as tied to a view of nature as other, and outside the human realm of reason.[49] According to Plumwood, female work (production), the female body (reproduction), and the labor of those understood as nature-like (e.g., people of color and the colonized) were, as "partly the result of chance and of specific historical evolution," excluded from "the master category of reason," and backgrounded with the Earth as the environmental "condition against which the 'foreground' achievements of reason or culture take place."[50]

---

[46] Val Plumwood, *Feminism and the Mastery of Nature* (London: Routledge, 1993), 6.
[47] Anna L. Peterson, *Being Human: Ethics, Environment, and Our Place in the World* (Berkeley: University of California Press, 2001), 2.
[48] Plumwood, *Feminism and the Mastery of Nature*, 4.
[49] Heather Eaton, *Introducing Ecofeminist Theologies* (London: T&T Clark International, 2005).
[50] Plumwood, *Feminism and the Mastery of Nature*, 4.

This understanding endures today, as Ivone Gebara points out.[51] Capitalism, she notes, has never valued breastfeeding, childrearing, and the domestic labor traditionally performed by women. Nor have male liberation theologians. Like the natural environment, women have long been understood as the "limitless provider without needs of its own."[52] Male liberation theologians' treatment of feminist liberation theologians parallels the subordination of nature and is deeply embedded in the economic system and modern social structures.

For centuries, viewing nature as non-agent and nonsubject has justified violating the right of Earth, and those considered closer to her, to exist as free subjects. Accordingly, human interactions are systemically characterized by a dynamic of domination and subordination. To prioritize the view of those supposedly identified with reason or intellect while subordinating the needs of nature and nature-like things came to be seen as "flowing from nature itself and the nature(s) of things," as Plumwood noted.[53]

I agree with Western feminists that projecting attributes that are valued and experienced within motherhood to the divine cannot facilitate women's empowerment and the Earth's liberation. I also agree that male liberation theologians sacrificed women's experiences of oppression because initially they could not see them as objects of oppression. However, one's ability to ignore others' struggles, even when made aware, only arises because one cannot see it as a moral imperative due to a lack of recognition of its existential significance.

Plumwood contested that dualisms have correctly been identified as "the construction of a devalued and sharply demarcated sphere of otherness."[54] However, she points out that previous analyses of dualistic binaries have not fully accounted for the dynamics of domination and subordination that underpin their formation.[55] In this light, I challenge the notion that dualisms are inherently

---

[51] Ivone Gebara, "Ecofeminism: An Ethics of Life," in *Ecofeminism and Globalization: Exploring Culture, Context, and Religion*, ed. Heather Eaton and Lois A. Lorentzen (Lanham, MD: Rowman & Littlefield, 2003).
[52] Plumwood, *Feminism and the Mastery of Nature*, 21–2.
[53] Plumwood, *Feminism and the Mastery of Nature*, 4–5.
[54] Plumwood, *Feminism and the Mastery of Nature*, 41.
[55] Plumwood, *Feminism and the Mastery of Nature*, 31.

oppositional and mutually exclusive. Rather, dispossessing the subordinated "other" of the dominant group's valued traits has allowed the dominator to deny reliance on those they subjugate. Plumwood asserts that this denial of dependency establishes a particular type of logical framework where the identities of both parties are shaped by the denial itself and the underlying relationship of domination and subordination.[56] Essentially, the dominator's identity is contingent on the continued subordination of others. I propose that such hierarchical dualisms persist through a mechanism of unacknowledged dependency on, and subordination of, the "other," perpetuated through our unrecognized participation in the dominator-subordinated dynamic inherent in the self-other relationship models.

The dominator-subordinated dialogue engaged by male liberation theologians and Western feminists demonstrates how the dominator identity of the master has become habitual due to its entrenchment in our consciousness as normative and paradigmatic. It is a manifestation of the reason-nature dualism: the persistent, dominant archetype governing human and nonhuman relations. My comparison of early male liberation theologians and Western feminism demonstrates that in our modern, globalized world, the lines between colonizer and colonized have become blurred due to our own unrecognized participation in the dominator-subordinated dynamic. This phenomenon is indicative of what decolonial scholars refer to as the coloniality of power and being.

Nelson Maldonado-Torres explains that coloniality and colonialism are different. Colonialism is "a political and economic" relationship, where "the sovereignty of a nation or people" is controlled by another nation, "which makes such nation an empire." Coloniality, by contrast, refers to enduring patterns of power arising from colonialism, which continue to "define culture, labor, intersubjective relations, and knowledge production" far beyond the confines of colonial rule. Coloniality outlives colonialism, as "it is maintained alive in books, in the criteria for academic performance, in cultural patterns, in common sense, in the self-image of peoples, in aspirations of self," among other facets of modern life. In essence,

---

[56]Plumwood, *Feminism and the Mastery of Nature*, 41.

"as modern subjects, we breathe coloniality all the time and every day."[57]

Our failure to recognize our own complicity in the structures we critique exposes our entanglement with what Sylvia Wynter terms "coloniality of Being."[58] More precisely, it reveals the coloniality of being in practice.[59] Wynter contends that any attempt to unsettle the coloniality of power will call for the unsettling of the "coloniality of Being."[60] One cannot dismantle forms of oppression "without a redescription of the human outside the terms of our present descriptive statement of the human."[61] In other words, a North/South dialogue between feminists and ecofeminists must take place inside and outside the study of religion and theology so that we can learn about our own entanglement in the webs of coloniality and actively contribute to the alternatives to our unsustainable models of survival. I am proposing a decological way to dialogue.

A Decological Way to Dialogue

The word decological is itself a portmanteau of the words decolonial, ecological, and pedagogical, forming a transdisciplinary approach that integrates decolonial theory, ecological ethics, and feminist pedagogy. It provides a guiding principle for fostering decolonial dialogue to collaboratively address climate change, coloniality, and the impacts of both.

Decological praxis is based on three premises. First, while we each contribute in differing degrees to the environmental crisis, the escalating consequences of climate change will spare no one. Climate change does not discriminate; however, societal structures

---

[57]Nelson Maldonado-Torres, "On the Coloniality of Being: Contributions to the Development of a Concept," *Cultural Studies* 21, no. 2 (2007): 243.
[58]Sylvia Wynter, "Unsettling the Coloniality of Being/Power/Truth/Freedom: towards the Human, after Man, Its Overrepresentation—An Argument," *CR: The New Centennial Review* 3, no. 3 (2003): 313–14.
[59]Walter D. Mignolo, "Os Esplendores e as Misérias da 'Ciência': Colonialidade, Geopolítica do Conhecimento e Pluri-versalidade Epistêmica," in *Conhecimento Prudente para uma Vida Decente: Um Discurso sobre as Ciências' Revistado*, ed. Boaventura Sousa Santos (Porto, Portugal: Edições Afrontamento, 2003), 669.
[60]Wynter, "Unsettling the Coloniality of Being/Power/Truth/Freedom," 260.
[61]Wynter, "Unsettling the Coloniality of Being/Power/Truth/Freedom," 268.

have positioned marginalized groups, particularly rural women in the Global South, at greater risk. As Neel Ahuja[62] reminds us, climate change and the social systems they impact are deeply intertwined. Thus, we must consider the political economy that feeds back into these issues. This is a deeply feminist and ecological issue.

Second, independently of diverse identities and histories, we are all entangled in a legacy of colonial relationships that have shaped our interactions with the Earth and its inhabitants. Our lifestyles and behaviors are embedded in a system that commodifies nature and people, often overlooking the intrinsic value of both. This shared history implicates us all in the ongoing exploitation of our planet and its diverse cultures, making this a decolonial, ecofeminist, and ethical matter.

Third, addressing each impact of these two realities requires a different means of healing. Walter Mignolo and Catherine Walsh explain the nature of different inflictions requires difference in its healing practices. To address coloniality we need to implement practices of decoloniality. Decoloniality is a process that involves both individual and communal efforts to identify and confront the enduring ontological and epistemological impacts left by colonization, with an emphasis on shifting the underlying premises of the dialogue. Decoloniality is about learning "'to resist re-existing' and/or 'to re-exist resisting.'"[63] Essentially, it is centered on learning to dialogue by resisting the reproduction of domination and subordination. As an educator, I see this as a critical pedagogical issue.

Ivone Gebara contends that critical knowledge of that which oppresses and marginalizes specific groups "is not enough to bring about actual change."[64] She further elaborates that in order to change the conditions that produce relationships of domination, there must be a collective process of education. I maintain that a collective process of education is the only way to strike at the root of the problem. To develop a feminist dialogue capable of generating a pluralistic

---

[62]Neel Ahuja, *Planetary Specters: Race, Migration, and Climate Change in the Twenty-First Century* (Chapel Hill: University of North Carolina Press, 2021).
[63]Walter Mignolo and Catherine E. Walsh, *On Decoloniality: Concepts, Analytics, Praxis* (Durham, NC: Duke University Press, 2018), 83.
[64]Ivone Gebara, *Out of the Depths: Women's Experience of Evil and Salvation* (Minneapolis, MN: Fortress Press, 2002), 69.

planet requires analyzing, engaging, rejecting, and providing an alternative to dismantling the colonizing ways to make sense of the world that we share. I advocate for a feminist scholarship and activism that is guided by a shared decological principle, informing our mutual learning and the way we contextualize our acquired knowledge. For those of us working in theological education, this is about developing shared theological criteria. Drawing on the insights of Carol Christ and Judith Plaskow,[65] this shared principle or criteria can be expressed in the self-reflexive questions: Does my epistemological position make sense of the world we share? Does this ontological view promote the flourishing of the world? Do our feminist ethics and praxis disrupt imperialistic models of human relations? Do they teach us to survive not at the expense of somebody else's survival?

As feminist scholars, we are all, in one way or another, educators and as such we possess the collective power to foster a culture of decoloniality. Recognizing that the historical linkage of "otherness" to nature has fueled human oppression and environmental destruction, we must critically examine our role in perpetuating these dynamics. We must ask ourselves, "How are we, as educators, working to reverse this syndrome?" Regardless of our diverse standpoints and geographical locations, we have a moral obligation to demonstrate the connections between climate change and the master model, thus, taking responsibility for our own roles in upholding these power structures. Although addressing the ways in which women contribute to oppression may be controversial, it is a necessary step if feminism is to help eradicate unsustainable ways of living.

Integrating the principles of decological dialogue into educational settings involves emancipating mindsets from the reason-nature dualism, envisioning a world where the false dichotomy between the dominator and the subordinated is replaced by a collaborative and mutually enriching relationship, one that honors the diversity of experiences and the shared responsibility for the well-being of our planet and its inhabitants. The term "interconnectivity" best encapsulates decological teaching and learning as it reflects the profound and holistic network of relationships entangling human

---

[65] Carol P. Christ and Judith Plaskow, *Goddess and God in the World: Conversations in Embodied Theology* (Minneapolis, MN: Fortress Press, 2016).

beings with each other, with nonhuman nature, and with the complex tapestry of colonial histories and contexts.

Inspired by practices modeled by Ivone Gebara—a willingness to interrogate her own positionality and integrity to change, and Anna Louise Keating's transcultural and post-oppositional proposal for dialogue through deep listening[66]—I strive to create a classroom environment that encourages my students to confront systemic power structures by embedding reflexivity into the inquiry process. This praxis, which scrutinizes the reproduction of colonial relationships, begins with self-reflection on our own experiences of coloniality. Such self-reflexivity is essential in decological learning as it acknowledges that teaching can perpetuate colonialism. By embracing decological dialogue, our classrooms can transform into spaces where both students and educators can reorient themselves to new ways of interacting with the Earth and the divine mystery. Considering the consequences of our actions on ourselves, other social groups and the broader Earth community calls for a critical evaluation of the ethical implications of our choices, making the act of self-reflection a personal and collective step toward transformation.

Many feminist scholars aspire to empower students to confront and challenge systemic power structures by raising awareness of these pervasive issues. However, only a few of us have gone as far as to embrace pedagogical strategies that create spaces for discussing how to bring awareness into daily practice. I have witnessed my students falling into a sense of despair upon recognizing their own racial, gender, sexual, able-body, and economic privileges. They often feel shame and loss, and become paralyzed with guilt. To navigate these challenges, I cultivate in the classroom dialogue practices that extricate colonial paradigms from our scholarly dialogue by addressing reason-body dualism. I encourage self-reflexivity and deep listening.

Latina theories of embodiment challenge Western epistemological and theological traditions. Their work demonstrates that bodies and senses, often viewed as distractions to be overcome to attain true knowledge, are in fact integral to our understanding of the world and crucial to the work toward collective liberation from the

---

[66] AnaLouise Keating, *Transformation Now! Toward a Post-Oppositional Politics of Change* (Champaign: University of Illinois Press, 2012).

master model. Maria Lugones called *limen*, "the place in between realities, a gap 'between and betwixt' universes of sense that construe social life and persons differently, an interstice from where one can most clearly stand critically toward different structures."[67] At the semester's outset, I explain the importance of listening to our embodied experiences as a significant self-reflexive lens toward moral action. I introduce decological dialogue, which prioritizes listening to each other's experiences with the intention to learn rather than to respond. My students engage in story-telling and are instructed to approach texts by authors from diverse cultures with openness and humility, paying close attention to any discomfort or defensiveness they may feel. I explain that these moments are opportunities for introspection and deeper self-awareness.

Instead of viewing moments of *limen* as a failure of intellect or a betrayal by our emotions, we could see them as instances of the fullness of human inhabitance. Perhaps, instead of shame, which can be counterproductive and reinforce harmful perspectives, we will be able to use these moments of realization to experience the complexity of human existence. This approach of staying with the boundlessness, the uncomfortable, can help us understand why many people resist behavioral change and why many become defensive. Instead, by naming and embracing the uncomfortable, we can pave the way for more constructive dialogues and actions, and turn to decological practices. Decological dialogue is not just about understanding one's position but also about actively working toward change. It involves the unraveling of affective knots that hinder the emergence of alternative possibilities for knowing, being, and relating, thereby fostering the growth of more generative relationships based on accountability, trust, respect, and reciprocity.[68]

Such a way of dialogue is crucial in advancing our decoloniality efforts. By creating a space where students and educators can share their narratives and learn from diverse experiences, we create opportunities for vulnerability and growth. This process not only

---

[67] Manuel Chávez Jr., "Toward a Decolonial Ethics," in *Speaking Face to Face: The Visionary Philosophy of María Lugones*, ed. Pedro J. DiPietro, Jennifer McWeeny, and Shireen Roshanravan (New York: SUNY, 2019), 185.
[68] Amanda R. Tachine and Z. Nicolazzo, eds., *Weaving and Otherwise: In-Relations Methodological Practice* (Sterling, VA: Stylus, 2022).

helps us understand how others are perceived as different but also how they have resisted such categorizations. This encourages learning in solidarity as the particularities of social contexts challenge normative or universal assumptions. In a time marked by profound grief—experienced by both the oppressed and those who knowingly and unknowingly perpetuate oppression—this approach contributes to decoloniality practices by fostering an ethics of care that emphasizes empathy, mutual respect, and the willingness to engage with and learn from the lived experiences of others. Decological dialogue is not merely an academic exercise; it is a commitment to an ongoing, collaborative journey toward healing, reconciliation, and the co-creation of sustainable futures. As we navigate the complexities of our shared human and nonhuman relationships, I invite feminists and ecofeminists to stay steadfast in our pursuit of a decological way to dialogue—one that honors the diversity of experiences and unites us in our common struggle for a just and thriving planet.[69]

Bibliography

Ahuja, Neel. *Planetary Specters: Race, Migration, and Climate Change in the Twenty-First Century*. Chapel Hill: University of North Carolina Press, 2021.

Althaus-Reid, Marcella. "'Let Them Talk …!' Doing Theology from Latin American Closets." In *Liberation Theology and Sexuality*, edited by Marcella Althaus-Reid, 5–18. Burlington, VT: Ashgate, 2009.

Biehl, Janet. *Rethinking Ecofeminist Politics*. Boston, MA: South End Press, 1991.

Chávez Jr., Manuel. "Toward a Decolonial Ethics." In *Speaking Face to Face: The Visionary Philosophy of María Lugones*, edited by Pedro J. DiPietro, Jennifer McWeeny, and Shireen Roshanravan, 175–94. New York: SUNY, 2019.

Chidester, David. *Religions of South Africa*. New York: Taylor & Francis, [1992] 2014.

Christ, Carol P. "Rethinking Theology and Nature." In *Weaving the Visions: New Patterns in Feminist Spirituality*, edited by

---

[69] I would like to thank Carolina Glauster, my research assistant, for her invaluable assistance with this chapter. Her dedication, meticulous attention to detail, and insightful contributions were instrumental in bringing this work to fruition.

Judith Plaskow and Carol P. Christ, 314–25. San Francisco, CA: HarperCollins, 1989.
Christ, Carol P., and Judith Plaskow. *Goddess and God in the World: Conversations in Embodied Theology*. Minneapolis, MN: Fortress Press, 2016.
Daly, Mary. *Beyond God the Father*. Boston, MA: Beacon Press, 1985.
Daly, Mary. *Gyn/ecology: The Metaethics of Radical Feminism*. Boston, MA: Beacon Press, 1978.
De Oliveira, Rosângela S. "Feminist Theology in Brazil." In *Women's Visions: Theological Reflection, Celebration, Action*, edited by Orfelia Ortega, 65–75. Geneva, Switzerland: World Council of Churches, 1995.
Eaton, Heather. *Introducing Ecofeminist Theologies*. London: T&T Clark International, 2005.
Eaton, Heather. "Women, Nature, Earth." In *Religion, Ecology and Gender: East-West Perspectives*, edited by Sigurd Bergmann and Yong-Bock Kim, 7–22. Berlin, Germany: LIT, 2009.
Eaton, Heather, and Lois A. Lorentzen, eds. *Ecofeminism and Globalization: Exploring Culture, Context, and Religion*. Lanham, MD: Rowman & Littlefield, 2003.
Eisler, Riane T. *The Chalice and the Blade: Our History, Our Future*. San Francisco, CA: HarperCollins, 1987.
Gaard, Greta. "Ecofeminism Revisited: Rejecting Essentialism and Re-Placing Species in a Material Feminist Environmentalism." *Feminist Formations* 23, no. 2 (2011): 26–53.
Gebara, Ivone. "Ecofeminism: An Ethics of Life." In *Ecofeminism and Globalization: Exploring Culture, Context, and Religion*, edited by Heather Eaton and Lois A. Lorentzen, 163–76. Lanham, MD: Rowman & Littlefield, 2003.
Gebara, Ivone. "Option for the Poor as Option for the Poor Woman." *Concilium* 194 (1987): 110–17.
Gebara, Ivone. *Out of the Depths: Women's Experience of Evil and Salvation*. Minneapolis, MN: Fortress Press, 2002.
Gimbuntas, Marija. "Women and Culture in Goddess-Oriented Old Europe." In *Weaving the Visions: New Patterns in Feminist Spirituality*, edited by Judith Plaskow and Carol P. Christ, 63–71. San Francisco, CA: HarperCollins, 1989.
Gross, Rita M. *Feminism and Religion: An Introduction*. Boston, MA: Beacon Press, 1996.
Gross, Rita M. "Buddhism and Ecofeminism: Untangling the Threads of Buddhist Ecology and Western Thought." *Journal for the Study of Religion* 24, no. 2 (2011): 17–32.

Hidalgo, Ann. "Weaving Ecofeminisms and Spiritualities Reflections from Latin American Women." In *Ecofeminism in Dialogue*, edited by Douglas A. Vackoch and Sam Mickey, 131–44. Lanham, MD: Lexington Books, 2018.

Hoel, Nina, and Elaine Nogueira-Godsey. "Transforming Feminisms: Religion, Women, and Ecology." *Journal for the Study of Religion* 24, no. 2 (2001): 5–15.

The Intergovernmental Panel on Climate Change (IPCC). "Climate Change 2007: Impacts, Adaptation and Vulnerability. Contribution of Working Group II to the Fourth Assessment Report of the Intergovernmental Panel on Climate Change." Cambridge, UK: Cambridge University Press, 2007. www.ipcc.ch/site/assets/uplo ads/2018/03/ar4_wg2_full_report.pdf, accessed April 8, 2024.

Keating, AnaLouise. *Transformation Now! Toward a Post-Oppositional Politics of Change*. Champaign: University of Illinois Press, 2012.

King, Ynestra. "Healing the Wounds: Feminism, Ecology, and the Nature/Culture Dualism." In *Reweaving the World: The Emergence of Ecofeminism*, edited by Irene Diamond and Gloria F. Orenstein, 106–21. San Francisco, CA: Sierra Club Books, 1990.

Kwok Pui-Lan. *Postcolonial Imagination and Feminist Theology*. Louisville, KY: Westminster John Knox Press, 2005.

Maldonado-Torres, Nelson. "On the Coloniality of Being: Contributions to the Development of a Concept." *Cultural Studies* 21, no. 2 (2007): 240–70.

Mallory, Chaone. "What's in a Name? In Defense of Ecofeminism (not Ecological Feminisms, Feminist Ecology, or Gender and the Environment) or 'Why Ecofeminism Need Not Be Ecofeminine—But so What If It Is?'" *Ethics & The Environment* 23, no. 2 (2018): 11–35.

Mellor, Mary. *Feminism and Ecology*. New York: New York University Press, 1997.

Merchant, Carolyn. *Earthcare: Women and the Environment*. New York: Routledge, 1996.

Mignolo, Walter D. "Os Esplendores e as Misérias da 'Ciência': Colonialidade, Geopolítica do Conhecimento e Pluri-versalidade Epistêmica." In *Conhecimento Prudente para uma Vida Decente: Um Discurso sobre as Ciências' Revistado*, edited by Boaventura de Sousa Santos, 667–709. Porto, Portugal: Edições Afrontamento, 2003.

Mignolo, Walter D., and Catherine E. Walsh. *On Decoloniality: Concepts, Analytics, Praxis*. Durham, NC: Duke University Press, 2018.

Nogueira-Godsey, Elaine. "A History of Resistance: Ivone Gebara's Transformative Ecofeminist Liberation Theology." *Journal for the Study of Religion* 26, no. 2 (2013): 89–106.

Nogueira-Godsey, Elaine. "Towards a Decological Praxis." *Horizontes Decoloniales* 1 (2019): 73–98.
Ortner, Sherry B. "Is Female to Male as Nature Is to Culture?" *Feminist Studies* 1, no. 2 (1972): 5–31.
Peterson, Anna L. *Being Human: Ethics, Environment, and Our Place in the World*. Berkeley: University of California Press, 2001.
Plumwood, Val. *Feminism and the Mastery of Nature*. London: Routledge, 1993.
Pulido, Laura. "Foreword." In *Latinx Environmentalism: Place, Justice, and the Decolonial*, edited by Sarah D. Wald, David J. Vázquez, Priscilla Solis Ybarra, and Sarah Jaquette Ray, ix–xvi. Philadelphia, PA: Temple University Press, 2019.
Ress, Mary Judith. "The Con-Spirando Women's Collective: Globalization from Below?" In *Ecofeminism and Globalization: Exploring Culture, Context, and Religion*, edited by Heather Eaton, and Lois A. Lorentzen, 147–62. Lanham, MD: Rowman & Littlefield, 2003.
Ress, Mary Judith. *Ecofeminism in Latin America*. Maryknoll, NY: Orbis Books, 2006.
Ruder, Sarah-Louise, and Sophia Rose Sanniti. "Transcending the Learned Ignorance of Predatory Ontologies: A Research Agenda for an Ecofeminist-Informed Ecological Economics." *Sustainability* 11, no. 5 (2019).
Salleh, Ariel. *Ecofeminism as Politics: Nature, Marx and the Postmodern*. London: Zed Books, [1997] 2007.
Sandilands, Catriona. *The Good-Natured Feminist: Ecofeminism and the Quest for Democracy*. Minneapolis: University of Minnesota Press, 1999.
Spretnak, Charlene. "Ecofeminism: Our Roots and Flowering." In *Reweaving the World: The Emergence of Ecofeminism*, edited by Irene Diamond and Gloria F. Orenstein, 3–14. San Francisco, CA: Sierra Club Books, 1990.
Spretnak, Charlene. *The Politics of Women's Spirituality: Essays on the Rise of Spiritual Power within the Feminist Movement*. Garden City, NY: Anchor Press, 1982.
Starhawk. "20 Years Later: How We Really Shut Down the WTO." *Starhawk's Website* (blog), November 29, 2019. https://starhawk.org/20-years-later-how-we-really-shut-down-the-wto/.
Tachine, Amanda R., and Z. Nicolazzo, eds. *Weaving and Otherwise: In-Relations Methodological Practice*. Sterling, VA: Stylus, 2022.
Tamez, Elsa. "Latin American Feminist Hermeneutics: A Retrospective." In *Women's Visions: Theological Reflection, Celebration, Action*, edited

by Orfelia Ortega, 77–89. Geneva, Switzerland: World Council of Churches, 1995.

Tully, Tyler M. "Native Futurities in an Age of 'Permanent Settler War': Conceptualizing Settler Coloniality as an Ongoing Ecological Structure." Paper presented at the 2020 Virtual Annual Meetings of the American Academy of Religion, November 29–December 10, 2020.

Wynter, Sylvia. "Unsettling the Coloniality of Being/Power/Truth/Freedom: Towards the Human, after Man, Its Overrepresentation—An Argument." *CR: The New Centennial Review* 3, no. 3 (2003): 313–14.

10

Re-membering Interdependency

Esther Parajuli

Around the globe, there is a rise in exclusionary politics. People are voting for representatives who stand on nationalist and xenophobic platforms that promise to protect their nation from threatening unknown others. With the rise of Hindu Nationalism in India and a resurgence of right-wing nationalism in Germany, Italy, Austria, France, Belgium, Spain, Sweden, Australia, Israel, Turkey, Myanmar, the United States, and more one would be hard-pressed to find a region of the world where hatred and anger for the other and fear of cultural dilution are not found.[1] There is an active mobilization to build a world for the self without "the other."

In the United States, Donald Trump won the 2016 election by chanting, "Make America Great Again" (MAGA) and, in the same breath, "Build a Wall." The sensibilities in these two slogans are not unrelated. "Make America Great Again" was not a prophetic call for the United States to embody the ideals of democracy and freedom to create a communal space where there is "right-to-difference-in

---

[1] See "Europe and Right-Wing Nationalism: A Country-by-Country Guide," *BBC News*, November 13, 2019, sec. Europe, https://www.bbc.com/news/world-europe-36130006 (accessed April 12, 2022).

equality."[2] Rather, it was instilled with a capitalist predilection for the "prosperity gospel" for selective citizens of the United States, and the companion slogan "Build the Wall" was a clear edict for the prioritization and preservation of white people in the United States, a concrete effort to keep out "the others." For Trump, MAGA and "Build the Wall" simply meant the quest to strengthen white supremacy. The slogan embodied a racialized understanding of national identity, one viewed through a continuity of hereditary linkages from some fictive "pure" Anglo-Saxon ancestry.

Belief in the purity of racialized national identity is never innocent. On the contrary, the illusion of pure white national identity contributes to the violent sequestration of people of color, who are perceived as a threat. There is a categorical relation between the wall, MAGA, anti-immigrant politics, and anti-Black culture. To the core, Trump's presidency was capitalist, xenophobic, and ableist. And, although he lost the 2020 election, we must wrestle with the fact that he received the second highest votes in the US presidential election history. People voted for Trump despite his exclusionary political views and, in many cases, because of his exclusionary views.

The rise of such exclusionary politics marked with machoism and racist rhetoric poses a huge challenge for postcolonial, feminist, theological commitment to incarnating collective liberation. So, what is manufacturing such a political landscape? The reasons behind people voting for divisive candidates like Trump are many and complex, but one main contributing reason is an understanding of "a self" in terms of purity and of others as a polluting difference, separate from the self. Put differently, the problem of exclusionary politics that deters mutual relationships is part of the deeper problem of the way we understand the self and the other. Who we think we are is a foundational force in shaping how we treat each other.

Postcolonial thoughts have extensively examined and offered myriad accounts of how empires endeavor to recolonize by shaping our understanding of identity, both individually and collectively. In this chapter, my intention is to provide further analysis of the fallacy of purism of self to offer a perspective of our inclination to construct exclusionary self by engaging with Mary Douglas's theory of purity and dirt. Furthermore, drawing on postcolonial feminist theologian

---

[2]Homi K. Bhabha, *The Location of Culture* (London: Routledge, 1994), xvii.

Wonhee Ann Joh and Black queer pleasure activist and emergent strategist adrienne maree brown, I challenge the purity vision of individualistic and xenophobic self by affirming a relational view of self, guided by jeong, that affects actions toward emergent modes of community building for collective liberation.

Purity and Pollution: Understanding the Logic of Exclusionary Self

Douglas's theory offers a framework to account for the kind of purity framework that crafts an exclusionary self that we encounter in the micropolitics of everyday life as well as in larger political processes. Through a complex reading of practices of different cultures in daily life, Douglas argues that there is no universal thing as "pure" or "dirt," but all human societies have their own notions of purity and dirt. She explains that the supposedly "pure" or "dirt" is not independent but a residual category of a given system. It is condensed with implicit meanings about the society and the cosmos. Therefore, Douglas writes, "where there is dirt there is system" and vice versa.[3]

Douglas's main argument is that (1) our ideas of dirt and purity depend on a system of classification, (2) both are social constructs, (3) and in terms of details, there are differences between what constitutes dirt and purity from one part of the world to another, (4) but the idea of dirt implies a "compendium of category[ies] for all events which blur, smudge, contradict, or otherwise confuse accepted classification,"[4] therefore, dirt is "matter out of place,"[5] (5) and the idea of purity implies that which remains within a determinate location, separated, and qualitatively homogenous.

Primarily, classification is an act of sense-making in a highly complex environment. To classify is to organize various elements such as spaces, entities both animate and inanimate, and encounters in a variety of classes through the processes of differentiation based on perceived similarity and difference. Of course, neither similarity

---

[3] Mary Douglas, *Purity and Danger: An Analysis of the Concepts of Pollution and Taboo* (London: Routledge & Kegan Paul, 1966; reprint, 2003), 44.
[4] Douglas, *Purity and Danger*, 109.
[5] Douglas, *Purity and Danger*, 35.

nor difference is a singular phenomenon, as there can be many iterations of what constitutes "similarity" and "difference." But when the classification process is driven by purity logic, which presupposes and necessitates a state of being unmixed, the categories get separated by fixed lines of demarcation. In this context, to be a member of a class in purity-informed classification, one must fully correspond to the class. There is no overlapping, and there is no space for boundary crossing.

Such demand for an unmixed, pure subject presupposes a nonrelational subject. At the core of purity's demand for the untouched subject is a view that *existence* is an individual occurrence: that an individual can exist and emerge alone; that any form of relationship with the other does not constitute an individual. This view of selfhood asserts an idea that the determinate individuals have "own-being"[6] or independent substance. It is a system that generates hyperindividualism, ableism, and homogeneity. Here, the different other is always *external* and *extraneous*. Bear in mind that it does not deny the existence of the other but does not view the other as part of the existence of the self. In fact, it views the touch of the other as a threat to the purity of the self. Within the purity matrix, the difference does not suggest particularity or heterogeneity without assumed or imposed hierarchy. Instead, it serves as a qualitative term employed for *othering*. Therefore, it requires a "wall" between the pure self-same and the polluting different other.

Such a conception of selfhood played a critical role in the modern classification of human beings, which continues to profoundly form and inform our present world. Purity discourse was at the center of the modern colonial social-political psyche. By the eighteenth century, the "taxonomies of human beings" based on visible difference, of which the skin was the prime signifier, were already a central theme within European anthropological discourse.[7] Colonial ideology further concretized the hierarchical construction of racial differences by asserting an intrinsic link

---

[6] "Own-being" is a translation of the Buddhist notion of *svabhava*. See Jan Willem de Jong, Chr Lindtner, and Adyar Library and Research Centre, *Nagarjuniya Mulamadhyamakakarika Prajna nama = Nagarjuna's Mulamadhyamakakarika Prajna nama* (Chennai, India: Adyar Library and Research Centre, 2004).

[7] See Michael P. Banton, *Racial Theories* (New York: Cambridge University Press, 1987).

between the biological features of a group and its psychological, cultural, and social attributes. Historian Romila Thapar shows that in the colonial discourse, there are a number of words used laxly and synonymously, such as race, religion, language, nation, ethnicity, people, and blood—words whose meanings, in today's context, would be very carefully differentiated.[8] This laxity means that the various forms of social collectivities such as kinsfolk, ethnicity, lineage, family, nationality, and home were often entwined with racial identity.[9]

The cultural and political scope of this set of arguments comes to focus when we hear the aggressive insistence on the interlink between national identity with racial and religious attributes—for example, in this context, the claim that "all United States citizens are white Christians" and the attendant fact that some are *not* white Christians creates anxiety and fear, which leads to various practices of control and punishment, namely stereotypical representations, discrimination, criminalization, invisibilization, and other fatal methods to patrol the border between the pure US citizens and the "polluting immigrants." The present-day political desire for "the Wall" is an iteration of the same white purity anxiety—the murder of Daoyou Feng, Soon Chung Park, Michelle Go, and many *other bodies* too because, in some imagination, they were "polluting" the purity of the US citizens. And that xenophobic imagination is so well understood in this white supremacist culture that those who kill or promise a wall out of the purity anxiety are rarely held accountable but rather are protected and rewarded by the white supremacist system.

When a society values purity, anybody who is "out of the accepted place"—geographically, economically, legally, politically, ethnoculturally, or in gender or sexual orientation—is treated like "dirt" that threatens the purity of the systems. It refuses to recognize the different other as a sacred being with whom self is in an inter-*dependent* relationship; instead, purity discourse constructs the other as "disposable bodies." It generates a discourse of humiliation aimed to dehumanize and degrade the other and, in turn, to discriminate. Thus, discrimination and humiliation are the two

---

[8] Romila Thapar, "The Theory of Aryan Race and India: History and Politics," *Social Scientist* 24, no. 1/3 (1996): 3–29, https://doi.org/10.2307/3520116.
[9] Thapar, "The Theory of Aryan Race and India," 6.

violent sides of the purity and pollution theory. Worst still is that the humiliation and discrimination against the other get justified as being ethical since it is a violence committed to protect the "pure self" from the "contaminating other." Such disavowal of our precarious life within a purity system and the violence committed on the other must be theologically accounted as sin. So, how do we imagine resistance in this context?

Imagining Resistance

The movie *Black Panther* offers fantastic imagination of resistance. The Black Panther story is based on a Marvel comic book series, set in Wakanda, a fictional African country that has never been colonized. The story's premise is that Wakanda houses the earth's only source of vibranium, which the rest of the world does not know about. The first black panther was an ancient warrior who ingested a "heart-shaped herb" affected by vibranium matter. Consuming it gave him supernatural abilities and made him the first king and Black Panther, "the protector of Wakanda." Over centuries, utilizing the resource of vibranium, Wakanda becomes a wealthy and high-tech country amidst the colonial exploitation happening in the world. Since the Wakandans knew that the colonial power would doubtlessly come to pillage their greatest asset and overthrow their carefully preserved way of life if they were "discovered," using the vibranium technology, they decided to hide and isolate themselves from the world.

The 2018 *Black Panther* movie is about T'Challa, son of the Black Panther T'Chaka, claiming the Wakanda throne as well as the mantle of the Black Panther. As the story unfolds, T'Challa is confronted with a choice between continuing the strategy of isolation amidst imperialism to protect Wakanda and its resources or actively participating in the world power blocks and becoming a catalyst for reimaging a better world for all beings beyond Wakanda.

Undeniably, the movie *Black Panther* makes great strides in presenting the fierce spirit of African and African American communities. The creative force of such representation amid the negative stereotypical images cannot be diminished. But, my issue with *Black Panther*'s story is an imagination of resistance emerging from a space untouched by colonialism. My postcolonial feminist gut is uneasy with any imagination of resistance from or toward pure presence, both at an individual and at a collective level. The problem here is not only that such imagination perpetuates purity logic even within anticolonial movements that continue to divide us and perpetuate a system of fear and control but that it also masks the present condition of the fierce resistance of the "postcolonial hybrid subjects."

Unfortunately, the iterations of purity logic within anticolonial movements are not only fantastic but historical. There are traces of purity sensibilities in India's Hindu Nationalist paramilitary organization, the Rastriya Swayamsevak Sangh (RSS), founded in 1925 to strategize anti-British colonial movements. The ruling political party in India under Narendra Modi, the Bhartiya Janata Party is the political wing of the RSS, which has played a crucial role in constructing an idea of Indian national identity, both in the past and in the present, as a Hindu nation. It has articulated an understanding of the Indian national movement as a restoration of Hindu rule.[10] Such an anticolonial imagination not only sanitizes the Indian identity as Hindu but also establishes it as normative.[11]

According to the RSS narrative, the Hindus are the authentic native Indians, and the Muslims and Christians are either colonizers or descents of colonizers or sympathizers of colonizers. The RSS refuses to wrestle with the long complex history of cultural and religious exchange between Hindus and Muslims and Christians and many other communities that have become part of the DNA of Indian selves. Rather, it presents a view that Indians should and can

---

[10] For more reading on the cultural political processes in the creation of India as a Hindu nation, see Ranjana Das and Ranjan Das, "The Nation and the Community: Hindus and Muslims in the Novels of Bankim Chandra Chatterjee," *Proceedings of the Indian History Congress* 73 (2012): 578–87; Meenakshi Mukherjee, "Anandamath: A Political Myth," *Economic and Political Weekly* 17, no. 22 (1982): 903–5.

[11] It is important to note that here I am focusing on one trope of anticolonial narrative. This line of thought agrees that our decolonization process ends in a nation-state. But there are also anticolonial activists like Rabindranath Tagore, who was critical of the idea of India as a nation. For further reading, see Rabindranath Tagore and Surendranath Tagore, *The Home and the World* (London: Macmillan, 1919); Rabindranath Tagore, *Nationalism* (San Francisco: The Book Club of California, 1917).

return to pure "Hindu self" untouched by the Other—"Make India Hindu Again." The current Islamophobic politics and Christian persecutions in India under BJP are part of that sanitization, or perhaps saffronization process.[12] We are witnessing iterations of purity violence in "postcolonial India." Today, in many ways, India's violence against its own community members is a direct result of the colonial trauma. Hence, it is urgent for us to heal and simultaneously reimagine the praxis of resistance that does not reproduce divisions and systems of segregation.

If the *Black Panther* imagines resistance from purity, then the Indian RSS is an imagination of resistance as a return to purity. Both forms of resistance fail a postcolonial hybrid subject. So how do we imagine resistance without falling into the cultural relativism that oversimplifies differences? How do we dismantle "the wall" between us and them? What kind of micropolitics of everyday life, as well as the larger processes, will help cultivate visions and commitment for collective liberation? For me, it entails *kenosis* and giving birth to a new view of human being, and this human being is characterized by interdependency.

Re-membering Self as Relational

Science journalist Ed Yong, in his brilliant introduction to microbes of the human body, writes "Every one of us is a … multi-species collective. An entire world."[13] These trillions of microbes in and on the human body form communities that are part of the ecosystem of the human body. The intricate symbiotic relationship with microbes has helped human bodies to persevere. Simultaneously, the human body is always dependent on the external ecosystem encompassing land, air, water, humans, and beyond human communities of care.

Right from the time of conception, a human being relies on environmental, familial, material, and social ecosystems to survive. In other words, at a very fundamental level, we know that the human being cannot sustain itself. It needs the ecosystems both

---

[12] See Ajay Gudavarthy, *India after Modi: Populism and the Right*, 1st ed. (Bloomsbury India, 2018).
[13] Ed Yong, *I Contain Multitudes: The Microbes within Us and a Grander View of Life*, reprint ed. (New York: Ecco Books, 2018), 3.

within and external to survive. So, principally, there is no "pure independent self-sufficient" human being. There is no *ex nihilo* creation of the self. Rather, all that we are, we have received. We are all characterized by interdependency, a principle that Paul reminds us before any scientists. He asks "What do you have that you did not receive? And if you received it, why do you boast as if you did not receive?" (1 Cor. 4:7, New Revised Standard Version). Our sacred incarnation tells us *existence is relational*, and therefore, self is a bio-psycho-social embodiment of multitudes of relations. We constitute each other—biologically, socially, economically, and politically. This also means the difference is both internal and external, contrary to purity logic.

The idea that an individual is a unit in and of itself, independent, and that "I" exist and end within my bodily border is erroneous and dangerous. It is an error because we depend on each other for survival. It is dangerous because by disavowing interdependency, purity logic attacks the fundamental basis of life, hence risks life itself. It puts survival at stake, a reason why a purity logic is a flawed and dangerous frame for understanding human beings and the world we participate in. Hence, it is urgent to re-member the principle of relationality.

Nevertheless, I also recognize that being aware of our interdependent reality does not in itself create life-flourishing conditions. Relationality is an ambivalent third space in which the question of ethics has to be deliberated perpetually. In so many ways, the COVID-19 situation revealed this point. During the COVID pandemic, we became more aware of our 'intra-active' lives, to use feminist theorist Karen Barad's word.[14] We now know, more viscerally, what happens in China affects those in the United States, India, Nepal, Ghana, and around the world. We are all interrelated. For some, this awareness has led to more ethical choices, but for others, the realization of interrelation has led to greater fear and hatred of the other. Across the United States, there were more than 2,500 reported cases of anti-Asian hate incidents related to COVID-19 between March and September 2020.[15] Interdependence means

---

[14]Karen Barad, *Meeting the Universe Halfway: Quantum Physics and the Entanglement of Matter and Meaning*, 2nd printing ed. (Durham, NC: Duke University Press Books, 2007).
[15]Zijia Eleanor Song and Jennifer Vázquez, "Study Shows Rise of Hate Crimes, Violence against Asian Americans during the Pandemic," *NBC New York*, n.d., https://

that we can not only nourish each other, but also harm each other. A self, nourished by the purity compost, will choose to focus only on the latter and eliminate the other for self-preservation.

But the principle of life as relationality suggests that it is impossible to preserve one's own existence without the presence of the other. Life inherently unfolds within a framework of interdependent relationships. Self cannot be free by eliminating the other. Rather, emancipation requires that we avow our conditions of interdependency, the theological principle "each is in each thing."[16] This means that our vision for life/liberation cannot ignore relationality because "I" cannot exist or be free without "you," and neither can "you" without "I." The assertion is that my vision of salvation cannot be solely for myself and/or for "people like me" but for the collective world, and you, too, bear similar responsibility in this regard. And this radical embrace of the principle of interdependent-becoming serves as a driving force for postcolonial strategies for collective liberation.

Such a proposal might meet many challenges. Commitment to collective liberation based on interdependency may be seen as an audacious claim because it suggests that I am not only in a relationship but must also bear the burden of imagining my oppressors' emancipation, who labeled me as disposal. Therefore, in such contexts, freeing oneself from such bonds seems desirable and an indispensable part of liberation. As a result, it might appear that severing the ties is a choice and, perhaps, liberation lies in repudiating relationality. But the principle of relationality that I am asserting here is not about two autonomous units coming together in self-interest. As a matter of fact, such an understanding of relationality between two separate autonomous entities is compatible only within a purity logic, where the other is always *external* and *extraneous*.

I am affirming the very condition of being interdependent on each other for life. It is not a voluntary commitment. My argument is that human beings are part of the relational planet, and we are

---

www.nbcnewyork.com/news/local/crime-and-courts/study-shows-rise-of-hate-crimes-violence-against-asian-americans-in-nyc-during-covid/2883215/ (accessed April 12, 2022).
[16] Nicholas of Cusa, *Nicholas of Cusa: Selected Spiritual Writings*, trans. H. Lawrence Bond (New York: Paulist Press, 1997), 140.

relational beings. I recognize that relationality is a space where we have experienced discrimination and humiliation. Nonetheless, the violence does not free us from each other. The conflict in the relationship is not the termination of the connection between self and the other. The violence of disavowal of relationality crafts not a self free from the other but an agonizing and wounded "self tethered to the other," as Homi Bhabha puts it.[17] So, the principle of relationality is not optional, and by asserting a relational self and collective liberation, I am acknowledging the laborious maxim that we need each other. However, we do have the agency to decide the question of ethics in this ambivalent field of relationality. In other words, we have agency to decide how we respond.

A Postcolonial Feminist Theology of Relationship: *Jeong* for Collective Liberation

Postcolonial feminist theologian Wonhee Anne Joh submits that relationality lubricated by *jeong* has the ethical force for collective emancipation. She writes, "Redemption emerges within relationality that recognizes the power and presence of *jeong* to move us towards life."[18] So what is *jeong*? Joh persistently emphasizes the difficulty in offering a precise translation of the Korean term *jeong* in any direct sense to one single English idiom. Hence, this description is my incomprehensive comprehension of the impossible *jeong*.

Joh writes: *jeong* is the

> Korean way of conceding an often-complex constellation of relationality of the self with the other that is deeply associated with compassion, love, vulnerability, and acceptance of heterogeneity as essential to life. It not only smooths harsh feelings, such as dislike or even hate, but has a way of making relationships richly

---

[17]Bhabha, *The Location of Culture*, 61–4.
[18]Wonhee Anne Joh, *Heart of the Cross: A Postcolonial Christology* (Louisville, KY: Westminster John Knox Press, 2006), xxi.

complex by moving away from a binary, oppositional perception of reality, such as oppressor, and oppressed.[19]

It seems to me that within Joh's theopolitical schema, *jeong* helps materialize the well-being of the collective by committing to with creative human emotions and presence. It is a proposal for working toward social change by attending to the affect, inspired by the bonds, to see the other in oneself and to love the neighbor the way one loves oneself (Mk 12:31).

To fully express the theoethical force of *jeong*, Joh reflects on its transformative power in the context of the division between North Korea and South Korea. Joh is keenly aware of the suffering and grief of Koreans caused by concrete border. Reflecting on her visit to the Demilitarized Zone (DMZ) between the Koreas, she writes, "My visit to DMZ was like a visit to an open grave. It was the first time I was able to participate in the collective *han* of my ancestors, of people who gave birth to me. I experienced grief for people I did not know intimately but who I realized then were part of my body and my memory."[20] Joh's autobiographical account of the DMZ visit speaks about *han* of neat division, and it also speaks about her connection with the present Korean communities and the past, which is not all available for her cognizance. The awareness of the community's *han*, leads Joh to avow the relationality that is beyond comprehension and narration. And this experience of collective *han* guides Joh to invite Koreans to be courageous, to cross military and ideological borders and risk their hearts by becoming vulnerable in the relationship. She argues that meeting the neighbor with *jeong* has the capacity to understand and hold space for difficult and violent histories that have shaped both our social and political lives in order to write our present into liberation. She argues, it is only the practice of "sticky" relationships that has the power to transform systems of oppression.[21]

It is important to note here that Joh's proposal of *jeong* as relational praxis is not a frail one. Joh notes that the patriarchal domestication of *jeong* tends to mask its force and risk.[22] She

---

[19] Joh, *Heart of the Cross*, xxi.
[20] Joh, *Heart of the Cross*, 29.
[21] Joh, *Heart of the Cross*, 120.
[22] Joh, *Heart of the Cross*, 127.

argues that, however, a postcolonial feminist appropriation of *jeong* demands courage and capaciousness to embody "hermeneutics of complexity," which our messy multitude of relationality demands. She suggests that such embodiment of *jeong* is not a powerless, uncritical, self-sacrificial, or toleration stance but a subversive, interruptive, interrogative, precarious, and oriented one toward abundant life for self and the other.

Joh further unveils the power and danger of *jeong* in the context of *han* by offering a reading of the event of the cross. She submits that "what is significant about the cross, then, is not that Jesus died on it but that because of his living out of *jeong*, he ends up de facto on the cross."[23] She explains that the cross embodies not just the suffering (*han*) but also the consequences of a radical form of inclusive love (*jeong*). Hence, she writes, "the cross then is not a symbol of love but of its risks, the risk taken by a whole lifetime lived on the edge."[24] By offering such examination of the event of the cross through the lens of *han* and *jeong*, Joh provides an understanding of the transformative power of the gospel rooted in the miracle of avowing interdependency, saturated with and by *jeong*, for collective emancipation. Joh is choosing and proposing the ethics of *jeong* to navigate the ambivalent field of relationality.

So, how do we embody this postcolonial theopolitical imagination of *jeong* for social change? My proposal is for us to practice *jeong* relational ethics in our most simple interactions until it creates an infinite intricacy of *jeong* fractals.

Creating *Jeong* Fractals

adrienne maree brown, a Black, queer, feminist social activist, wants us to reconsider our approach to the work of social justice and our connections to movements through the lens of emergent strategies. brown explains that emergent strategy emphasizes the idea that "complex systems and patterns arise out of a multiplicity of relatively simple interactions."[25] Elucidating further, brown

---

[23] Joh, *Heart of the Cross*, 106.
[24] Joh, *Heart of the Cross*, 106.
[25] adrienne maree brown, *Emergent Strategy: Shaping Change, Changing Worlds*, reprint ed. (Chico, CA: AK Press, 2017), 15.

proposes six key elements of the emergence strategy in her book. I would like to focus on *Fractals*.

brown writes: "A fractal is a never-ending pattern. Fractals are infinitely complex patterns that are self-similar across different scales. They are created by repeating a simple process over and over in an ongoing feedback loop."[26] Using this metaphor of fractal, brown illustrates how systems are constituted through a series of simple and everyday interactions. She writes:

> When we speak of systemic change, we need to be fractal. Fractals—a way to speak of the patterns we see—move from the micro to macro level. The same spirals on seashells can be found in the shape of galaxies. We must create patterns that cycle upwards. We are microsystems ... . Our friendships and relationships are systems. Our communities are systems. Let us practice upwards.[27]

This means, if we change our everyday interactions, it will metastasize into large-scale change. It is the idea that if we practice ethical relationality in our most simple conversations and connections, that seemingly decimal change in our way of treating one another will create an infinite *jeong* fractals at the local, regional, state, national, and global levels. The emergent fractal strategy focuses on the revolutionary power of the individualized, not individualistic, and local practices to incarnate collective liberation. Bear in mind that the emphasis on the micropolitics is not a move away from the urgent work of large-scale community organizing for resistance, but as brown reminds us, we need to "practice upwards." It is an invitation to cultivate *jeong*-infused interactions in our everydayness, generating life-fulfilling-patterns for inter-liberation.

Creating *jeong* fractals can take the form of openness and hospitality toward that one neighbor who is different from self; to a simple conversation of care and respect with a stranger; to being intentional to keep deepening with our kins, beyond species and sentients; to doing the hard work of healing from interpersonal and systemic trauma so that we show up better in our

---

[26]brown, *Emergent Strategy*, 54.
[27]brown, *Emergent Strategy*, 61.

conversations and connections at home, playgrounds, and work spaces; to practicing the ministry of compassionate presence with someone who is traveling the gender/sexual wilderness; to initiating story-telling with the community, where people from different backgrounds can hear each other's experiences and perspectives, fostering friendship and solidarity; to individuals committing to advocacy work and promoting social justice at the local spaces. Practicing *jeong* is to honor the fundamental principle of life—interdependency. It is an invitation to re-member that human beings are relational selves who have the potential to create complex *jeong* fractals every day. This postcolonial feminist theological invitation extends to all who desire collective liberation.

Bibliography

Banton, Michael P. *Racial Theories*. New York: Cambridge University Press, 1987.
Barad, Karen. *Meeting the Universe Halfway: Quantum Physics and the Entanglement of Matter and Meaning*, 2nd ed. Durham, NC: Duke University Press Books, 2007.
Bhabha, Homi K. *The Location of Culture*. London: Routledge, 1994.
brown, adrienne maree. *Emergent Strategy: Shaping Change, Changing Worlds*, reprint ed. Chico, CA: AK Press, 2017.
Das, Ranjana, and Ranjan Das. "The Nation and the Community: Hindus and Muslims in the Novels of Bankim Chandra Chatterjee." *Proceedings of the Indian History Congress* 73 (2012): 578–87.
de Jong, Jan Willem, Chr Lindtner, and Adyar Library and Research Centre. *Nagarjuniya Mulamadhyamakakarika Prajna nama = Nagarjuna's Mulamadhyamakakarika Prajna nama*. Chennai, India: Adyar Library and Research Centre, 2004.
Douglas, Mary. *Purity and Danger: An Analysis of Concepts of Pollution and Taboo*. London: Routledge & Kegan Paul, 1966; reprint, 2003.
"Europe and Right-Wing Nationalism: A Country-by-Country Guide." *BBC News,* November 13, 2019, sec. Europe. https://www.bbc.com/news/world-europe-36130006, accessed April 12, 2022.
Gudavarthy, Ajay. *India After Modi: Populism and the Right*. New Delhi: Bloomsbury India, 2018.
Joh, Wonhee Anne. *Heart of the Cross: A Postcolonial Christology*. Louisville, KY: Westminster John Knox Press, 2006.
Mukherjee, Meenakshi. "Anandamath: A Political Myth." *Economic and Political Weekly* 17, no. 22 (1982): 903–5.

Nicholas of Cusa. *Nicholas of Cusa: Selected Spiritual Writings.* Translated by H. Lawrence Bond. New York: Paulist Press, 2005.

"Study Shows Rise of Hate Crimes, Violence against Asian Americans during the Pandemic." *NBC New York*, n.d. https://www.nbcnewyork.com/news/local/crime-and-courts/study-shows-rise-of-hate-crimes-violence-against-asian-americans-in-nyc-during-covid/2883215/, accessed April 12, 2022.

Tagore, Rabindranath. *Nationalism.* San Francisco: The Book Club of California, 1917.

Tagore, Rabindranath, and Surendranath Tagore. *The Home and the World.* London: Macmillan, 1919.

Thapar, Romila. "The Theory of Aryan Race and India: History and Politics." *Social Scientist* 24, no. 1/3 (1996): 3–29.

Yong, Ed. *I Contain Multitudes: The Microbes within Us and a Grander View of Life.* Reprint ed. New York: Ecco Books, 2018.

11

Queer Intimacies and Art as the Necessary Work of the Soul

Su Yon Pak and Alicia R. Forde

How do we practice new feminist praxis in our ordinary and everyday lives? What is the role of art and intimacy in feminist praxis? This chapter does not propose a defining response to these questions. Rather, it is a reflection and exploration of our engagement in the artistic space. This chapter is a feminist praxis in creative nonfiction that was born out of our pandemic practice of poetry writing. It is a witness to the friendship that was becoming in and through our practice. As coauthors, much like friendship itself, we allow our voices to dance together in this piece in a variety of forms. You, the reader, are invited into this journey with us. At times, you'll wonder: *whose voice is this?* It will not always be clear. As coauthors, our ideas and writing are commingled in ways that are not necessarily easy to tease apart. We suspend the idolatry of "ownership" to explore what happens when we do not try to possess and discipline our words, our thoughts, our ideas. Knowledge is always cocreated and coconstructed. It is never singular. It is never individual. By this way of writing, we push against and disrupt the hegemonic forces that mandate that scholarship, for it to mean something, must be a single-authored monograph.

During the height of the pandemic, we decided to write poetry in the spirit of Jacqueline Woodson's *Brown Girl Dreaming* (Note: the book is published with title in lower case). Even though we'd only met once in person (pre-pandemic), we craved a different and deeper way of connecting in that chaotic and liminal time ... much like many others who sought community and connection through different rituals using Zoom. Some started Zoom dinner parties, Zoom cooking classes, and some even mailed around sourdough starters from house to house.

Alicia and I decided to write poetry and share them on Zoom. We did not know what to expect. We did not know what would flow from our pens (or our keyboards) and what stories yet to be remembered and voiced would find their way to our pages. We did not know how our relationship would be transformed from colleagues and acquaintances to friends and sisters, or whether that was even a conscious goal.

After our initial "getting to know" Zoom calls, we decided to embark on this pilgrimage of poetry writing together. Inspired by Woodson, we wrote poetry from the perspective of the age of that which we were writing about. It was an autobiographical creative exercise. Our shared journey was exploring what our *childhood self* would see and understand of pivotal/impactful childhood events. Su began her first poem that told of her ten-year-old self's experience as an immigrant coming from South Korea to the United States. Alicia began with her seven-or-eight-year-old-self pretending to be American while still in Tobago, flipping her grandmother's wig this way and that like in a L'Oréal commercial.

Much like our poetry, in this chapter, we have been deliberate in staying with our experiences and reflections. We allow ourSELVES to take up space in these pages. We do not engage in art criticism/theory or literary criticism/theory. We are not attempting to arrive at a particular destination or map a single process for others to follow. We are sharing truthfully as one way of modeling how we have embodied and practiced doing "the work our souls must have." It is queer. It is intimate.

The Work Our Souls Must Have

It wasn't without trepidation that I boarded my flight from the Denver International Airport, Colorado, to the LaGuardia Airport, New York, for a visit with Su. Our relationship has been largely mediated by screens—chest up—even though we'd previously met twice in person. This third in-the-flesh reunion felt different. Five/six days; me in Su's home. Multiple geographies, languages, time zones, commingling between us with the expressed goal of coauthoring this chapter, which demanded our undivided attention. What if, I wondered, our burgeoning friendship unraveled? What if, in our time together, I—or we—were transformed in ways that neither one of us yet envisioned? Could I surrender to such an unknown? Was it within my reach to keep trusting in the sacred pull that accompanied the intimacies we've shared?

It's hot and bright outside of the airport. Su is waiting and waving. There's a confidence in my step that I don't quite feel. I'm aware that—in person—we have few norms, scant histories, languages, or storied ways of being. We are interdependent beings who now exist in a temporal reality that was yet to be created while simultaneously existing in a verdant indefinite/intangible reality, made fertile with the ongoing exchange of the deepest parts of our selves ... selves revealed and coconstructed through our shared poetry practice. In multiple ways, Su already occupied a home in my heart and was my soul's companion. It was with Su that I'd undertaken a pandemic pilgrimage, companions in the dynamic meaning-making of our many selves and lives.

Within the boundaries of Su's home, we arrived at an unfolding— or jointly mapped—temporal landscape. We explored new daily rituals, familiar to each of us in different contexts and new to us in the "retreat time" configuration of this visit. We did what we do best: we turned to poetry, wrote ourselves separately, and made meaning collectively as we explored the major and minor themes of our singular and intertwined being and becoming ... And what were we becoming?

///

"You must call me *Unni* (older sister)," I declared to Alicia as we sat down for our last dinner of our writing retreat together. By this time, we had spent five days in constant proximity. There was no escape from each other except for sleep and occasional calls to our partners and work colleagues. Each day began with breakfast followed by poetry reading and free writing, and a long walk. We spent time researching and writing, thinking through ideas and directions that this chapter would take. We had written together before, so we were familiar with each other's terrains of thinking, working style, and singular and shared trenches.

I don't usually express my love and care through words or hugs. Food, for me, is the language of love, and I express love through my cooking. Alicia's delight in the food we prepared together, especially the way she ate *kimchi* (with everything) unlocked a tightly secured chamber of my heart—the chamber that holds my sisters. It was these small details, small acts of surprise and delight that moved me. It was the way in which I felt so familiar and comfortable, as if we had grown up in the same family. The way she cleaned and chopped vegetables, the way we watched *Ms. Marvel* or *Kotaro Lives Alone* after a long day's work, the way she threw mini tantrums about something that she was bothered by. It was so familiar, navigating a well-worn groove of my heart. Yes, we had many intense and vulnerable conversations, not only about this chapter-writing but also about our lives. And yet, what remains in my memory of our time together is the way she wrapped a piece of grilled mackerel with *kimchi* and popped it in her mouth with delight, savoring the flavors balancing the rich oily fish and the spicy, slightly tart, fermented *kimchi*. Like *Babette's Feast*, our intensity of writing and sharing was held together by the joyful, grateful, and convivial ritual of our cooking, dancing, and eating. Through this, she was becoming my *dong-saeng* (younger sister), and I, her *unni*.

///

Compulsory heteronormativity—and similarly homonormativity—continues to be defining characteristics of intimate relationships. In our artistic undertaking, we rejected those forms of normativity as our foundation, and we (perhaps unknowingly, at first) queered both our relationship and our art itself. We took what is typically a solo pursuit and through our practice insisted that it be communal and collaborative. It was imperative that our work was cocreated, cointerpreted, and that meaning was jointly constructed. Our "poetry pilgrimage" could be likened to a perichoretic dance of the Trinity. In our creating, there were always at least three of us and at times more. That third was an ever-shifting cast of integral others: the Spirit, the spirit of Alicia's sister, the spirit of Su's mother, and sometimes all of them, or some of them. Generativity whirled between us as well as between us and those whose lives had shaped our own. We were defining and redefining ourselves, individually and collectively—and defining and redefining ourselves in relation to those who have gone before us and continue to mold us.

Our practice of writing poetry together has been foundational to our soul work. This practice raised several questions about what it is that we are doing. Foremost, is art necessary for our living? How do we know what we know? How does art and relationship help us name and claim what we know? How is it a feminist praxis? How does relationship and art as processes create *"something new in the world that changes the world to allow itself to exist"*?[1] And finally, *how is art as self-care also political warfare?*[2]

Art as Necessary

To claim something as necessary is to claim that it is vital for becoming. It is essential for survival. It is not a luxury or an elective or optional, but rather it is a basic requirement—a thing that one must have, make, create, be to exist. In our view, art, to paraphrase Audre Lorde, is not a luxury but a matter of survival. Art demands that we pay deep attention—with the entirety of our being—to what is. The imaginative potential and power of art can offer us a visceral experience of what is not readily apparent through the normative social conditioning of our lives. Paying attention to *what is,* then, is a radical act of survival. Paying attention shifted the totality of our being. What was once tight and locked, loosened and rearranged itself to embrace/enfold; what we once thought we knew about our stories, our roles, and our selves untangled and rebraided; mental memory muscles on the verge of atrophy, exercised, exorcized, resurrected, and restored to life.

---

[1] Amy Whitaker, quoted in Makoto Fujimura, *Art and Faith: A Theology of Making* (New Haven, CT: Yale University Press, 2021), 8. Emphasis added.
[2] Audre Lorde, *A Burst of Light, Essays* (London: Sheba Feminist, 1988), 95.

There is tremendous temptation and pressure to think of the "self" as a cohesive entity that exists as it has always existed. We narrativize our being, viewing our present self as an extension of the meanings we've made of our past self. We tell ourselves stories, daily, about who we are and how we came to be. The practice of journeying together from the soul allowed for an unfolding that upended what we *think* we know about who we are. Such a practice—such a pilgrimage—can unravel the carefully constructed narratives we hold about who and why we are. And yet, it is that very practice of paying attention to *what is,* that makes us whole. It is counterintuitive—and it is a radical act of survival. This practice of journeying together, from the soul, was and is a pilgrimage.

Like any pilgrimage, this practice can be unsettling. It invites us into a liminal realm where we are asked to be unguarded, unmasked, vulnerable, guileless, to connect to another, whether "another" is a person, the divine, or nature. We are compelled to remove the very boundaries that have afforded us safety, protection, understanding self, and community. These boundaries define us, they give our bodies and emotions shape and meaning. They offer us a narrative frame that gives us a sense of identity, and we impose (knowingly and unknowingly) a plumbline on a collection of experiences and memories that then tells us who we are and by what standards we live. Like good fences, boundaries can delineate what constitutes family, community, and normative ways of inhabiting our gender, racial, sexual orientation identities. Such spaces also have immense potential to hold memories, practices, and identities. And yet, in these (potentially) prescriptive and protected spaces, we can over rely on role, on preconceived social/normative expectations, that predetermine who we think we are supposed to be. Intimacy can dissolve the veneer of a self/identity to expand beyond what we know. This way, as Mary Hunt has written, we challenged the heteronormative understanding and practice of friendship by inviting each other into a practice of intimacy that gave us new ways of understanding our past and present.[3] Yes, "*a work of art is something new in the world that changes the world to allow itself*

---

[3]Mary Hunt, "Love Your Friends: Learning from the Ethics of Relationships," in *Queer Christianities: Lived Religion in Transgressive Forms,* ed. Kathleen T. Talvacchia, Michael F. Pettinger, and Mark Larrimore (New York: New York University Press, 2015), 140.

to exist,"[4] and we claim that intimacy is a practice that changes the world in order for something new to come into being. This is not without risk.

Relationship and Art as Processes

Who dances on pilgrimage? In August 2022, when we gathered at Su's home for a writing retreat, we lived this question fully. In Su's kitchen, we play song after song, cooking, and dancing. Su is telling stories about her siblings and the music they love. We discover songs we like together. We discover new rhythms that one or the other of us was unaware of before. We shake and shimmy. The beats are loud and provide a wild soundtrack to the sizzling and bubbling on the stovetop. There isn't much time to think. Just *be(come)* in the moment as it is. There is something ancient and emergent about the dance: a dash of this, a splash of that, plates wheeled out to the table, waters, beer, wine, singing, wordlessness, and music—bodies navigating space without colliding as if we have always done this. As if we have lived this scene repeatedly. As if we were always this free.

In those moments, we danced with the Divine.

Early on in our writing practice, Alicia wrote a piece that embodies the paradoxical dance with the divine "who exists in all fears and in trembling boldness" (*Thunder: Perfect Mind*).[5] After only three writing-sharing sessions, Alicia wrote "Confession" that embodies both her desire and fear for intimacy, both as an agent and as a recipient of Divine invitation, both shameless and ashamed. She begins the poem with one (humorous) confession—about her being vain—but leads the reader through scars mapped in her body to another confession as she argues and pleads with God for that intimacy. "In trembling boldness," Alicia lays bare her vulnerability, perhaps as a challenge to the two of us to step into this space of risk and freedom that art and art of friendship demand.

///

---

[4]Fujimura, *Art and Faith*, 8. Emphasis added.
[5]Hal Taussig, ed., *A New New Testament* (Boston, MA: Houghton Mifflin Harcourt), 184.

Confession

19 Sept 2020

The funny thing is,
        I am secretly vain
I am stuffed with vanity
I know this because
I want to get to heaven with my breasts still perky.
I know—there's something comical … almost perverse
about that
        and also
impossible.
Let's face it: gravity is definitely not on my side.
Never mind that heaven isn't real and the two tattoos
I have guarantee that I'm not ascending with
my body unscathed, unscarred, and in mint condition.
But still,
        it's what I think about when I think about heaven.
That,
        and
the scars on my left arm
made by my right hand and a razor
when words weren't enough to express the pain
pulsing from the wounds unhealed inside of me
I remember the last time sitting in
my first car; that light blue chevy cavalier
four neat lines carved on my upper arm.
Blood   beading,
… heart rate slowing,
… breath moving
back
to even again
panic quietening when the opposite
should have been happening.

I'll go to God with these fading scars and say:
        This is what I did when you left me
This is what I did to make it through
the next minute, next hour, next day.

And God will know that what I'm really saying is:
Forgive me, forgive me, forgive me. I was drowning.
Everything was too much then.

God will know that
what I really want is a chance to mourn
because I am still so ashamed that I failed myself
for not being strong enough
courageous enough
compassionate enough
enough

God will know that what I need is
redemption
                        in the form of being held so close
that my heartbeat syncs with the rhythm of the Universe
and the music we make remind me that
no matter
                    I am perfectly formed
scars,
              tattoos
                    sagging breasts (eventually)
and all.

///

"Why do you do that?" is a question that Su has asked more than once, usually when I (Alicia) am making a practice of minimizing my competence or presence. It speaks to an implicit commitment she holds to my healing/development; to her ability to see my edges, and the beauty of those edges so that the "delusions" can be sloughed away while the distinctive terrains of pain, life, and even trauma are held sacred. Let edges be edges. Let smoothed parts be smoothed. In other words, not all edges need to be chipped away. Shared pilgrimage is about discerning together that which no longer serves us and that which needs to be (re)surfaced and shined. We do this for each other: hold a commitment to develop, to live intimacy as a practice of freedom.

These words open Su's poem *Journey I*:

Following you was the beginning of my journey
back home

though queer and labyrinthine …
You knew, I would come.

In this poem, she creates and describes her dance with the Divine, with her grief, with her mother's love, and her mother's death. She writes and rewrites herself as being in process, and by joining her, I (Alicia) be-come a partner in that perichoretic dance, not only holding heart but also as a companion to eventual acceptance. In this moment of encounter, both Su and I—through Su's poem (which is something new in the world)—cocreate a world that can hold our full existence. We ourselves are "re/ordered" in this honest exploration of grief, loss, and desire for a transcendent love. Su writes of "duty and grace" as her spirit guides, and they were, in a very real sense, also *our* spirit guides in navigating the trepidation that comes with the demands of intimacy and in accepting the invitation for soul-commitment.

///

Journey I

12 March 2021

Following you was the beginning of my journey
back home
though queer and labyrinthine.

It was duty
and grace—
two wings that grew in the muck of my doubt
as my spirit guides
that allowed me to fly
to you
and to see in the dark
courage as my heart-sight
to your dis/re/ordered
jumbled up, re/membered life-world-reality
    broken shards reassembled a mosaic of
      supernatural memory mocking the linear
rhythm of chronos

tumbling into the eternal now
stretching and bending
fixed, ordered spatial-temporal relations
to find you there, waiting.

You knew, I would come.

Your mothering instinct as a North Star,
homing through your Alzheimer-ravaged brain
willing one final lesson for your daughter,
perhaps the most important one—
your legacy.

Following you was journeying by heart.

Where the mind flies it reaches the heights
of imagination and soars
through meaning making,
theologizing,
systematizing,
untangling the knotty problems
of the whys.

Why my mother?
Why me?
But to follow by heart is to move through to the center
of my body until it reaches
my belly button where
umbilical cord tethers your world (your womb) to mine.

To follow you is to suspend
my mind's chest-thumping chatter
however clever it may be
to aches, pains, joys, and delight.
To know what my body knows.

It spares not thorns that rip open
my soft places because to journey by heart
means to crawl through the thicket and under brushes
of razored history we have with each other
overgrown with hurt, disappointment,
and missed opportunities to say,
I am grateful

I understand
and yes, I will listen to your stories
again as if for the first time.

Because a time will come
when I will want nothing more
than to hear your voice again
puffs of breath enlivening those dry-boned stories.

I found you there, waiting
in the clearing
where the dementia has done its work of logging
felling trees that marked your life's moments
though traces like ghosts shimmer
just beneath the surface

You knew I would come.

Fervent prayers for your wandering daughter
inexorably pulled me toward you protecting me
against the gravitational force
of normativity
because to follow you
was to follow the deep desires of my heart
forty years of searching
for my way back home
to that ecstatic communion with God

To follow you into your demented world
was to practice journeying by heart
spacious, timeless, soulful,
and queer
the very practice that led me
back to the heart of God

It's been four years now
since you left your earthly body
I now understand your final lesson
that this journey was a gift
from a loving mother whose prayer
was nothing more, nothing less
than her daughter afire with God.

///

We are hearts afire with God on this shared poetry pilgrimage. In each other's presence, we take off our shoes because the ground we are on is sacred. How is pilgrimage different from everyday practices? What boundaries, rituals, frames, creates this liminal space? How is this a feminist praxis?

Art as Feminist Communal Radical Praxis

We entered into this poetry pilgrimage intuitively and we knew we were being guided. We sought to reflect on the question of how we were cocreating a world that did not yet exist between us. What were the guideposts that allowed for the emergence of that which did not exist?

Hilary Bradbury and Shakiyla Smith offer a helpful articulation of our instinctive journeying in this pilgrimage. In their work, "Relational Action Inquiry," they explore the interpersonal skills and heart-orientation required for transformation of self and community. Bradbury proposes that "convivial, co-creative relating" is about holy play, sharing power, intimacy, reaching toward/yearning, risk-taking, mutual questing, and being in inquiry.[6] This convivial, cocreative relating—a relational process—mirrors the process of artmaking. As such, friendship itself is an *artistic* process. The beings in friendship are the art. We are the ones who become something new that exists in the world. Our becoming more fully human/spiritually aware/divine is the art itself. We are the craft and crafters in God's studio, always creating the art/artistic process that did not exist before. Through these relations, each is changed, always. We are practicing "becoming-selfhood-in-relation."[7]

---

[6]Hilary Bradbury and Shakiyla Smith, "Relational Action Inquiry: To the Heart of the Learning," in *Cooking with Action Research: Stories and Resources for Self and Community Transformation*, digital ed., 2017. AR+ https://actionresearchplus.com/wp-content/uploads/2017/08/Cooking-with-Action-Research.pdf, 153 (accessed April 8, 2024).
[7]Kathleen T. Talvacchia, *Embracing Disruptive Coherence: Coming Out as Erotic Ethical Practice* (Eugene, OR: Cascade, 2019), 8.

Of course, one risk in this is boundary crossing, especially when we are living/residing/working in a realm that actively seeks liminality and breaks down boundaries. Counterintuitively, the presence of boundaries established a playground that was vast, and yet constrained. This allowed for deeper exploration. We found that with constraints and a guiding set of ethics/principles, one finds ways to play within that vastness. In fact, our art of becoming was because there were internal and external boundaries that we, though not explicitly stated, maintained. It was an intuition that we were both guided by and only in writing this chapter together are we able to articulate and explicitly explore the dynamics at play. As Hunt posits, "friendship includes love and power, embodiment, and spirituality. … Friendship becomes the bedrock of all love relationships."[8]

"Becoming-selfhood-in-relation" is not a fusion of self with the other. It demands emotional and spiritual maturity that includes operating within a clear ethical framework and with trust. The impact of our actions extends beyond ourselves. Trust is communal. Trust is a commitment to communal relations. Trustworthiness is often a product of attending to one's own wounds and healing (ongoing, never finished). As such, the growth of the moral and ethical self is something that happens in relationship, in community—and includes the presence of boundaries as a way of orienting oneself to self and others.

I am not you, but I am not not you.
I am not divine. I am not not divine.[9]

Being willing to be acted upon by another, having enough core self and core identity, one is willing to be acted upon and be changed without giving oneself away. We have agency to both act and be acted upon. For example, as poets, we write by listening to the deepest parts of ourselves and the world we live in for what is asking to be written. Words and images have a way of emerging and presenting themselves. Our task is to pay close attention to

---

[8]Hunt, "Love Your Friends," 140.
[9]Adapted from James Finley's quote of Romano Guardini, "Although I am not God, I am not other than God either" to which he adds his own, "Although I am not you, I am not other than you either." James Finley, *Jesus and Buddha: Paths to Awakening*, disc 6 (Center for Action and Contemplation: 2008).

what is seeking expression, breathe into what stories are longing to be liberated and heard. It is a collaborative relationship between the words and the writer.

Our shared art, as friends, then, is the practice of being willing to be acted upon by another, removing the masks and protective boundaries that we put in place to keep ourselves safe. Then it's a risk, not a random risk, to know and be known. It's a model of the kind of freedom that one wants with God: to be fully known, even the parts of ourselves that seem completely unlovable, and perhaps even unknowable. To do that, you need to risk being seen and heard. It feels like you are finally not hiding in secret. And it can also feel vertiginous having removed the anchors that held you in place. It can be difficult and painful. A shaking of the foundation that you have identified yourself with. And yet, this freedom, this willingness to be known, is a necessary condition for soul work.

Art as Political Warfare: A Dialogue

It's not a secret: *People like us were never meant to survive.*

Our bodies encase and emerge from myriad intergenerational trauma to include the legacy of imperialism and colonialism that eventually brought us to the US where we continue to labor under the pervasive reality of white supremacy that seeks to diminish who we are—and how we are—because we are.

What does it mean to say we were never meant to survive? To claim art/poetry as political warfare?

Su: Alicia, this world driven by capitalism and white supremacy did not dream of my existence. It does not have my well-being in mind, does not have the way I wish to live out my life in mind.
I think of how much I work—fueled in part by a lie that I can attain value in this society if I work toward perfection. Driving myself to work in order to prove my worth. It's almost as if I feel the need to apologize for taking up space. As an Asian American in the US, I am fighting against being erased while also seeking a sense of belonging. This undergirds that impulse to

work hard, not be a burden, this sense that, unless I buy into this world of white supremacy, it is not a place for me. And yet, I *am* in this world, and I am complicit in its machinations. I derive status and benefit from it even as it is detrimental for my physical, emotional, and spiritual well-being. I am not without privileges. Even our practice of writing and sharing poetry was made possible because during the pandemic, the type of work we do allowed us to stay at home and work comfortably. Many others simply did not have that choice. I had a job that gave me a sabbatical. That gave me the space and time to reflect, to pray, to take walks, and to write. My spiritual and political discernment is how not to be deluded by that privilege ... really, by that lie.

Alicia: I hear you, Su, especially around the felt need to apologize for taking up space as well as the notion that this world is not created for us. I am constantly stunned by what it took for me to be here. Somebody had to survive captivity on the African continent. Somebody had to survive the middle passage. Somebody had to survive the auction block, the passage from Barbados to Trinidad & Tobago. Somebody had to survive labor in the fields, in the sun, under whips, just for me to be here. This is angering and their survival is miraculous, extraordinary. This system of white supremacy, of capitalism, sought to render those who came before me disposable. Their thriving, their well-being was not part of the equation. And yet, they kept going. Being generative. Creative. For the present, current and next generation. What, then, is my responsibility? What is our responsibility? If not to be generative ourselves? Creative? For me, generativity and creativity is (in part) using art, using what we have, to resist, to burn down, to rebuild.

Su: Generativity, yes! Poetry, for me, is the act of putting words into experience. That, in itself, allows me to make meaning of my experiences. Alice Walker was formative for me. Her work gave me permission ... no not permission, *confidence* to write poetry. Because she kept it real. Her poetry wasn't "pretty." It was free and freeing. She spoke plainly about her experiences and the experience of her people in the rhythm and music of her own. It made me yearn for what Homi Bhabha calls "third space"[10]—and what Rita Nakashima Brock calls, "interstitial integrity"[11]—where I too could find my rhythm and feel whole. It allowed me to experiment with images, words, metaphors, both Korean and American, both religious and secular. It was a space where my hyphenated identity was being real/ized. It allowed me to author myself into being. Her poetry gave me the confidence to give voice to my rage against the pervasive whiteness, to the impact of being erased, the impact of being a target of injustice, of being in the wilderness of immigrant life where we swallowed the bitter bile of survival. My first poetry was a "litany of wilderness" that I wrote for the Easter vigil when I was at a seminary in the early 80s. It was my first public performance of anger.

I write to know what I feel for myself, from the inside out. Poetry, writing poetry, is a way of giving attention to ourselves that necessarily takes attention away from "proper objects"[12] as a way to resist the fact that we were not meant to survive. This. This is an act of political warfare.

Alicia: Su, we were never meant to survive. We live in a society that is intent on diminishing who we are; poetry is a way to push back against that diminishment. While serving in the military, I found this community of misfits who also wrote poetry—we became kin. Writing kin who, for a time, were able to create community across surface differences. There was so much that conspired against us in terms of being in community, and ... and,

---

[10] Homi Bhabha, *The Location of Culture* (London: Routledge, 1994).
[11] Rita Nakashima Brock, "Cooking without Recipes: Interstitial Integrity," in *Off the Menu: Asian and Asian North American Women's Religion and Theology*, ed. Rita Nakashima Brock, Jung Ha Kim, Kwok Pui-lan, and Seung Ai Yang (Louisville, KY: Westminster John Knox Press, 2007), 126.
[12] Sara Ahmed, "Selfcare as Warfare," in *Feminist Killjoys*, https://feministkilljoys.com/2014/08/25/selfcare-as-warfare/ (accessed April 8, 2024).

	our being in this space of poetic heart connection, was a practice of changing the world we live in by impacting each other. In a sense, we were co-creating kin-dom[13]; I think that poetry as political warfare has the potential to create kin-dom right here on earth.
Su:	Kin-dom. Yes, Alicia. Isn't that what we have created through our poetry sharing? We are not meant to be friends. The social, political, and historical realities in the US pit our communities against each other. The Black-Asian conflict, and more specifically, Black-Korean conflict and animosities have played out in many ways from anti-Black racism of Asian American communities to anti-Asian racism of Black communities. Both communities have been used to further the agenda of white supremacy, seeding division and stoking fear for its own gain. And yet, through our poetry, we see a glimpse of a kin-dom that we aspire to. This kin-dom is sort of queer; we are not meant to be family. We are not meant to survive. We create queer bonds—modes of survival in an otherwise hostile world. Creating our own family, a particular kind of family arrangement—moving against the grain as a way to thrive.
Alicia:	Sometimes I think that *brown girl dreaming* [Jacqueline Woodson] is the luxury that we are not afforded. To shift attention away from "proper objects" [Sara Ahmed] to reflect, to think, to write, to feel is not a luxury that is associated with this body. Our bodies, Su, are meant to labor. Lorde says, and I wholeheartedly believe that poetry is not a luxury at all … it's a necessity. It is a way to take up space. It's a way of breathing, of being revealed *and* revealing—reveal a world/inner world and reveal to the world that our very existence and thriving matters. It is a way of claiming space in the here and now and beyond.

---

[13] Ada-Maria Isasi Diaz, "Kin-dom of God: A Mujerista Proposal," in *In Our Own Voices—Latino/a Renditions of Theology*, ed. Benjamin Valentin (Maryknoll, NY: Orbis Books, 2010), 171–90.

Su: Alicia, I am thinking back to your question, what it took for you to be here. For me, my families on both sides had to survive Japanese colonization, the division of the Korean peninsula, the Korean war, and immigration to the US. I know that many did not survive. Writing poetry allows me to unearth the deep, often disattended materials. When I was writing "Gifts from Okinawa," I was remembering my father's gifts fondly from his trips abroad. But what surfaced was something unexpected and haunting.

Gifts from Okinawa

Circa 1965/6
9 October 2020

He comes homes again
        with bags full of gifts
           from Okinawa after weeks away
for military reconnaissance.

We sit expectantly as my father brings out
        a string of pearls, for my mother
           (we later learn that they are fake)
two white faux leather vinyl coats, for my sister and me
the latest children's style
by Japanese fashion,
A-shaped, pointy collared, with pockets for knick-knacks.

Amidst the chorus of oohs and aahs, in quick movements we
        push our arms through the sleeves.

The resistance of this
stiff, scratchy, and flattened
like cardboard cut-out for a dress-up doll
        two-dimensional coat
           too strong for my small but three-
   dimensional body
with shiny metal toggles that I struggle to fasten
against the biting Seoul winter.

This innocuous fatherly gift
        balks at my body's natural rhythm
of bending, jumping, and running,
        to show my good fortune to coveting friends

Picture-perfect though impractical
        modeling the latest and the newest
        asymmetry of form and function
gleaming white muddied in an instant
        against the dirty city streets

Like the generation before me, I lose
        the battle
against this imperious Japanese coat that
        disciplines, disrespects, and discards
straightjacketing me to colonial powers.

///

Alicia: "Disciplines, disrespects, and discards," I've always found this poem of yours so powerful, Su. The contrast between the celebration and coveting the fashion of a colonial power, and the attempted resistance of your own body—as if you knew, instinctively, that such fashion was not made for you. And further, you had more to offer than succumbing to a restrictive way of being that sought to define and determine the limits of your existence. You were—and are—three dimensional with a culture, history, and trajectory that refuses to be subverted.

It starts early, this seeding, this occupation of the mind and body by standards of whiteness and colonial power. In one of my first poems to you, I reflect on the desire to be other than I am. I reflect, too, on my desire to inhabit "American-ness"—an escape from the world we inhabited. It is an insidious form of violence that takes root in the body and mind. I've spent much of my adult life trying to uproot and resist that violence.

13 August 2020

Even before we arrived, we were already here.

It started with our granny's wigs.
She had a collection that she used to cover
her "good hair."
Hair that was curly, and felt soft beneath my fingers
my older sister Jacqueline and I each selected
long haired wigs.
Hair without kink
straight
reaching our shoulders
Outside on the concrete red porch steps
we smiled wide
        just like the Black girls on t.v.
flicked our hair
our wig hair
over our shoulders
We were American
        just like the girls on Sesame Street
with American accents
nasal not resonant

dialect ironed letters over-pronounced
The neighborhood boys pitching marbles in the yard
bought it
Jason, Kenneth, and Nigel (where are they now?)
We'd fooled them
pretending to be our own cousins
in Tobago for a visit

///

Su: This poem is a bitter-sweet reminder of my own childhood play. We too, pretended to have long "blond" hair—sinister colonial legacy that shaped our childhood imagination. Though separated by thousands of miles, the haunting shadow of the US empire formed us. "Even before we arrived, we were already here." And yet, this memory—innocent, playful, and trusting—unearthed a sense of connectedness despite the vast differences between us.

Our shared art has been—and is—the practice of doing the work our souls must have. Diving, delving, dancing, on the rhythms of self, is becoming-selfhood-in-relation to each other [Kathleen Talvacchia], to our memories, and to the forces that have, and are, shaping us. It's an opportunity to examine and reexamine the many meanings we make.

Conclusion

Pilgrimages like art are never truly complete. Both are dynamic and continue to unfold new meanings with ongoing exploration and interaction. This is also true of the work of the soul. There is no one destination, only the necessary practice of practicing, whether kneeling, walking, dancing, praying, cultivating relationship with self and other, the work of the soul is a process. We write, explore, and heal together. We grow our souls together.

Unni and *dong-saeng*. The identity of each is dependent on the identity of the other. Existing, becoming, making meaning, in relation to.

We are clear that the work of the soul isn't always easy, though necessary. Our art is necessary. Even as we craft this conclusion, we're aware that the demands of our lives have interrupted our poetry pilgrimage, and we feel the cost of that interruption. To not make time for art or soul-work is to reject the invitation to make space for something vital and new to exist in the world. It is to reject the invitation to be both intimate and vulnerable with the Divine.

Our commitment to art-making and the feminist praxis of becoming-selfhood-in-relation is an antidote to accepting individualism and heteronormativity as the norm. Our practice is not perfect. We ourselves are perfectly imperfect; willing to keep dancing, writing, and living against the grain so that we thrive in a world not meant for us to survive. Art and artists: a queer embodied cocreation that opens up new possibilities in the world.

Bibliography

Ahmed, Sara. "Selfcare as Warfare." In *Feminist Killjoys*. https://feministkilljoys.com/2014/08/25/selfcare-as-warfare/.

Bhabha, Homi. *The Location of Culture*. London: Routledge, 1994.

Bradbury, Hilary, and Shakiyla Smith. "Relational Action Inquiry: To the Heart of the Learning." In *Cooking with Action Research: Stories and Resources for Self and Community Transformation*, digital ed. 2017. AR+ https://actionresearchplus.com/wp-content/uploads/2017/08/Cooking-with-Action-Research.pdf, accessed April 8, 2024.

Brock, Rita Nakashima. "Cooking without Recipes: Interstitial Integrity." In *Off the Menu: Asian and Asian North American Women's Religion and Theology*, edited by Rita Nakashima Brock, Jung Ha Kim, Kwok Pui-lan, and Seung Ai Yang, 125–44. Louisville, KY: Westminster John Knox Press, 2007.

Finley, James. *Jesus and Buddha: Paths to Awakening*, disc 6. Albuquerque, NM: Center for Action and Contemplation, 2008.

Fujimura, Makoto. *Art and Faith: A Theology of Making*. New Haven, CT: Yale University Press, 2021.

Hunt, Mary. "Love Your Friends: Learning from the Ethics of Relationships." In *Queer Christianities: Lived Religion in Transgressive Forms*, edited by Kathleen T. Talvacchia, Michael F. Pettinger, and Mark Larrimore, 137–47. New York: New York University Press, 2015.

Isasi Diaz, Ada-Maria. "Kin-dom of God: A Mujerista Proposal." In *In Our Own Voices—Latino/a Renditions of Theology*, edited by Benjamin Valentin, 171–90. Maryknoll, NY: Orbis Books, 2010.

Lorde, Audre. *A Burst of Light, Essays*. London: Sheba Feminist, 1988.

Talvacchia, Kathleen T.. *Embracing Disruptive Coherence: Coming Out as Erotic Ethical Practice*. Eugene, OR: Cascade, 2019.

Taussig, Hal, ed. *A New New Testament*. Boston, MA: Houghton Mifflin Harcourt.

Whitaker, Amy. *Economics of Visual Arts: Market Practice and Market Resistance*. Cambridge: Cambridge University Press, 2021.

CONTRIBUTORS

Toni M. Bond is an associate professor of ethics at the Methodist Theological School in Ohio and one of the founders of the reproductive justice movement. She received her doctor of philosophy degree from Claremont School of Theology in California.

Alicia R. Forde is an ordained minister who serves with the Unitarian Universalist Association as the director of the International Office. She is a certified spiritual director and has a strong interest in health and wellness. She is a graduate of the Iliff School of Theology and currently lives in Boulder, Colorado.

Margaret D. Kamitsuka is the Francis W. and Lydia L. Davis professor emeritus of religion at Oberlin College. She is the author of numerous books, including *Feminist Theology and the Challenge of Difference*; *Abortion and the Christian Tradition: A Pro-choice Theological Ethic*. She also edited *The Embrace of Eros: Bodies, Desires, and Sexuality in Christianity* and co-edited the *T&T Clark Reader in Abortion and Religion: Jewish, Christian, and Muslim Perspectives*. Kamitsuka serves as the editor for the American Academy of Religion's academy series, which partners with Oxford University Press to publish new revised dissertations.

Mónica A. Maher is the founding director of the Ecuadorian Faith Network for human rights advocacy and visiting professor of sociology and gender studies at the Latin American Faculty of Social Sciences (FLACSO)–Ecuador. With María Pilar Aquino and María del Carmen Servitje Montull, she is co-editor of the upcoming interdisciplinary, interreligious, and international volume, *Religion, Sexual Violence and Peacebuilding: Feminist Perspectives of Intercultural Transformation*. She is an ordained minister in the United Church of Christ and Zen Sensei.

Elaine Nogueira-Godsey is an assistant professor in religion and society at the Drew University Theological School. She is a Latina ecofeminist scholar, working on the intersection of religion and ecology. Her research and pedagogical practices focus on advancing decolonial ecofeminist ethics and perspectives from the Global South. Her recent publications are "A Decological Way to Dialogue: Rethinking Ecofeminism and Religion (2022)" and "Race, Religion and Environmental Racism in North America (2024)." She is currently working on the book tentatively titled "Roots of Resistance: Ivone Gebara and the Journey of Latin American Ecofeminism."

Keun-joo Christine Pae is a professor of religion/ethics and women's and gender studies and chair of the Religion Department at Denison University in Ohio. Her research and teaching interests include transnational feminist ethics, religious ethics of peace and war, feminist spiritual activism, and Asian/Asian American feminist theologies and ethics. She is the author of *A Transpacific Imagination of Theology, Ethics, and Spiritual Activism: Doing Feminist Ethics Transnationally* (2023), and co-editor of *Embodying Antiracist Christianity: Asian American Theological Resources for Just Racial Relations* (2023).

Su Yon Pak is the vice president of Academic Affairs and the dean of the Union Theological Seminary in the City of New York. She is also a spiritual director grounded in contemplative traditions. Her life and research passion include contemplative practices, chaplaincy education, the elderly and spirituality, women's leadership, and integrative, embodied, and critical pedagogies. Her most recent book is *Sisters in Mourning: Daughters Reflecting on Care, Loss, and Meaning* co-edited and co-authored with Rabbi Mychal Springer (2021).

Esther Parajuli is an assistant professor of Christian theology at the Lexington Theological Seminary in Kentucky. Her work explores the ways in which notions of purity, defilement, and danger are woven into our perceptions of sameness and difference, further shaping our understanding of the self and the other.

Heike Peckruhn is a German native with biracial parentage. She teaches courses in religious studies and theology at the Eastern Mennonite

University in Virginia. Her scholarly interests pivot around bodily life, especially at the intersections of gender, sexuality, and disability and the ways in which embodiment and experience create meaning and meaningful action in the world. She is the author of *Meaning in Our Bodies: Sensory Experience as Constructive Theological Imagination* (2017).

Charlene Sinclair served as interim publisher of Colorlines (colorlines.com), a leading source for accessible media on race, power, and democracy, and as an associate director of BlackPAC and the Black Progressive Action Coalition (BPAC). Influenced by James Cone's Black liberation theology, Sinclair is committed to fashioning strategies that embrace a liberationist approach to faith and spirituality in the context of popular struggles for racial, economic, and gender justice. She received PhD in Christian social ethics from the Union Theological Seminary in the City of New York.

Nikia Smith Robert is an assistant professor of religious ethics and social justice at the University of Kansas and the founder and executive director of Abolitionist Sanctuary. Her expertise as a womanist abolitionist scholar focuses on theological, ethical, and sociopolitical responses to the criminalization of impoverished Black motherhood and emancipatory interventions for social transformation. Robert's scholarly contributions expand canonical thought in religious studies, gender and women studies, and African(a) American/Black studies.

Kathleen T. Talvacchia is a contextual theologian with interest in practical theology, Christian practices of marginalized communities, and queer theology. She was previously an associate professor of Ministry and Theology at the Union Theological Seminary and an associate dean for Academic and Student Affairs at the New York University Graduate School of Arts and Science. She authored *Embracing Disruptive Coherence: Coming Out as Erotic Ethical Practice* (2019) and co-edited *Queer Christianities: Lived Religion in Transgressive Forms* (2015). She is also a conflict mediation facilitator and a spiritual director in the contemplative tradition.

INDEX

abolition, ethic of 7, 79–82
abolitionist 32
abolitionist sanctuary 67–83
abortion 30–1, 33–6, 48, 59–61
Abya-Yala 136
"Acts of Paul and Thecla" 51
agency 40
   moral 32, 41, 44
Ahuja, Neel 178–9
Althaus-Reid, Marcella 16–17, 19–20, 22–6, 145–7, 149, 166–7
ancestral spirituality 123, 133, 137
Andes 136
Anselm (St. of Canterbury) 71, 80
Aquino, María Pilar 124, 129, 135, 136, 137
Arias, Patricio Guerrero 126
art
   as feminist communal radical praxis 217–19
   as necessary 209–11
   as political warfare 219–23
   relationship and 211
   shared 219–26
Augustinus, Aurelius 70–1, 80–1
autonomy 31–2, 36–7, 40–5
Aymara 124, 134, 136

becoming 14, 40, 54, 168, 194, 200, 205, 208–9, 217–18, 225–6
Belser, Julia Watts 114
Berne, Patty 109

Betcher, Sharon V. 102
Bhabha, Homi 199, 221
Bhagwati, Anuradha 151
Biehl, Janet 170, 173–4
Black, Indigenous, and People of Color (BIPOC) 145
Black feminist thought 32
Black motherhood 49. *See also* Black womanhood
Black Panther 194, 196
Black womanhood 67–83
   policing 68–70
   respectability politics 75–9
   sin 70–5
   stereotypes of deviance 70–5
   womanist ethic of abolition 79–82
Black women 1, 7, 29–32, 73, 76–8
   death due to pregnancy-related causes 37
   as deviant and sinful 79–80, 82
   embodied existence 38–41
   moral worthiness 79
   policing 68–70
   role in coining of the term reproductive justice 29–30
   welfare queens 91
Black Women for Reproductive Justice (BWRJ) 35, 35 n.14
body 131–6
Bradbury, Hilary 217
Brock, Rita Nakashima 152–3, 221

INDEX

brown, adrienne maree 201–2
Brown, Lydia X. 109
Burdette, J. Dexter 68–9

Cabnal, Lorena 133–4
Cáceres, Berta 137
Calvin, John 71–2, 80
Cannon, Katie 1
celibacy 52–4, 60
childhood experiences 206
Chipana, Sofía Nicolasa 124, 127–8, 130, 132, 133, 134, 136
Christ, Carol 180
Christian theology 7–8, 14, 22, 100, 123, 128, 156, 159, 165
cis-heteronormative theology 21–3
Clinton, Bill 87
Clinton administration 30
collaboration 107
coloniality 177–8, 181
colonial legacy 165, 225
community feminism 123, 133
"Confession" 212–14
connection
   community and 206
   to feminist theology 100–1
   poetic heart 221–2
Cooper, Anna Julia 78–9
Cooper, Brittney 76–80
Cooper, Thia 23
Copeland, M. Shawn 39
corazonar 128, 137
Cortez, Marc 40, 44
Cottom, Tressie McMillan 2
creative nonfiction 8, 205
critical physicality 145, 145 n.7

decological praxis 178–83
decoloniality 179, 180, 182–3
decolonization 127–30
deification 80
de l'Incarnation, Marie 55
desire 2–3, 4, 14–15, 23–7

dialogue 127–30, 164, 177, 178–83, 219–33
Dingle, Shannon 59
dirt 190–1, 193
disability(ies) 96–113
   connections to feminist theology 100–1
   emergence and legacies 101–5
   engaging in 97–100
   feminism and 105–7
   imagination 97, 101, 103, 111–12
   intersectional disability justice 110–13
   justice 107–10
   limits model of 99
   medical model of 98
   social model 98–9
   tragedy model of 98
disability justice movement 96–7, 109, 111–13
disability studies 97, 98–3, 107–8
disability theology 97, 100–2, 105
Dobbs v. Jackson Women's Health Organization 33, 48
dominator-subordinated dialogue 177
dominator-subordinated dynamic 165, 175–8
Dorrien, Gary 73
Douglas, Mary 191
Drewermann, Eugen 127

Eaton, Heather 172
Ebel, Jonathan 155
ecofeminism 163–83
   decological praxis 178–83
   dominator-subordinated dynamic 175–8
   essentialism and 167–71
   experience 164–6

feminist liberation
    theology 166–7
liberation theology 166–7
religion and 167–75
spirituality and 167–71
Ecuador 123–4, 134
Eiesland, Nancy 100–2, 104, 105
Eisenstein, Zillah 151
embodiment autonomy 7, 29, 39
emergence and legacies,
    disability 101–5
Enloe, Cynthia 153
environmental justice 171
erotic theology 18–19
essentialism 167–71
ethics 197, 201
    of care 183
    feminist 180
    theological 101–2
European Enlightenment 39–40
exclusionary self 191–4
experience 164–6

faith-based activism 4
feminism 105–7
feminist differences 6
feminist ecumenism 124–6
feminist liberation theology 166–7
feminist praxis 8, 205, 209, 226
feminist theoethicist 7, 88
feminist theology 1–8, 13–27,
    47, 100–1
    cis-heteronormative
        theology 21–3
    disability connections to 100–1
    intercultural framework for 129
    Latin American 124, 136,
        164, 171
    methodological base
        points 16–17
    of motherhood 60–2
    of peace as radical
        praxis 143–59

postcolonial 199–201
queer desire as praxis of
    justice 23–7
queer experiences of gender and
    sexuality in 18–21
Feng, Daoyou 193
fetus, personhood of 48
First Nations 55
Fox, Matthew 74–5
fractals 201–3
freedom 23, 25, 31, 72, 73, 170
    democracy and 172
    human sacrament and 39
    risk and 211
free will 32, 40–1

Gaard, Greta 168, 173–4
Gbowee, Leymah 143–4
Gebara, Ivone 124–5, 128, 135–7,
    165, 179, 181
gender
    labor based 8
    presentation 15
    in queer experiences 18–21
    studies 4, 15
    violence based on 3
gender and sexuality 16, 18–21, 35
    in peace 149
    in soldiering and
        prostitution 150–4
gender-based violence 152
gendered capitalism 87
"Gifts from Okinawa" 223–6
Gimbutas, Marija 169
Gingrich, Newt 87
Global South 8, 108, 168, 171–
    3, 178–9
Go, Michelle 193
God, described 135
God Behind Bars (research
    project) 86
Golubski, Roger 68, 82
governmental obligations 36–7

INDEX

Gregory of Nyssa 52
grief 111–13, 214
  of Koreans 200
  profound 183

Harriot, Michael 68
healing 4, 128, 131–6, 138–9, 159, 170, 179
health care reform 30
hero-mythmaking 154–6
heteronormativity 3, 15, 22, 26, 43
heterosexuals
  assumptions 25
  binary systems 17
  cisgender 25
  ideological stance 22
  ideology 19
  normativities 16
  theological constructs 20
Heyward, Carter 18, 19
Higginbotham, Evelyn 75–7, 79–80
Hines, Darlene Clark 78
human embodiment 29
human identity 29, 42, 43
human rights 31, 32, 36–7, 41
Hunt, Mary 151, 210

identity 29–44, 50, 109, 210, 218, 221, 226
  biological 61
  cultural 130
  discourses 110
  dominator 175, 177
  gender 149
  national 190, 193, 195
  racial 193
  social experience and 97
imagination
  anticolonial 195
  constructive 101
  creative 111–12
  hegemonic 79
  prophetic 97
  theological 102–3
  imagination of resistance 194–6
imago Dei 39–41, 43, 80, 101–2
"Imbabura Woman Mountain Deity" 126–7
immigrant experience 206, 221
incarceration of women 30, 37, 76–7, 86
indecenting 17, 19, 20, 23
indecent theology 19, 24, 145
individual human rights 36–7
interculturalism 127–30
interdependency 189–203
  exclusionary self 191–4
  imagination of resistance 194–6
  jeong for collective liberation 199–201
  jeong fractals 201–3
  postcolonial feminist theology 199–201
  self as relational 196–9
interreligious 127–30
intersectionality 6, 15, 24
  disability justice 110–13
intimacy 8, 205, 210–11, 213–14, 217

jeong 199–201
  for collective liberation 199–201
  fractals 201–3
Joh, Wonhee Anne 199–201
"*Journey I*" 214–17
Julia, Anna 78

Kang, Namsoon 2
Kant, Immanuel 39
Keating, Anna Louise 181
Kemp, Margery 54–5
Kichwa 123, 124, 126, 136
King, Karen 92
Kwok, Pui-lan 143

Ladin, Joy 20–1, 26
land territories 131–6
Latin American feminist theology 124, 136, 164, 171
Lee, Debbie 158
Lee, Jin-kyung 150
Lettini, Gabriella 152–3
LGBTIQ+ 16, 23, 24
  communities 14 n.2
  experiences 15
  perspectives 15
LGBTQ 61
liberation theology 19, 81, 101, 128, 145, 166–7
liminality 206, 210, 217–19
lived experience 1, 2, 6, 15, 17, 22–4, 31–2, 67, 71, 75, 97, 100, 108, 111, 112, 144, 166
loss 111, 113, 133, 181, 214
Lugones, Maria 182
Luther, Martin 53–4

Make America Great Again (MAGA) 189–90
making meaning 223–6
Malcolm X 74
Maldonado, Tsaywa Samay Cañamar 124
Maldonado-Torre, Nelson 177
Mallory, Mary 172–3
marginalized groups
  oppression of 70
Martin, Marie 55
Mary Magdalene 7, 88–93
maternal duties 51–3
maternal mortality 48
McIntyre, Rosie 68–70, 74, 82
memory 130, 132, 200, 208, 209
Mena-López, Maricel 135
mental health
  motherhood 56–8
Merchant, Carolyn 170
methodological diversity 5–6

methodology 102, 124, 165
Mignolo, Walter 179
Mikhail, Hanna 148–9
Milburn, Stacey Park 109
militarized labor 154
militarized masculinity 153, 154
military prostitution 153–4
Mills, Charles 39
Mingus, Mia 109
miscarriage 59, 61
models of disability 97–100. *See also* disability(ies)
Modi, Narendra 195
Moorehead, Terra 68–9
moral agency 32, 41, 44
moral injury 152–3
motherhood. *See* presumptive motherhood
mothering tragedies 56–8
movements for economic justice 88

necropolitical labor 150–1, 153–4, 158–9
Nenquimo, Nemonte 138
New Testament 51
Niebuhr, Reinhold 72, 80

original sin 71–2, 74, 81
othering 192

Palestine 147–9
Park, Soon Chung 193
passion-arousing 145–6, 149
pedagogy 178–9, 181
Perpetua 51
Piepzna-Samarasinha, Leah Lakshmi 109
pilgrimage 210–11
  pandemic 207
  of poetry writing 206, 208
  shared poetry 213, 217, 226
  spiritual 54
Plaskow, Judith 180

Plumwood, Val 174–7
poetry pilgrimage 208–9, 217, 226
poetry writing 205, 206, 221
policing Black womanhood 68–70
pollution 72, 191–4
population control 32
postcolonial feminist theology 199–201
postpartum depression 57–8
practical nonviolence 149
praxis of justice, queer desire as 23–7
presumptive motherhood 7, 47–62
  current scenario of 56
  feminist theologies of 60–2
  maternal duties 51–3
  mental health and 56–8
  mothering tragedies and 56–8
  prolife-prochoice binary 59–60
  resistance to resurgence of 53–6
  women's historical counter-stories 50–1
prisons 51, 58, 69–70
prolife-prochoice binary 59–60
prostitution 150–4, 157
  military 153–4
Pulido, Laura 171
purity 191–4

queer friendship 205, 207, 210–11, 217–18
queer intimacies 205–26
  art as feminist communal radical praxis 217–19
  art as necessary 209–11
  art as political warfare 219–23
  "Confession" 212–14
  "Gifts from Okinawa" 223–6
  "*Journey I*" 214–17
  relationship and art 211
  souls 207–9
queer/queering 7
  cisgender woman 15

  desire as praxis of justice 23–7
  gender and sexuality experiences in 18–21
  life 15–16, 26
  theology 16, 17, 22
Quinn, Niko 69–70, 74, 82

race 38–41
racialized capitalism 87
radical polypraxis 136–9, 143–59
  described 144–9
  gender and sexuality in peace 149
  gender and sexuality in soldiering and prostitution 150–4
  hero-mythmaking 154–6
  redoing theology 156–9
radical praxis 5–6, 8, 15, 24
radical resurgence 146–7
Rastriya Swayamsevak Sangh (RSS) 195
reason-nature dualism 166, 175, 177, 180
redoing theology 156–9
relationality 19, 42–4, 103, 197–202
relationship and art 211
religion 167–75
religious biodiversity 124–6
reproduction 29, 38, 42
reproductive and sexual justice (RSJ) 29–32
  Black women's embodied existence 38–41
  founding members of movement 30 n.1
  governmental obligations 36–7
  individual human rights 36–7
  paradigm shift caused by 31
  principles of 32–5
  theological and anthropological doctrine of 41–4

theory 36
women 3
respectability politics 75–9
Ress, Judith 171
right not to have a child 33–4
right to have a child 32–3
right to parent the child(ren) one already has 34–5
right to sexual pleasure 35
ritual 80, 134, 139, 159, 208
Roe v. Wade 34, 48
Roll Call 30, 30 n.2
Roman, Gabriel Garcia 23
Runa feminisms 121–39
 body/land territories 131–6
 decolonization 127–30
 feminist ecumenism 124–6
 "Imbabura Woman Mountain Deity" 126–7
 interculturalism 127–30
 interreligious 127–30
 radical polypraxis 136–9
 religious biodiversity 124–6
 "To Write" 130–1

sacredness 148, 207, 213, 217
Schaberg, Jane 89
self as relational 196–9
self-care 209
self-determination 41, 42, 45
self-reflexivity 181
sex 43
 commercialization of 153
 education 35, 37
 gender and 17
 premarital 44
 pro-sex space 35
 sex-phobic early church 52
sexuality
 gender and 16, 18–21, 35
 in queer experiences 18–21
sexual justice. *See* reproductive and sexual justice (RSJ)

sexual pleasure 32, 35–7, 40, 41
shared art 219–26
Simpson, Leanne Betasamosake 146
sin 70–5
SisterLove 35
Smith, Shakiyla 217
social sin 73
soul-commitment 214
souls 207–9
soul work 209, 219, 225–6
Sousa Santos, Boaventura de 131
Spiritual Exercises of Saint Ignatius 25
spirituality 167–71
St. Augustine. *See* Augustinus, Aurelius
Stella, Mãe 80–1
stereotypes of deviance 70–5
Sunlit Center 157
survival 87, 138–9, 163, 175, 197, 209–10, 220–2

tapestries 124–6
Thapar, Romila 193
theological anthropology 7, 40
theology 80–2, 87. *See also* feminist theology
 Christian 7–8, 14, 22, 100, 123, 128, 156, 159, 165
 continued challenges 105–7
 erotic 18–19
 indecent 19, 24, 145
 intersectional disability justice 110–13
 intersectional visions 107–10
 liberation 19, 81, 101, 128, 145, 166–7
 queer/queering 16, 17, 22
 redoing 156–9
 Totalitarian Theology (T-Theology) 22

Thistlethwaite, Susan 145, 154, 156
Tillman, Pat 155–6
Tonstad, Linn Marie 23–4
Totalitarian Theology (T-Theology) 22
Townes, Emile 73
"To Write" 130–1
transformation 18, 73, 108, 111, 134, 181, 217
Trump, Donald 93, 189–90
trust 182, 207, 218, 225

United States
  Black women in 38
  children in food insecure homes 34–5
  Health Security Act of 1993 30
  maternal mortality in 48
  Supreme Court 36

Virgin Mary 88, 91
von Bora, Katharina 53
vulnerability 70, 110, 112–13, 182, 199, 211

WADRJ 31
Walsh, Catherine 179
war 1, 8, 143–5, 148–54, 157, 158–9
Washington Post 30
welfare 30, 33, 87–90, 91
  punitive 38, 73
West, Traci 91
white supremacy 3, 32–3
Williams, Ophelia 69–70, 74, 82
Willis, Winnette 35 n.14
womanist, ethic of abolition 79–82
Women for Genuine Security 158 n.45
women-nature nexus 163, 167
women's historical counter-stories 50–1
Wong, Alice 109
Woo, Soon Duk 157
Woodson, Jacqueline 206
Wynter, Sylvia 178

Yates, Andrea 56–8
Yong, Ed 196

Zaru, Jean 147–9